Music In — and On — The Air

Lloyd Schwartz

introduction by Jan Swafford

Music In—and On—The Air
© 2012 Lloyd Schwartz

ISBN-10:0989237206
ISBN-13:978-0-9892372-0-8

Cover Art: Ralph Hamilton
portraits of Klaus Tennstedt, Annie Fischer,
Elliott Carter, Pierre Boulez, Phyllis Curtin, and John Harbison

Original cover design Nathaniel Forsythe
Initial book design Erica Mena
Adapted to accommodate this print edition

A duet by
Arrowsmith Press
11 Chestnut Street Medford, MA 02155
arrowsmithpress@gmail.com
&
PFP Publishing
144 Tenney Street Georgetown, MA 01833
publisher@pfppublishing.com

For David Stang, who tirelessly continues to listen to music with me and keeps me alert and keeps me honest

I'm very grateful to the following people. First of all, to the extraordinary Terry Gross, for inviting me to be part of *Fresh Air*, which for twenty-five years has been one of the happiest experiences of my life. And to *Fresh Air*'s executive producer, Danny Miller, for his longstanding support. For nearly two decades, Phyllis Myers has cast her penetrating eye over every word I've written for the show and made sure that I was writing words that *spoke*. Before Phyllis, Naomi Person helped make each piece better. Deepest gratitude to my friend and colleague Askold Melnyczuk, the very model of a modern man of letters, for deciding to publish this book, and for persisting in seeing it through. And to the people who did the hard work: designer Erica Mena, cover designer Natty Forsythe, and organizer Sam Cha.

My abiding thanks, too, to the friends with whom I first listened seriously to music, and who opened my ears and mind to what makes the great performances: Frank Bidart, and the late Robert Garis and George Curran.

LS

Contents

A Note On the Text by Jan Swafford

Contemporary Classics

John Harbison	1
Peter Sellars's *Don Giovanni*	8
Klaus Tennstedt	11
Akhnaten	13
Lutoslawski	16
Arvo Pärt	18
Jorge Bolet	20
Ives	22
Ensemble Alcatraz	24
Arlene Auger and Dalton Baldwin, *Love Songs*	26
Dubravka Tomsic	28
Kurtág	30
Adriana Lecouvreur	32
Alkan	34
Kleiber Waltzes	36
Gubaidulina	39
Busoni Concerto	42
Horowitz	44
Music in Time of War	46
Boston Chamber Music Society, Brahms Quintets	48
Josephine Barstow, *Opera Finales*	50
Giulio Cesare	52
Krenek	54
Leon Fleisher	56
Angela Gheorghio and Roberto Alagna	58
David Helfgott	60

CLASSICS FOR DUMMIES 63
Kurt Weill, *Die Bürgschaft* 65
Dresden Music Festival 67
Samuel Barber 70
Alcina 72
Ida Haendel 74
Christmas Records 76
Marin Alsop 78
Sarah Caldwell 80
Ruby Elzy 83

Pop Kulcha

Eskin's Rags 87
Kiri Sings Gershwin 89
Jonathan and Darlene Edwards 91
Gershwin, *Of Thee I Sing* and *Let 'Em Eat Cake* 93
Into the Woods 95
Irving Berlin/Elizabeth Welch 97
Lotte Lenya Sings Kurt Weill 99
Bernstein at 70 101
Mary Martin and Ethel Merman 103
She Loves Me 105
Bulgarian folk music 107
Show Boat 109
Anything Goes 111
Leroy Anderson 113
Smithsonian American Musical Theater Collection 115
Bernard Herrmann 117
D'Oyly Carte Gilbert & Sullivan 119
Crossover 121
Mary Martin Sings—Richard Rodgers Plays 123

Decca Original Cast Albums	125
Fernwood 2-Night	127
The Original All-American Sousa!	129
Tippecanoe and Tyler Too	131
Cole Porter	133
Elvis Costello	135
Barbra Streisand, *Back to Broadway*	137
Spike Jones	139
Passion	141
Oscar-winning Songs	143
Germaine Montero	145
Kurt Weill, *From Berlin to Broadway*	147
Ira Gershwin at 100	149
Porgy and Bess	151
Follies	153
Threepenny Opera	155
Three Mo' Tenors	157
Gosford Park	160
Jerome Moross Centennial	163
Forgotten Broadway numbers	165
My Fair Lady on DVD	167
Alloy Orchestra	169
Abbott & Costello	171
The Triplets of Belleville	173
Around the World in 80 Days	175
Marx Brothers	178
Judy Garland	180
Movie Themes	182
Thin Man Collection	184
Unfaithfully Yours	187
Fred Astaire and Ginger Rogers	189
The Nicholas Brothers	191
Busby Berkeley	194

Betty Hutton 196
Lubitsch musicals 198
Sinatra DVDs 200
Gypsy: 50th Anniversary 202
Porgy and Bess 204
A Damsel in Distress 207
Car 54 209

My Parnassus

Artur Schnabel 215
Elliott Carter 219
Benita Valente 232
Pierre Boulez 236
Otto Klemperer 243
Arturo Toscanini 248
Leon Goossens 253
Mieczyslaw Horszowski 255
Maria Callas 257
Glenn Gould 263
Mravinsky Tchaikovsky 265
Jussi Björling 267
Pablo Casals 269
Cortot, Thibaud, Casals 272
Casals Festival at Prades 274
Kolisch Quartet 276
Lorraine Hunt Lieberson 278
Stravinsky 287
COLH 289
Annie Fischer 291
Szigeti/Bartok 293
Szigeti on DVD 295

Ravel's Bolero	297
Dinu Lipatti	299
Comparisons	301
Beecham's Haydn	303
Conchita Supervia	304
Roland Hayes	307
Hindemith	309
Opera Originals	311
Eleanor Steber	313
Kathleen Ferrier	315
Hollywood String Quartet	317
Benjamin Britten and Peter Pears	319
Brain, Kell, Goossens	320
Karl Muck and Early BSO Recordings	322
Maggie Teyte/Heddle Nash	324
Four Saints in Three Acts	326
Budapest String Quartet at the Library of Congress	328
George Copeland	330
Erich Kleiber	333
Patricia Brooks	335

Discography

A Note On the Text
Jan Swafford

I came to know Lloyd Schwartz gradually, first on paper as an aficionado of his music criticism, then in person. Two moments stand out in our early acquaintance. One was at a meeting of a literary panel, when Lloyd broke an impasse with a plea for giving our award to a poet in danger of neglect, which we did. Later we ran into each other at a publisher's shindig, and I shared with him a favorite Shakespeare line I'd been talking about in my classes: *the dark backward and abysm of time.* I'd always assumed a line that shadowed came from one of the tragedies, but Lloyd corrected me: "No, it's from *The Tempest*. It's one of my favorites too, and in the play it's a throwaway." In the middle of a noisy cocktail party we parsed the phrase word by word.

That's where I began to learn not only Lloyd's varied passions and his range of knowledge, but also his personality of a quietly relentless enthusiast. He's not only a prizewinning poet and likewise music critic, but as this book details, he's a collector of old records and forgotten musicians, the sort of person who in college sat into the night with friends comparing recorded performances. In recent years our friendship has developed over food and wine and laughter as much as anything, but part of our mutual appreciation is based on sharing a good many tastes, with enough disagreement to keep it interesting.

Lloyd has published three books of poems, his other works including co-editing the Library of America collection of Elizabeth Bishop's work. In 1994, his criticism won a Pulitzer Prize. This collection traces his radio pieces since 1987 from NPR's *Fresh Air*.

The book is in three parts, which is to say three ranges of

interest: *Contemporary Classics*, pieces on current classical musicians; *Pop Kulcha*, pieces on musical theater and film and other popular entertainments; and *My Parnassus*, his reflections on performers and composers, some from old and rare recordings. As all these short pieces reveal, though Lloyd only officially studied music on violin when he was five, and later took several college courses, he has a musical sensibility honed from a lifetime of fervid listening and comparing.

I'm a composer who has spent much of my last twenty years writing biographies of composers, and especially in working with Brahms and Beethoven I noticed a particular kind of person who used to be essential to the life of music: the passionate, knowledgeable musical amateur. In the later 18th and 19th century, these were often the people buying the tickets, writing the reviews, sometimes—if they played—collecting the sheet music that was the only way music was transmitted. Many of these people were polymathic in their artistic concerns, knowledgeable about literature and the visual arts as well as music. Often they inhabited the inner circles of composers. One of Brahms's closest friends was the famous surgeon Theodore Billroth, who played viola; some of Beethoven's closest companions in later life were journalists.

Through the lens of my own discipline, Western classical music, I see Lloyd as one of that vanishing breed—and to the degree it vanishes, music suffers. I've never asked him, but I'm sure he considers himself first a poet and a teacher (of English, at the University of Massachusetts). His three books concerning Elizabeth Bishop have occupied much of his time and concern. His warm, calm voice is familiar on radio, reviewing records on *Fresh Air*. For good measure, now and then he's acted in the theater, sharing the stage with Tommy Lee Jones and Stockard Channing. Many nights for the last twenty-five plus years he's sat in the audience of a concert hall, listening always critically and always hopefully.

As a writer, journalist, and longtime teacher of writing I'm perennially interested in my colleagues' prose, and for many years I've had a particular curiosity about the prose of writers who are essentially poets. Lloyd's poems are noted for plain-spokenness, not only in their subjects but in their style. This is from his "Leaves":

> You'll be driving along depressed when suddenly
> a cloud will move and the sun will muscle through
> and ignite the hills. It may not last. Probably
> won't last. But for a moment the whole world comes to.
> Wakes up. Proves it lives. It lives—
> *red, yellow, orange, brown, russet, ocher, vermilion,*
> *gold.* Flame and rust. Flame and rust, the permutations
> of burning. You're on fire. Your eyes are on fire.

The prose in Lloyd's criticism is inevitably different in style, less intimate and provoking than his poetry, but not different in temperament. Here he is on one of his recent discoveries of obscure musicians from the dark backward and abysm of time:

> I'm an optimist about the arts. I want to believe that what's really good will eventually come to light. You'll see an old movie on television and say: Who was that actress?—she's so real. Then you begin watching for her. One of the most important things a critic can do is remind people of the existence of lost treasures. At dinner recently a friend said that he'd been meaning to ask me for years if I'd ever heard of a pianist named George Copeland. I was astonished. When was the last time I'd heard that name, except from a few fanat-

ic record collectors? George Copeland didn't record very much, but I've loved the few recordings I've heard. He had an extraordinary touch—feathery, pearly, glistening—and instantly recognizable. He specialized in French impressionism yet there's nothing merely "impressionistic" about his playing. You can hear every note distinctly—nothing gets washed away in a watery blur.

Note the word "love" here. How many critics in any of the arts use that word so often and so intimately as Lloyd? At the same time, note his sense of responsibility: What's important for a critic to do for his readers. His opinions can be fierce—quietly fierce—but he's not snobbish in his tastes. Writing about his enthusiasm for the *Thin Man* movies, he reminds us why the leading actors were an ideal duo:

> I've often had the feeling about great chamber music that it was like listening to the animated give and take of dialogue. And sometimes, seeing a play or a terrific movie, the dialogue seemed like listening to chamber music. The epitome of that conversational elegance was the repartee between William Powell and Myrna Loy in the dozen or so movies they made together, especially their six *Thin Man* films, made between 1934 and 1947. They were the perfect team—both so intelligent and witty and teasingly sexy. Their timing never missed a beat. Loy said that her dialogue with Powell reflected the ease and spontaneity of their real-life conversations. Powell said they weren't actors, just two people in perfect harmony. Their deep underlying affection lights up the screen.

He brings the same attention to the classic 1950s TV series *Car 54, Where are You?*

> I didn't watch it until I got hooked on it in syndication long after it was originally aired. So I was very happy to see the complete series of sixty episodes released on two DVD boxed sets. The episode in Season 2, "I Hate Capt. Block," about trying to teach a recalcitrant parrot to talk, and the way people are not much smarter than parrots, is one of the most hilarious things I've ever seen on television, maybe as inspired as Sid Caesar's foreign film parodies or Carol Burnett's version of *Gone with the Wind*.

I'm looking forward to telling Lloyd, next time I see him, that *Car 54* was William Faulkner's favorite TV series. He'll appreciate that literary tidbit more than anybody else I know.

Inside you'll find pieces on Groucho Marx, Judy Garland, Stephen Sondheim, Abbot and Costello, and all sorts of unexpected figures, some of them largely buried in the cultural memory. The bulk of the book is a twenty-five year tour of Lloyd's passions and discoveries in classical music old and new. Here in memorable prose he joins his own life with a record of discovery, all enfolded in storytelling:

> Artur Schnabel isn't as well-known for his Mozart or Bach as for his Beethoven and Schubert, but this has nothing to do with his artistry. He's the greatest Mozart pianist I've ever heard—his touch, his phrasing, his insights are as searching as they are in Beethoven and Schubert . . . I remem-

ber a Schnabel record I found years ago. I was spending a summer in Santa Fe trying to preserve a relationship that was going sour. I had lost my teaching job, and at summer's end I would have to return to Boston, probably alone and unemployed. One of the uncomplicated pleasures of Santa Fe was a small record shop run by a former classical music disc jockey from Chicago who was forced to retire because of his heart condition. He had wonderful out-of-print records—and great stories . . . A few days before I left, a record turned up that I'd been wanting for years: a long-out-of-print LP of Artur Schnabel playing two of Mozart's very greatest piano concertos—the powerful D-minor and the heartbreaking, heartbroken C-minor. . . . With practically my last cent, I bought it. I played it as soon as I got back to Boston—and it was everything I imagined.

These were among the most profound, moving performances of Mozart—of anything—I'd ever heard. They actually helped me see my life from a new and longer perspective. Later, my mother called to tell me that . . . a job had opened up, I wasn't going be destitute, and I had my Schnabel!

One of my favorite paragraphs in the book, and one of the most poetic, begins his memorial for the great mezzo Lorraine Hunt Lieberson after her early death in 2006:

Lorraine Hunt Lieberson had everything. Her sumptuous voice could turn from blue velvet to molten gold. Her uncanny ability to enter the spirit of whatever music she sang also allowed her to identify completely with every character she played. She went from triumph to triumph yet never became a diva, never lost her sense of humor about herself. I was lucky to hear her from the beginning of her vocal career, especially in a couple of the famous Mozart and Handel productions staged by Peter Sellars, as well as with the Boston Symphony Orchestra, and in leading roles at the Metropolitan Opera. As Dido, Queen of Carthage, in Berlioz's epic opera *The Trojans*, she achieved a truly tragic stature. She was such a regal presence that her suicide when Aeneas deserts her was all the more heartbreaking. As Carmen, a role she sang only once, she was a scintillating, charismatic, complicated heroine, not a hip-swinging cliché.

Reader, I'll leave the rest for you, except to opine that all this is criticism at its best: fierce when it needs to be, but mostly a record of love and a love of sharing his passions with readers. I'm happy to report that he's the same in person, and in person as good a listener as talker. Polymath that he is, Lloyd Schwartz has found success in poetry, the most considered and disciplined kind of language, and in the writing-on-deadline world of music journalism. That makes him a unique and irreplaceable voice in the ongoing dialogue among artists, public, and critics. No one else brings a warmer, more committed, more literate voice to that dialogue.

Contemporary Classics

John Harbison

May 27, 1987

This year's well-deserved Pulitzer Prize in music went to John Harbison's darkly radiant *The Flight into Egypt*—a Christmas cantata whose spiritual message is less about Christmas than the plight of the homeless. This intersection of the spiritual and the realistic is typical of the paradoxes in Harbison's music. He's been called both a "radical conservative" and a "conservative radical," a "New Romantic," a "tune man." I think this means that his music combines sophisticated modern techniques—polyrhythms, tone-rows, palindromes—with such current anomalies as melody and harmony. He writes chamber music, symphonies, concertos, song cycles, and even operas. His musical imagery embraces mysticism and ritual as well as jazz and popular music (Harbison himself plays both classical viola and jazz piano). He actually seems to want to write music that is both beautiful and moving.

The two pieces of his on a new Northeastern record were composed five years ago, but they demonstrate his continuing fascination with the earthy and the sublime. The *Mirabai Songs* are settings of six poems by the 16th-century Indian mystic poet, Mirabai. When her husband died, she took to the streets instead of the funeral pyre—singing and dancing with alluring sensuality her own witty, erotically spiritual poems about Krishna.

The superb musicians for John Harbison's *Mirabai Songs* are members of Collage, the group of mostly Boston Symphony players that Harbison co-directs (he's also been composer-in-residence with the Los Angeles Philharmonic for the past two years). The soloist, mezzo-soprano Janice Felty, is one of the six dedicatees of these six songs. She's a dedicated singer, but she lacks Mirabai's volatility, her "Dancing Energy," the sense of ecstatic "fun" these songs require. You can also hear a good deal of strain in her voice, and too often you can't make out the words. I wish the record had been made with the extraordinary Susan Larson, who sang the premiere of the original—and even more exciting—version with only piano accompaniment.

The unqualified joy of this new Harbison CD are the Variations for violin, clarinet, and piano. They seem completely abstract but they were actually inspired by a sculpture of a Canaanite fertility goddess, dancing (like Mirabai). In 15 brief variations plus Finale and Epilogue, Harbison mixes his three instruments in every conceivable combination, tempo, and style (there's even a waltz). These variations build a musical arch that reaches an ecstatic climax and then dies away into introspection, and elegy, as at the end of the waltz and the beginning of the haunting 14th variation. The players on John Harbison's Variations are David Satz on clarinet; Ursula Oppens, piano; and the brilliantly expressive violinist, Rose Mary Harbison, who isn't on this record only because she happens to be married to the composer.

December 19, 1990

John Harbison's wonderful cantata, *The Flight into Egypt*, is a setting of the passage in the Gospel of Matthew where an angel comes to Joseph in a dream and warns him that Herod is determined to destroy his child. Joseph takes Mary and the infant Jesus to Egypt, where they remain until the death of Herod. In the meantime, Herod orders the slaughter of all children under the age of two. Two years later, in Egypt, the angel reappears, and the Holy Family returns and settles in Nazareth. Harbison says that this work grew out of conversations he had with the dedicated musicmakers at Boston's Emmanuel Church. For years, I think they've been among the true moral voices of the city—and not only in musical matters. Harbison says that in their discussion about the experience of counseling during the Christmas season, especially counseling the homeless, they agreed that given the widening gap between the fortunate and the less fortunate, the darker side of Christmas needed to be represented. *The Flight into Egypt* is as much about homelessness as it is about the gospel. You can hear that sense of desolation in the winding, wandering music for two oboes and English horn that the cantata opens with.

The Flight into Egypt was commissioned by the Boston choral group The Cantata Singers and their music director David Hoose. Harbison himself used to lead this group. And they are privileged with the first recording. Here are the two radiant soloists, baritone Sanford Sylvan singing the Evangelist and soprano Roberta Alexander as the Angel telling to Joseph to arise and take his family to Egypt.

With its traditional solo obbligatos and compact lyricism, *The Flight into Egypt* is a kind of contemporary equivalent of a cantata by Bach or Heinrich Schuetz. But Harbison adds a trombone to the instruments of a Bach chamber orchestra and organizes his material around the most modern of musical techniques, the tone row. Some of the most wonderful passages are reserved for the chorus, in which Harbison competes with Bach and Schuetz on their own turf. Here are the Cantata Singers led by David Hoose in the wondrous chorus singing the prophetic words, "Out of Egypt I have called my son."

This recording also includes two other recent works by Harbison. A song cycle called *The Natural World* is Harbison's tribute to the landscape of rural Wisconsin, where he does most of his composing. Harbison himself conducts mezzo-soprano Janice Felty and the Los Angeles Philharmonic New Music Group in this setting of three American poems by Robert Bly, Wallace Stevens, and James Wright. There's also the exhilarating Concerto for Double Brass Choir and Orchestra. Harbison calls this music "public, blunt, and ceremonial." He says he composed it to celebrate the brass section of the LA Philharmonic, and they respond brilliantly under the guiding hand of Andre Previn.

July 11, 1992

In the esoteric world of contemporary classical music, composer John Harbison has increasingly come to be recognized as a major figure. He's won numerous awards, including a Pulitzer Prize and a MacArthur "genius" grant. This summer, he's composer-in-residence at Tanglewood.

I like John Harbison's music in any form, but it's his chamber music that I seem to keep coming back to most. A new recording features all his chamber music for string ensemble: his two string quartets and an extraordinary piece for piano and string trio called "November 19, 1828." The first quartet is an intimate work, easy to follow though emotionally complex. It ranges through movements marked, sometimes rather deceptively, "amiable," "bitter and intimate," and "fugitive." The haunting main theme of the "amiable" first movement suggests Harbison's long interest in Indian mysticism.

The second quartet is more complex in design, with five movements based on the formal patterns of classical and preclassical music. The third movement, called Recitative and Aria, embodies what I love most about Harbison's music: its quietly heartbreaking melodies and emotional openness.

"November 19, 1828" is one of Harbison's, or anybody's,

most original inventions. The title refers to the date that Schubert died. The piece is a touching memorial to Schubert seen darkly through 20th-century eyes. The second movement is called "Schubert finds himself in a hall of mirrors." It's a brief suite of enchanting Schubert imitations played rightside-up and then upside-down.

In the third movement, Harbison actually uses an original Schubert theme—an early Rondo. This, Harbison writes, is the only music in this piece that was "composed by Schubert in his first life."

A week before he died, Schubert went to a music theorist for advice. He was assigned to write a fugue on his own name. Harbison ends his piece by composing the fugue that Schubert never lived to write. The performances here are all flawless. The Lydian String Quartet is one of America's finest chamber groups. From their inception, in 1980, they've balanced classical music with a concern for what is being written today. Three of the original four women remain—violinist Judith Eissenberg, violist Mary Ruth Ray, and cellist Rhonda Rider. Early-music specialist and noted Ives expert Daniel Stepner is the new first violinist. The loving pianist here is the distinguished composer Yehudi Wyner. I think they must all love playing this wonderful music as much as I love listening to it.

December 23, 1999

World premieres at the Metropolitan Opera House are far rarer today than in the days of Puccini. The latest—the first in seven years—is John Harbison's *The Great Gatsby*. F. Scott Fitzgerald's 1925 novel of the jazz age had only a small cult following among writers until it was, as the composer John Harbison says, "rescued from the literary junkheap." Thanks in large part to the enthusiasm of Edmund Wilson in the 1950s, *Gatsby* is now generally regarded one of the greatest American novels of the 20th-century—by some people the greatest. It tells one of the archetypal American stories: the hero of obscure origins who makes a shady fortune and gives his life (finally quite literally) to his pursuit of an ideal that finally can't help but betray him. It's also a story about the confrontation between the moral Mid-West and the moneyed East of New York and Long Island, the tyranny of beauty, and the brutality of the upper classes.

But if *The Great Gatsby* is a masterpiece, it's because it has some of the century's most dazzling writing, racing non-stop, in under 200 pages, from one breathtaking image to the next. "The lights grow brighter as the earth lurches away from the sun," writes Fitzgerald's narrator and alter ego, Nick Carraway, in a famous passage about one of Jay Gatsby's lavish parties, "and now the orchestra is playing yellow cocktail music, and the opera of voices pitches a key higher." There are certainly operatic elements in this book, with its prose arias, its tone of yearning, and heated melodrama. John Harbison succeeds in capturing a lot of that blend. His most fruitful idea is to mix the idioms of opera and pop music. Opening night at the Met, people around me audibly relaxed as the music in the Overture moved from the chromatic, almost discordant angst of operatic yearning into a suddenly flippant foxtrot.

The whole score is punctuated with original '20s-style songs and dance tunes played at parties or sung over the radio—tangos and Charlestons and foxtrots. The lyrics by Murray Horwitz (who was the originator of Broadway's *Ain't Misbehavin'*), mirror the emotional situations of the main characters, like the production numbers in Stephen Sondheim's *Follies*. And Harbison's melodies are infectious: people were leaving the Met humming the tunes. This might be the first opera to emerge with hit songs rather than famous arias, though there are also exquisite lyrical passages in the modern-classical mode. Stage director Mark Lamos, though, doesn't make enough of this brilliant musical juxtaposition—or of any of the opera's other dramatic confrontations—so this first production remains frustratingly static, despite James Levine's conducting, the scintillating playing by the amazing Met orchestra, and some strong performances by Susan Graham as Jordan Baker, heroic tenor Mark Baker as Daisy Buchanan's wealthy, narrow-minded, and "hulking" husband Tom ("I hate that word, 'hulking,'" he sings), and the stunning Lorraine Hunt Lieberson, in her overdue Metropolitan Opera debut, as Tom's earthy and doomed mistress, Myrtle Wilson. Soprano Dawn Upshaw and tenor Jerry Hadley are less successful as Daisy and Gatsby. Occasionally, Harbison has to resort to some pretty dated exposition to turn the novel's narrative into stage action. But some of the most awkward dramaturgy has some of his most beautiful music. You can hear the opera for yourself on New Year's Day, when the Saturday matinee will be broadcast live from the Met. Until it gets the production it deserves, John Harbison's noble collision with Fitzgerald's masterpiece may actually work better on the radio than in the opera house.

Peter Sellars's Don Giovanni

July 22, 1987

1987 marks the bicentennial not only of the American Constitution but of another, more ambiguous statement about liberty: Mozart's *Don Giovanni*. "Viva la liberta!" Mozart's revolutionary Don Juan makes everyone repeat at his wild party. Probably no one has ever taken more liberties with our preconceptions of this opera than Peter Sellars, the young American director who, with his collaborator, conductor Craig Smith, has been changing the face of 20th-century opera production. *Don Giovanni*, at PepsiCo Summerfare, is their latest adventure.

Sellars worked on *Don Giovanni* once before—seven years ago. It was his first complete professional opera. And like all his later work, it was both controversial and a knockout. One of his images for "Life in the fast lane" was a Big Mac at Don Giovanni's elegant Last Supper. The contemporary updating demystified the supernatural ending, turning heavenly retribution into a practical joke on the Don perpetrated by his victims. But Sellars has deepened his ability to mix styles and blend the realistic with the visionary. The Big Mac is still there—now joined by Chicken McNuggets—and so is the sinister practical joke, the handguns and hypodermic needles. But he also brings back Mozart's apocalyptic, supernatural ending, and with overwhelming theatrical and moral power.

The new setting, brilliantly designed by George Tsypin, is a street corner in Spanish Harlem, the intersection of, say, 117th Street and the 7th Circle of Hell. There are burning trashcans, a church with a white neon cross, corrugated metal storefronts, a gaping excavation with blinking warning lights, and a three-story tenement with windows that light up and open like an

Advent calendar designed by Hieronymus Bosch. The lighting by James F. Ingalls works like crosscutting in a movie—a brilliant solution to Mozart's cinematic scene shifting. It both dazzles and keeps us in the dark. Sometimes you can barely make out what's going on. This is a dangerous night world. There are no rules, and life is cheap.

Don Giovanni here is a free-spending, sex-obsessed drug dealer, young but already burnt-out. Not the least perverse of Sellars's ideas is that the notorious libertine is almost completely passive. He makes women run after him, and he's especially fond of little girls. Here's Kurt Ollmann elegantly singing the famous serenade. The noise in the middle isn't a set change but Don Giovanni falling off his chair when a mysterious little girl suddenly appears in a second-story window—the same one who'll re-materialize at the end of the opera and pull him down head first through an open manhole into hell.

Sellars consistently avoids class distinctions. Leporello is more the Don's henchman than his servant. Donna Anna is not an aristocrat but a heroin addict who's been having a secret affair with Don Giovanni. Not all of this works, and some of the casting is weak. But Lorraine Hunt as Elvira, who looks like Madonna and sounds like a major new opera star, gives a devastating, no-holds-barred performance as the woman wronged who still wants to save her lover's soul. Janet Brown as Zerlina is heartbreaking in the fragile beauty of her voice and demeanor, especially in her soothingly sexual wedding night reconciliation aria. And José Garcia is extraordinary as both her exuberantly demonstrative husband, loving yet violent, and the imposing Commendatore who returns as a ghostly statue. Craig Smith's conducting is magnificent, spacious (like Klemperer) and full of ironic contrasts. He builds the whole opera inevitably and enthrallingly to its shattering conclusion.

What's most extraordinary about this production is that in

spite of all its ideas—maybe too many for its own good—its vision is basically instinctual; it reaches you on a profoundly emotional level. I've never seen a *Don Giovanni* that comes to grips so fully with the vision of Hell, and the Hell we make of our lives, that Mozart created in his sublime and dangerous music.

Klaus Tennstedt

October 21, 1987

Klaus Tennstedt, the East German conductor who established himself in the West as one of the last major musicians in a disappearing European tradition, is very ill. He has resigned his directorship of the London Philharmonic, the orchestra with whom he recorded his complete Mahler cycle, and he's had to cancel his American tour. If he has, in effect, truly retired, he'll be deeply missed not only by his extremely devoted following, affectionately called the "Klausketeers," but by anyone who loves the mainstream of Austro-German symphonic music, especially Mahler.

It seems that great performances of the so-called standard repertory are getting rarer and rarer. But you could count on Tennstedt—especially his live performances—which had a kind of manic power. His gangly figure, his arms hovering and flapping like a giant flamingo, were an extraordinary, almost comical sight. But he could galvanize the most jaded of orchestras. His recordings, somehow, don't always capture the concert-hall experience. They're too much of the studio—often the playing is limp or even sloppy.

But the last of his Mahler recordings may be his best. It's the impossible Eighth Symphony, the "Symphony of a Thousand," Mahler's most rhetorically inflated and least melodically inspired major symphonic work. Few good performances, let alone good recordings, are known to exist. In joining an elaborate choral setting of the Catholic hymn "Veni, creator spiritus," the first part of the symphony, with the final transfiguration scene of Part II of Goethe's *Faust*, the symphony's second part, Mahler had hoped to make this his largest statement about the union between creativity and love. But what emerges is an overstated, abstract, yet rather corny theology with an occasional passage of quiet beauty to temper the relentlessly worked-up ecstasy.

Tennstedt succeeds in injecting the Mahler Eighth—Mahler's most impersonal symphony—with his own personal urgency and warmth. It begins ferociously but not melodramatically, and never lets up. Which I think is what gives those extended passages of uneasy repose such moving, and haunting, conviction. Typically, the slew of vocal soloists doesn't rise to the exalted level of the Philharmonic's choir, the Tiffin School Boys' Choir, or the marvelous orchestra, but French alto Nadine Denize, Finnish baritone Jorma Hynninen, and German bass Hans Sotin make some eloquent contributions. We can only hope that Tennstedt will get well enough at least to make more records. But if he can't, this one will be the most powerful reminder of the kind of musician he's been.

Akhnaten

January 14, 1988

Traditional opera tells a story, and the book, the libretto, is there to further the plot through soliloquy, dialogue, and ensembles, and to give the music something to hang on to. The words can be very poetic, especially in the arias, the soliloquies. The dialogue is usually quite banal, especially since opera plots themselves are so conventional and mechanical. Of course, there are exceptions. Da Ponte's librettos for Mozart's great Italian operas are literate and dramatically subtle and interesting.

In an interview with Terry Gross on *Fresh Air* last December, Philip Glass admitted that he wasn't much interested in opera when he was growing up in New York. And in his own operas, especially in his three so-called portrait operas—*Einstein on the Beach*, *Satyagraha* (about Gandhi), and *Akhnaten*—you can see his impatience with traditional operatic conventions. In most operas, the plots are merely an excuse for the music, something to hang the music on. So Glass banishes the story—if there is any—to the background, an outline in a program book, while symbolic images take over the stage. Glass is the first to admit that these operas are real collaborations, a long process of working out the scenes that are to be presented. At the same time, the music itself takes heretofore undreamed of precedence. There's no filler, no dull recitative that has to further the plot, and connect the great numbers. It's all meat.

Of course, this is something like what Wagner wanted too—music to break down the conventional pattern of aria and recitative. Something that flowed, non-stop, from beginning to end. And Wagner used the orchestra to convey layers of mean ing, ironies, subconscious references, commentaries on what the singers were saying, directed at the audience, often without the character's knowledge or awareness. But even at his most abstract and ideological, Wagner always based his ideas on characters, the interplay of personality. Even *Parsifal* and *Tristan* tell stories.

Philip Glass's *Akhnaten* has a great story behind it, the story of the Egyptian Pharaoh who "invented" monotheism and brought it to his kingdom for one brief shining moment. Seventeen years, actually, before the overwhelming forces of tradition, conformity, and conservatism destroyed him. Organized in conventional operatic scenes, *Akhnaten* could have turned into a hyper-romanticized Hollywood epic like *The Egyptian* (which told the same story).

So Glass and his literary and scenic collaborators, Shalom Goldman, Robert Israel, and Richard Riddell, give us the story in a printed plot summary and present instead a spectacle of symbolic images—sung, recited, mimed, and danced. The libretto consists of disconnected passages, drawn mainly from ancient writing. They're sung or spoken in English, wordless vowels, and a modern rendering of ancient Egyptian, Akkadian, and Biblical Hebrew. On records, *Akhnaten* seems a kind of symphonic cantata or oratorio, with solo and choral passages surrounded by extended minimalist tone poems: the funeral of Akhnaten's father; Akhnaten's coronation; Akhnaten pulling down the roof of the old temple. Vocal highlights include Akhnaten's love duet with his wife, Nefertiti; a Trio announcing the dawn of the new age; and Akhnaten's Hymn to Aten, the new god. Glass calls this ecstatic, almost pop-music-pretty aria the central moment of the opera and wants it to be sung in whatever language the audience speaks. At the end, a present-day guide leads tourists through the ruins, and the ancient ghosts finally join the funeral procession the opera began with.

Glass clearly realizes that the minimalist style doesn't work with conventional operatic recitative or dialogue. Its repeated modules seem more appropriate for ritual than drama. Ironically, it also reminds me of movie music. The main recurrent theme is like Bernard Herrmann's haunting music churning and churning ominously under the main titles of *Vertigo*. (Could he—or Alfred Hitchcock—have been the real father of minimalism?)

I don't think Glass's orchestration has ever been more dazzlingly colorful. Sometimes it's almost schlocky in its easy excess (the fall of Akhnaten sounds like a cross between Borodin's Polovtzian Dances and the Triumphal Scene from *Aida*). Dennis Russell Davies conducts the orchestra and chorus of the Stuttgart State Opera with amazing precision and passion. The soloists, especially early-music countertenor Paul Esswood, negotiate the intricate, insinuating harmonies brilliantly. Actor David Warrilow, as the Scribe (*The Egyptian* also begins with a Scribe), gets a bit portentous on the orotundity though.

This is one of the main problems with *Akhnaten*. For all its variety of texture and pace, the overall tone is oppressively solemn (very different from the wit of *Einstein on the Beach*). And because the music sometimes doesn't seem very deep or genuine, that solemnity often seems pretentious or melodramatic. So for all its exciting and even moving passages, the whole thing feels a little like being in church for two hours. Or like a Hollywood version of church.

Lutoslawski

February 24, 1988

Lately, I've been overcoming my preconceptions about contemporary Eastern European music—my fear that it's going to batter my eardrums with clangy church-and-shipyard music, or people's-party propaganda. I've been listening to Lutoslawski, who turns out to be more interested in beautiful textures and unusual but comprehensible structures. He even has a sense of humor. His recording *Lutoslawski Conducts Lutoslawski* includes an impressive live performance of his 1970 Cello Concerto, with the brilliant cellist Heinrich Schiff. Another important cellist, Mstislav Rostropovich, who encouraged Lutoslawski to write it, thinks it's the greatest cello concerto ever written. I can't think of a major concerto in which the solo instrument is more independent. It seems to be going through a series of adventures, like an argonaut, or an astronaut. In its long opening soliloquy, the steady ticking is like a heartbeat. But the outside world insists on intruding. The orchestra is the constantly metamorphosing enemy. A traffic jam of honking brass, a pizzicato rainfall, a jam session with the plucked cello as double bass. These interruptions keep recurring, but the ticking continues, as if time itself couldn't stop—or be stopped—for anything.

Lutoslawski is probably best known for his use of "aleatoric" or "chance" music. At certain places carefully indicated in the score, the notes may be played at whatever speed or tempo each player in the orchestra wishes. But it's more a free fall than a free-for-all. Time, at least the kind of timing you've gotten used to, is temporarily suspended. If the first section of this single-movement piece is earth, the second is air. It's filled with eerie textures: swarming birds or insects, or interstellar winds. It also has the cello's most rhapsodic music.

The last section is more confrontational, and more disjointed. The cello argues with the orchestra, at another point it seems to be chuckling to itself, or sighing, maybe even dying. It reminds me of the death of Don Quixote in Richard Strauss's tone poem (Strauss's hero is also played by a cello). Our hero recovers, but the ending is ambiguous: defiant yet also resigned.

The earliest work on the album dates back to 1955, five very brief Dance Preludes—delightful folk pieces for solo clarinet and chamber orchestra, picking up from where Bartok left off. The album ends with the tricky, ironic Double Concerto for oboe and harp, completed in 1980 and commissioned by Heinz and Ursula Holliger, its two dazzling soloists. With the composer conducting there's no questioning the authenticity and authority of these performances.

Arvo Pärt

June 1, 1988

I was driving home one night and listening to the car radio. The announcer was introducing the *Stabat Mater* by the Estonian composer Arvo Pärt. I dimly recalled seeing his name on the stark but elegant jackets of a couple of ECM records. But I'd never heard a note, and taking the line of least resistance I kept listening. I'm glad I did. What I heard was a piece of unearthly beauty—almost literally. It seemed otherworldly in its purity, in its spare means. Simple broken chords slowly repeated over and over, yet without the steely calculation or worked-up energy of minimalism. Its deep sincerity got under my skin, like a kind of modern Gregorian chant.

Pärt has said that "it is enough when a single note is beautifully played. This one note, or a silent beat, or a moment of silence, comfort me." Minimalism has never been this minimal. Pärt has written that he builds his music out of "the most primitive materials, with the triad, with one specific tonality. The three notes of the triad are like bells." He calls his method "tintinnabulation."

He composed the *Stabat Mater* in 1985. It's 25-minutes long and scored for a string trio and three very high voices—soprano, tenor, and countertenor. The performers on the recording are the well-known Russian violinist Gidon Kremer, a longtime champion of Pärt's music, violist Vladimir Mendelssohn, and cellist Thomas Demenga; the soprano is Lynne Dawson, and the two male voices belong to David James and Roger Covey-Crump of the Hilliard Ensemble, a group best known for singing early music but that has also worked extensively with Pärt. The *Stabat Mater* is a 13th-century poem in which the poet prays to identify with the suffering of Mary at the foot of the cross, and Pärt's uncanny textures and out-of-the-cradle-endlessly-rocking rhythms capture both its ecstasy and its deep poignance.

Pärt has alternated between periods of high productivity and periods of introspection and withdrawal. In the '60s he wrote primarily orchestral pieces and experimented with 12-tone music that aroused official criticism. Later his style was transformed by his exposure to early Church music. His best-known work is *Tabula Rasa*, from 1977, and the ECM recording of that was a surprise best-seller. The seven pieces on this new album, *Arbos*, were composed between 1976 and 1986. The brief title cut, *Arbos*, represents to Pärt the image of a growing tree. It's performed twice on the album, once at the beginning and once just before the Stabat Mater. It's a kind of hieratic fanfare, played by the Brass Ensemble of the Stuttgart Staatsorchester and its celebratory sound world is something like Janacek's Sinfonietta.

But it's the *Stabat Mater*, one of Pärt's three longest compositions, that is the jewel of this album. It guarantees Pärt his solitary place beside Josquin, Palestrina, Pergolesi, Haydn, Rossini, Dvorak, Liszt, and Verdi, other composers who were also moved to respond to these still moving words.

Jorge Bolet

August 17, 1988

Jorge Bolet is a familiar name on the concert circuit. He's been on it for years. Yet he's never become a great celebrity. I seem to recall his reputation as a young Turk. Lately, though, perhaps with a new revival of interest in the Romantic repertoire he excels in, Bolet has suddenly emerged as an old master—concertizing and recording more actively than ever. He's probably best known for his vibrant performances of Liszt, much of which he's recorded in the past few years for London records. There's an especially interesting Liszt CD on the Priceless label, originally recorded in 1960. His latest release is a Chopin album, including the Four Ballades, the Barcarolle, and the F-Minor Fantasy. Bolet is digitally secure, elegant, intelligent in every way. He conveys the atmosphere and the structure of each of these intricate works. He does all the right things. He builds the magnificent F-minor Fantasy, for example, to a great climax, then pulls back at the end to reveal its quiet almost childlike innocence, then a somber finality.

And yet, when I compare some of these performances with my own favorite versions, I find something lacking here—some extra ounce of interpretive giving, some little personal fillip that makes a phrase get under my skin. Take the first Ballade. Ballades are Chopin's own invention. The title sounds like a poem—a narrative poem. And Chopin's Ballades have an episodic quality—not looseness of structure so much as a sense of one event leading to another. Chopin may have derived this form from the epic poems of his Polish contemporary, Adam Mickiewicz. Bolet's pianism at the beginning of the first Ballade is lovely, but there's no impulse to make the notes sound any thing beyond lovely. Then listen to the way Czech pianist Ivan Moravec begins to tell us the story of the first Ballade.

But there's at least one great performance on the new Bolet album: the Barcarolle. What makes Bolet's version so remarkable is his daring slow tempo. There are plenty of "interpretive" readings of this wonderful piece: Venice, the Grand Canal, passion in a gondola. But Bolet is not just depicting a slow gondola ride. He seems to be making a conscious musical decision to get away from the usual programmatic, story-telling content—different, it seems to me, from his complacency and reticence in the Ballades, where the story-telling is built into the music. Here, what he tells us, *tells* us, is that the Barcarolle can be heard as pure music, that it works magnificently if you just listen to it slowly unfold its musical secrets. That neither the concert hall nor the recording studio have to turn into Venice for this piece to be understood and appreciated. If Bolet has neither the impetuosity and Italianate lilt of an Alfred Cortot, nor Dinu Lipatti's rapture or sublime grace, the insights he brings are profoundly revealing and completely convincing on their own terms.

Ives

August 31, 1988

In non-musical circles, Charles Ives may still be better known as the founder of an insurance company rather than as a composer. But gradually through the century, his music has been reaching a larger and larger audience. He may or may not be the *greatest* American composer, but he must be the most *American*. Fragments of popular songs, folk songs, ragtime, and hymn tunes pervade his music. His innovations in tonality and rhythm at the turn of the century have a peculiarly American sound. He probably developed his layered, overlapping, contrasting, and sometimes conflicting musical effects from the sound of his father's town band in Danbury, Connecticut—and all the noises going on around it. Ives's experiments influenced composers as diverse as John Cage and Elliott Carter. Or think of a Robert Altman movie like *M-A-S-H* or *The Long Goodbye,* where not only the leading actors but also phones ringing, cars honking, and other people talking in the background are equally important.

It's as if for Ives, America itself was a kind of collage—a collage of sounds and cultures, clashing and, finally, merging. His *Holidays* Symphony is one of his richest, most moving and beautiful works, and one of his most American. It's in four movements, each celebrating an American holiday. The first movement is Washington's Birthday, and what it first celebrates is the bleak beauty of winter (the symphony has sometimes been referred to as Ives's *Four Seasons*). The climax, however, is in a different mood—a rip-roaring barn dance. There's even a Jew's harp. Then the ending gets quietly nostalgic to the tune of "Goodnight, Ladies."

This pattern of quiet beginnings, lively, sometimes comic mid-sections, and inward-turning endings is repeated in the following movements. The greatest, I think, is the second: *Decoration Day*—the holiday commemorating the Civil War dead that eventually became Memorial Day. The most moving passage is the sounding of Taps before the march home from the cemetery.

The remaining movements represent a complex and boisterous Fourth of July, complete with "explosions," and a solemn and tender Thanksgiving. The symphony didn't get its first complete performance until nearly a half-a-century after it was written, April 1954, a month before Ives died.

The performance here, and of two short, complementary Ives orchestral works, *Central Park in the Dark* and *The Unanswered Question*, are by the Chicago Symphony conducted by Michael Tilson Thomas, and it's impossible to imagine anything more refined or loving or deeply imagined. These are the first recordings of the symphony from the recent critical edition of the score. *The Unanswered Question* even appears in two versions—one reconceived by Ives some thirty years after it was first written. But if this is a landmark recording, it's not just for historical or technical reasons. Tilson Thomas and the orchestra succeed in capturing the most appealing—and haunting—eccentricities of this quintessential American genius.

Ensemble Alcatraz

September 14, 1988

On the cover of *Visions & Miracles*, the new album of 13th-century Spanish music by the Ensemble Alcatraz, there's a painting of the Madonna and child with St. Sebastian and other saints. At first it looks like a medieval Spanish painting, then like a Salvador Dali. It was actually painted eight years ago. As their name suggests, this vocal and instrumental group that specializes in medieval Spanish music is based in the San Francisco Bay area, but the twist is that "alcatraz" is also an early Iberian word for "pelican." It was an old belief that the pelican fed its children with its own blood, and so it was a potent symbol for early Christians (a myth debunked as recently as the 17th-century by the great English author Sir Thomas Brown in his *Pseudodoxia Epidemica*, or Vulgar Errors). So the Ensemble Alcatraz itself combines contemporary points of view and scholarship with a devotion to early music and performance practice.

This delightful album, however, wears its scholarship lightly. Most of the pieces here are from the Cantigas de Santa Maria, the ballad-like songs in the Galician dialect commissioned by Alfonso the 10th, called the Wise, to praise the miracles of the Virgin Mary. These are fascinating pieces, with some surprisingly comic overtones. The funniest one tells the story of the heretic who stole a beautiful picture of the Virgin and "put it in his privy—then he sat down there and he made a great mistake." The devil kills him and the picture is rescued by a good Christian who is surprised to discover that in spite of its unhappy surroundings it still has a heavenly smell.

The most beautiful Cantiga narrates the story of the

workaholic seamstress who sews on Saturday despite her promise to the Virgin not to. The Holy Mother paralyzes her in punishment, and finally cures her at Chartres. The refrain, repeated after every verse, says: "Every promise that is made to the Virgin, it is just and right that it be upheld."

Some of the songs are 10 or 15 minutes long and they're all structurally repetitious, but there's a slippery shifting of rhythm and color. Besides which, the Cantigas evidently derive from so many different cultural layers—Spanish, French, Moslem, and even Jewish—that they provide a continual sense of discovery. And the performances by the five-person Ensemble are full of energy and variety, especially Susan Rode Morris, the extraordinarily resourceful soprano who can sound like a recorder or a choir boy one moment and a peasant the next. The album also includes two moralizing Church songs in Latin and a long hypnotic instrumental suite arranged from various melodies from the Cantigas. Who can say if performers sounded like this in the 13th century. Could they have been nearly as good?

Arlene Auger and Dalton Baldwin, *Love Songs*

September 28, 1988

The soprano voice of Arleen Auger is one of the loveliest on the international concert and opera scene. It has something of the sweet-cream richness of Dame Kiri te Kanawa, and Auger too made one of her most significant appearances singing at a British royal wedding (she's the only American ever to do so)—the wedding of Prince Andrew and Fergie. But Auger is a more adventurous singer than te Kanawa, and a more sensitive one. Her new album on the Delos label, called *Love Songs*, has an ominously icky cover: a clean-cut, preppy couple with their arms around each other in a field of wildflowers. But the 25 selections on the CD have been chosen with more care and intelligence than the usual recital of love songs. There are songs in German, French, Spanish, and Portuguese besides the ten in English. There are relatively familiar songs by Schumann, Mahler, and Richard Strauss and some unjustly neglected songs by Aaron Copland, a Stephen Foster gem called "Why No One To Love?", and songs by Roger Quilter, Frank Bridge, and Charles Gounod's forgotten, enchanting "Serenade."

There's a dreadful fully derivative, practically anonymous setting of Elizabeth Barrett Browning's "How Do I Love Thee, Let Me Count the Ways" by Edouard Lipp, who was head vocal coach at MGM during the Jeannette McDonald/Nelson Eddy days (Eddy was one of Lipp,'s students). You might want to program your CD player to skip over this band after you've heard it once. But there are also several theater songs that Auger seems to have special affinity for: Noel Coward's "I'll Follow My Secret Heart" and Lerner and Loewe's "Before I Gaze at You Again," Gwynevere's farewell to Lancelot in *Camelot*, which Auger turns into one of the most touching art songs on the album.

Auger's accompanist is the estimable and elegant Dalton Baldwin, probably best known for his collaborations with French tenor Gerard Souzay as well as his work with sopranos Elly Ameling and Jessye Norman.

But this album of Love Songs also reveals some of Auger's limitations, and perhaps helps to explain why she isn't more of a superstar than she is. For all the intelligence and sensitivity, the gift for languages and good diction (though she does tend to alter vowels to make her high notes come out easier), and the sheer loveliness of her sound, she tends to sing each of these 25 selections with a certain sameness, a sameness of both mood and vocal color. Everything is lovely, in fact, extremely lovely, but nothing makes you jump with excitement or melts you with charm or breaks your heart. Except for maybe the Stephen Foster and the *Camelot* number, few of the selections haunt my memory or infiltrate my sleep. Still, Auger is one our most valuable performers, even if she has yet to become one of our most cherishable.

Dubravka Tomsic

October 12, 1988

A few months ago my friend George Curran, an adventurous record collector, picked up an extremely low-priced CD on the Stradivari label. It was an album of Bach played on the piano—not so common since the early-music movement started insisting that Baroque harpsichord music should be played on the harpsichord. My friend was impressed and called to ask if I knew anything about the pianist, Dubravka Tomsic. I didn't. I called my colleague, the *Boston Globe's* music critic Richard Dyer, who is especially expert on keyboard artists. He had received several review copies but he hadn't heard them yet. When he did, he was so impressed that he called Stradivari records in Hackensack, New Jersey, and the director suggested that he telephone Tomsic herself in Yugoslavia.

Tomsic, it turns out, was born in Dubrovnik forty-eight years ago and had been a child prodigy. At 12, she came to study at Juilliard; at 15 she won a competition and played the Grieg Concerto with the New York Philharmonic; at 17 she made her solo debut at Carnegie Hall; and at 19, she returned to Yugoslavia, where she got married, had a son, and settled down to become a Yugoslavian celebrity.

Perhaps the most remarkable part of her story concerns pianist Arthur Rubinstein. When the money to continue her studies ran out, Rubinstein himself took up her cause with the Yugoslavian ambassador. As a result, no less a personage than Marshall Tito, President of Yugoslavia, agreed to subsidize Tomsic's musical education with his own money—provided that Rubinstein agree to become her teacher—which he did.

Tomsic's recordings are certainly remarkable—fleet, elegant, extremely lyrical, yet sometimes hair-raising in their manic energy, as at the opening of Beethoven's *Waldstein* Sonata. Tomsic has a glorious singing tone—a little like Rubinstein's—yet with a musical sensitivity that reminds me more of musicians as profound in their different ways as Dinu Lipatti, Glenn Gould, Artur Schnabel, and especially Harold Samuel, the great Bach pianist of the 1930s. At the moment, there are some ten compact discs of her recordings available on two labels, Stradivari and the Vienna Master Series on PMG. Several of the pieces are on both labels. They demonstrate a remarkable range: Bach, a Mozart concerto, Scarlatti, Beethoven (three sonatas and two concertos), Chopin, Tchaikovsky, and the Grieg Concerto. She plays a nearly 9-minute Scarlatti sonata in F-minor whose repeated phrases I find so haunting and mysterious I can't stop listening to it.

Her performance of the Grieg Concerto is one of the best I've ever heard—maybe the best. Her name is missing from the record label and the liner notes, but Stradivari records promises that this omission will soon be corrected. Besides, anyone who's come to know Dubravka Tomsic's work from her other recordings will soon realize that the fresh, imaginative phrasing and lilting, rippling sweetness of these thrice-familiar tunes couldn't be by anyone else.

There are several new Dubravka Tomsic recordings in the works and next summer she's returning to America to open the Newport Music Festival.

Kurtág

November 9, 1988

Last summer at the Monadnock Music festival, in New Hampshire, and a week later at the Festival of Contemporary Music at Tanglewood, the hills of New England were alive with the sound of György Kurtág. Audiences were treated to—or confronted with—the first American performances of the Hungarian composer's song cycle *Kafka Fragments*, sung by Adrienne Csengery, the soprano for whom they were written and who seems to be Kurtág's Muse. I couldn't get to those performances, but people were excited about them. There isn't much Kurtág on records, but I did find an LP on the Hungaroton label made a couple of years ago that included Csengery in two earlier Kurtág song cycles: *Messages of the late R.V. Troussova* and *Scenes from a novel*.

Like the Kafka series, which contains many short fragments excerpted from Kafka's letters and diaries, both of these cycles consist mainly of short, Haiku-like poems in Russian by the poet Dalos Rimma. *Messages of the late R.V. Troussova* is the more ambitious of the two cycles: 21 poems divided into three sections: Loneliness, A Little Erotic, and the longest section, Bitter Experience—Delight and Grief. The poems reticently trace the progress of an extremely sensual, occasionally tender, but ultimately unhappy relationship. The vocal line owes a lot—maybe too much—to the hyper-Romantic Expressionism of Berg and Schoenberg (there's even a little bit of the musicalized speech inflections Schoenberg called "*sprechstimme*"). Csengery, who has sung Mozart heroines at Glyndebourne and gone on to heavier roles, is a powerful interpreter. But there's even greater variety, freshness, and delicacy in the accompaniment, played on this recording by the greatest chamber group in the world, the Ensemble InterContemporain under the direction of its founder, Pierre Boulez. There are also solo passages for the cimbalom, a Hungarian version of the dulcimer, a stringed instrument struck with hammers. The soloist, Marta Fabian, makes it feel both sinister and nostalgic.

Here are two consecutive poems from the Bitter Experience section, complete. The first, "Love me," says: "Love me,/Forgive me—/ My wishes are so simple." The second, called "Account," says: "An eye for an eye,/love for love;/And then/the sweet shame/of the balance/paid/by installments." The cycle ends with more resignation than bitterness: "For everything/we did together at some time—/I'm paying."

The other cycle on the album, *Scenes from a novel*, uses only three instruments—cimbalom, violin, and double-bass. Kurtág's inventiveness undercuts the poetic melodrama—he even makes jokes. The album closes with an independent song, the brief "Farewell," poignantly sung by Csengery, who is accompanied this time by the composer himself.

Adriana Lecouvreur

July 10, 1989

Cilea isn't a composer I'd ordinarily cross the street to hear, but in 1973 a friend of mine talked me into driving from Boston to Newark, New Jersey, for a production of Cilea's most famous opera, *Adriana Lecouvreur*. Or rather, for the soprano in the title role—the legendary Magda Olivero, the singer Cilea preferred over all others in this part. Olivero had been a major star in Italy before she retired in 1941. Cilea himself wanted to see her as Adriana one more time. But when she finally returned to the stage, Cilea had died. It was this second leg of her career that brought her to America. When she appeared in Newark, she was at least 63 years old. You'd better see her now, my friend advised, you'll probably never have another chance. Who could have guessed that her career was far from over, that two years *later* she'd make her Metropolitan Opera *debut* as Puccini's Tosca? But she never made a commercial recording of *Adriana Lecouvreur*, and this performance turned out to be her farewell to this role. Fortunately, just as in the movie *Diva*, someone in the Newark audience snuck in a tape recorder. That performance has just been released by Legato Classics on a set of compact discs. So we now have Magda Olivero as the 18th-century French actress Adriana Lecouvreur, singing "I am the humble servant of the creative Genius," the aria every soprano believes is about herself.

Adriana Lecouvreur was composed in 1902, two years after *Tosca*, and they're both cut from the same melodramatic cloth. Both are about stars whose lovers are out of favor with the ruling political powers. Both heroines are destroyed by their own mistaken jealousy. Floria Tosca leaps off a tower, Adriana inhales flowers poisoned by her rival. Cilea's opera isn't as dramatic or as inventively orchestrated as Puccini's. I think it has only two real tunes, repeated over and over. And so on.

The tunes, though, are pretty and gratifying to sing. Like *Tosca*, *Adriana* was a major vehicle for Caruso. The big tenor aria even sounds like the big tenor aria in *Tosca*. Olivero's tenor in Newark was the young Placido Domingo, and I've never heard him sound more spectacular. He created such an uproar he had to sing one of his arias twice, something the Met would never have allowed.

The sound is obviously not ideal—a nearby seat squeaks louder than some of the singing. But the performance is unforgettable. Olivero was a great diva in the 19th-century tradition. Every gesture made a large theatrical point. I can still see her shawl draping around her shoulder in time to the music, as if she had trained it to do that. You can hear the grandeur of her poses in her evaporating pianissimos and swelling climaxes. At 63, she could still give even her stupendous young co-star a run for the roses.

Alkan

July 19, 1989

The composer Alkan, whose real name was Charles Henri Valentin Morhange, is probably better known for how he died than for anything he wrote. A recluse most of his life, he was apparently crushed to death when he was reaching up to the top shelf for a volume of the Talmud, the encyclopedic collection of Jewish civil and religious law, and the entire bookcase collapsed on him. Alkan was considered one of the great piano virtuosos of the 19th-century, sometimes spoken of in the same breath with Liszt. His music, too, is extremely difficult. There's a piano concerto, for instance, for piano alone, that is, the piano itself also plays the part of the entire orchestra. One of the reasons Alkan is now so little known may be his dedication to playing and writing for an instrument that had only a very brief history—the so-called "pédalier" or pedal-piano. This is something like a grand piano rigged up like an organ with a pedal board so the bass notes can be played with the feet. Some of Alkan's later music is for either pedal-piano *or* organ. A new album of this forgotten music has been released on the Nimbus label. The performer is the young British organist Kevin Bowyer, and the music is fascinating.

Alkan tended to compose in shorter forms. The longest of the Thirteen Prayers is under seven minutes. The second selection on this album are the eight Little Preludes on the Eight Modes of Plainchant, and all eight together last little over seven minutes. But they are all delightfully inventive and, like all the other pieces on the album, beautifully structured. These little preludes are the only works Alkan published directly for organ. Ironically, they're just for keyboard, no pedals.

The longest piece on the Alkan album is the powerful fourteen-minute Impromptu on Luther's "A Mighty Fortress Is Our God." And even this piece, probably Alkan's last and greatest work for pedal-piano, builds to its magnificent final fugue from a series of brief but intricately woven variations on Martin Luther's famous hymn.

All these pieces are vividly played by Kevin Bowyer on the Salisbury Cathedral organ. But what's most impressive about these selections is their astonishing variety of feeling and color. They are celebratory and sinister, grandiloquent and naive. Some seem conservatively rooted in the 19th-century. Others sound astonishingly modern with their fascinating textures and harmonies. There are even premonitions of minimalism, though no minimalist I can think of ever wrote anything so short. Nimbus gives us a generous playing time of almost 74 minutes. Unlike minimalism, when it's over, you want to hear more.

Kleiber Waltzes

September 6, 1989

No one can trace the history of the waltz with absolute certainty. The word "waltz" itself comes from the Latin "volvere"—to turn. Couples who were willing to risk a public display of intimacy between the sexes were circling the dance floors before the end of the 18th-century. In 1819, Carl Maria von Weber's *Invitation to the Dance*, for piano, was probably the model for all subsequent concert waltzes. But of course it's the Strauss family that we associate most with the Viennese waltz. Papa Johann was a violist and conductor. He was a largely self-taught musician, trained as a book-binder; he died at 45. His older son, also Johann, became the Waltz King. His more melancholy younger son, Josef, died at 43. The Strausses didn't invent the Viennese waltz, but they developed it into the elegant, complex, and richly colorful form we know.

Strauss waltzes are no less than symphonic tone poems. They can evoke a poetic setting—like the Vienna woods or the beautiful blue Danube—or an entire social order. What more vivid symbol of the Hapsburg monarchy than the *Emperor Waltz?* It's a far cry from the beer gardens where Viennese waltzes first caught on. If you've ever heard any of the old recordings by the great Viennese conductors—Bruno Walter, Felix Weingartner, Erich Kleiber—you know what buoyant and magical—even profound—experiences the best waltzes can be, not at all the stainless steel oom-pah-pahs of today's Pops concerts.

This new Strauss album, which was recorded live at the Vienna Philharmonic's 1989 New Year's Concert, gives me some hope for the future of Viennese light music. The conductor is Carlos Kleiber (Erich Kleiber's son), a wonderful musician who doesn't seem to like recording studios or crossing the Atlantic (he made his Metropolitan Opera debut only in 1988). One of his few recordings is his much admired version of Johann Strauss's most famous operetta, *Die Fledermaus*. The Overture to that is one of the delights of this new recording, as is a selection that includes not only famous waltzes but such rarities as Josef Strauss's *Chatterbox*, the *Jockey*, and the *Dragonfly* polka.

Carlos Kleiber has many of his father's gifts. These performances balance discipline and flexibility. They have that teasing lift on the second beat—that instant of weightlessness most modern orchestras can't seem to get right. Individual moments keep their special delicacy, yet each piece seems built on a large and expansive scale. On some of those old recordings from half a century ago, though, I also hear a quality of tenderness in the playing, a knowing affection for the style that gives the upswings a little more zip, that makes the nostalgia a shade more mysterious and sad. Those old records remind us that some things may be lost forever. Carlos Kleiber, in his moving performance of *Artist's Life*, proves he's learned *that* from his father too.

Gubaidulina

October 18, 1989

In the spring of 1988, controversial opera director Sarah Caldwell engineered an enormous three-week festival of Soviet music and dance in Boston called *Making Music Together*. It was a tremendous cooperative effort, with both American and Soviet artists performing a phenomenal range of contemporary Soviet works. For me, the big discovery was Sofia Gubaidulina, the only woman composer represented. I think the single greatest work performed at the festival was her violin concerto, *Offertorium*. It's a hypnotic and deeply spiritual work in one movement, just over half an hour long. It begins with her setting of the famous "royal theme" from Bach's *The Musical Offering*, which sounds like Anton Webern's famous 1935 orchestration of it. But just as the orchestra approaches the last note of the theme, the solo violin interrupts and launches into its own complex variation.

The Russians translate "Offertorium" as "sacrifice." Each time Gubaidulina repeats the Bach theme, it loses a note. She calls this "the theme offering itself up as a sacrifice." Finally, the theme is reconstructed in reverse. The concerto ends with a heartbreaking hymn. The last fading violin sound is the high D, played three octaves higher, that was missing from the end of the very first statement of the theme.

The recording is very much an international venture. The Soviet violinist Gidon Kremer is the soloist. Gubaidulina wrote the piece for him ten years ago, and it's the greatest performance by him I've ever heard. The Swiss conductor Charles Dutoit leads the Boston Symphony Orchestra, and it's a stunning achievement for everyone.

The other Gubaidulina piece on this CD is her 1987 *Hommage . . . T.S. Eliot*, for octet and soprano. This marvel of invention in seven movements is based on passages from Eliot's deepest spiritual testament, *Four Quartets*. Much of Gubaidulina's music tends to have a religious, even mystical aspect—something that turns out not to be as rare as you'd think in Soviet music. Interestingly, she earns her living by writing movie music, which she says helps give all her music a sense of character. Fascinating sounds and textures punctuate everything she writes. Her adventurous technical vocabulary makes a lot of electronic music sound pedestrian in comparison. The splendid American soprano Christine Whittlesey sings Eliot's "frigid purgatorial fires/Of which the smoke is roses and the flame is briars," flames we can hear in Gubaidulina's creepy pizzicatos.

In the Russian festival, Sofia Gubaidulina had the quietest voice. And the strongest.

November 29, 1989

A little over a year ago, I never heard of Sofia Gubaidulina. Now I can't wait to hear more of her remarkable compositions. For me, she was the major discovery of last year's Soviet-American Music Festival in Boston. More of her music has recently become available. On the new Art & Electronics label, distributed by MCA, there are three of her works that feature the cello and a Russian folk instrument called the bayan, which looks and sounds like an accordion. But instead of having buttons on one side and a keyboard on the other, the bayan has buttons on both sides. Gubaidulina uses this instrument to create an extraordinary range of sounds, from flights of innumerable bees to eerie, *Twilight-Zone* effects, in which the bellows move but no keys are pressed. It's like someone breathing.

Gubaidulina's music is often deeply religious. One reason she chose these particular instruments is that playing them suggests an image of crucifixion—the bayan moving across the chest, the cello bow crossing the strings. A piece called *Et expecto*, for solo bayan, is about the Second Coming. The ending is like an exhalation. The cello and organ crossing paths in *In croceis* means to suggest the cross itself. The most ambitious piece on the album, *The Seven Last Words*, is a seven-movement work for bayan, cello, and string orchestra and depicts the last moments of Christ on the cross. It was suggested by—and quotes from—*Die sieben Worte*, a Passion by the great pre-Bach composer Heinrich Schütz. In the Soviet Union, the religious element is downplayed and Gubaidulina's *Seven Last Words* is known only as "Partita for Cello and Bayan." But the musical program is quite explicit. We hear the earthquake in the rumbling, shaking tremolos of the bayan; Christ's spirit ascends from the cross as the cello bow moves up the strings to the bridge, then passes beyond it. The climax of *Seven Last Words* is one of the most harrowing depictions of physical and spiritual suffering in music.

These works build with a creepy, terrifying intensity toward cosmic struggles between good and evil, life and death. The bayan player is Friedrich Lips, and he's one of the most expressive instrumentalists I've ever heard. He can make his bayan sound like anything from a grand organ to a voice crying in the wilderness. He's even written a book called *The Art of Accordion Playing*. The cellist, Vladimir Tonkha, is equally impressive. Another great cellist, Yo-Yo Ma, plays Gubaidulina's *Rejoice!* with violinist Gidon Kremer on a new album for CBS. Joy, Gubaidulina says, is the transition to another plane of existence. She embodies this idea in her use of harmonics. That's where you change the pitch on a stringed instrument by changing not your place on the string but the amount of pressure on it. In a movement called "Rejoice with joy," Joy has been only tentatively achieved. Gubaidulina's music, though, suggests that joy may never be exactly what we expect it to be.

Busoni Concerto

November 22, 1989

One of the most mysterious and original figures in modern music is the turn-of-the-century Italian piano virtuoso and composer Ferruccio Busoni. He was born in 1866 and died in 1924, the same year as Puccini. They even both wrote operas called *Turandot*. But there's very little further similarity. Puccini was purely a man of the theater, a popularizer. Busoni was an idealist, a theorist, an internationalist, and a great teacher. His favorite composers were the unlikely duo of Mozart and Liszt. Today recordings of Busoni playing the piano are rare and his major compositions are rarely performed. He's probably known best for his Bach transcriptions and his other ferociously difficult work based on Bach, the *Fantasia contrappuntistica*. One of Busoni's most notorious pieces is his Piano Concerto, and there's a new recording by the Cleveland Orchestra under Christoph von Dohnanyi with pianist Garrick Ohlsson that may give it a new lease on life.

Busoni completed his Piano Concerto in 1904, and it immediately broke new ground. Most piano concertos had only three movements until Brahms added a fourth to make the concerto more symphonic. Busoni's concerto has five. Beethoven used a chorus in his Ninth Symphony and a piano in his ambitious Choral Fantasy. But no one before (or, to my knowledge, after) Busoni has employed a chorus in a piano concerto. This grandiose 70-minute work, according to Busoni's original Mahler-like outline, depicts the ages of man. Before he dropped the titles, Busoni was going to call the first movement "Expectation before the Glory, the Mystery and the Call to Life." The second and fourth movements, based on the same tarantella, are manic scherzos: "Youth with Its Thousand Fantastic Plans" and "The Final Refuge of the Wild Lust of Life." These movements surround a mystical slow movement: "Maturity with Its Serious Struggle for Inner Concord." Busoni said this movement was inspired by the melody he once heard entering the Strasbourg Cathedral at sunset.

The last movement is the "Conscious and Dispassionate Withdrawal into the Infinite." An unseen male chorus sings passages from the Danish poet Adam Gottlob Ohlenschläger's Alladin: "Lift your hearts. Feel Allah near."

The music may not be consistently inspired, but the performance is consistently gripping. Dohnanyi holds the entire massive structure together. He can even make the Cleveland Orchestra sound vulgar when he has to, and that's when the Concerto is the most fun. Ohlsson plays with extraordinary finesse, yet has astounding reserves of energy. He once said playing the Busoni Concerto was like playing three Brahms concertos in a row, but his effort always sounds effortless. He gives one of the most stupendous keyboard performances on record.

Horowitz

May 23, 1990

Vladimir Horowitz was probably the most famous concert pianist of this century. He died last November at the age of 86. Sony Classics, which used to be CBS, has just issued an album called *Horowitz: The Last Recording*. In the liner notes, pianist Murray Perahia writes about a performer who, he says, "gave himself completely through his music and who confided his deepest emotions through his playing. His tone, especially if heard live, had such a dramatic presence—a speaking quality—that you felt you were listening directly to his most private thoughts."

Horowitz, however, was not a pianist I associated with deep emotions, private thoughts, or a speaking quality. I think of Horowitz as representing just the opposite—a phenomenal virtuosity whose brilliant surface reveals almost no interest in the psychology, the philosophical meaning, or the structure of the music.

Perahia goes on to say that Horowitz's playing "was always changing, always evolving." But this recording made just before his death reinforces the impression that throughout a career of more than seventy years, Horowitz hardly changed at all. He played practically everything in the same style. Or two styles. Anything that didn't require drop-dead virtuoso display, he delivered with a precious, small-scale daintiness, as if Mozart composed only for musical-snuff-boxes.

Would you be surprised if I confess that I've never been a great fan of Vladimir Horowitz? I think the mellowing some people heard in his later years was more the result of diminishing strength, even a diminished technical capacity, rather than new and searching insights. In the piano music I love most, there's never been a piece I didn't prefer played by someone else. Still, you can't deny the Horowitz fascination—the unmistakable color of his sound, his nervy energy. What I admire most about *The Last Recording* is that Horowitz plays only works he never recorded before, including an edgy version of Chopin's famous *Fantaisie-Impromptu*.

The musical curiosities are two items by Liszt. Horowitz could be an astonishing Liszt player. But here, instead of dazzling virtuoso pieces, he plays two obscure works based on themes by other composers. There's Liszt's transcription of Wagner's "Liebestod," the "Love-Death," from *Tristan und Isolde*. But Horowitz—with Liszt's help—makes Wagner sound less erotic than melodramatic and sentimental. I prefer Liszt's melancholy variations on Bach's Cantata No. 12, *Weinen, Klagen, Sorgen, Zagen* ("weeping, wailing, sorrows, and fears").

Sony offers virtually no information about the music itself—not even a translation of the Bach title. The only commentary is the unqualified tribute, in four languages, by Murray Perahia, who also happens to record for Sony. Maybe because this album doesn't emphasize the big bravura showpieces, it seems a little dull, elegant but monotonous. Of course, for some listeners, just the fact that it's Horowitz will be interesting enough.

Music in Time of War

January 30, 1991

I've been very moved by the way musicians in Boston have responded to the war. The cast of the Peter Sellars production of *The Marriage of Figaro* at the Boston Opera Theater has a statement in the program about how the opera's war between the sexes "holds a small mirror to all the brutality, bullying, greed, and self-righteousness of the larger world." They say Mozart tells us that although it seems impossible to say no to war, peace is within our reach. At the annual Mozart Birthday and AIDS benefit concert at Emmanuel Church, pianist Russell Sherman, speaking against the war, said he found in music a source of balance and reason we need to hear. In a time of crisis, great art becomes more, not less, important.

The night after the first Scud missile hit Israel, I wasn't much in the mood for music. But one of my favorite groups, the Cantata Singers, was doing one of my favorite pieces, Arnold Schoenberg's choral work "Friede auf Erden" ("Peace on Earth"). So I went. Conductor David Hoose led an unusually clear and unusually impassioned performance. There was a warm round of applause. Then an amazing thing happened. The applause wouldn't die down. The audience began to stand, one by one. There were handkerchiefs in many hands. It's as if it were slowly dawning on us what this sublime, spiritual music really meant, and how much we all needed to be there together, listening to it. Then without even looking at us, Hoose returned to the stage and signaled the chorus to sing it again. This time, we all understood from the beginning.

The Cantata Singers concert had been planned long before war broke out. But it was clear that in some deep way, the music was responding to the world crisis, that making and listening to music was a way of responding to world crisis. Two days later, there was a benefit concert by the Boston Philharmonic. This is a remarkable community orchestra conducted by Benjamin Zander. The special guests were Yo-Yo Ma, who has performed with Zander numerous times, and pop star Bobby McFerrin, who conducted the orchestra in a jubilant performance of the Scherzo movement of the Beethoven Ninth Symphony. Then Ma and McFerrin teamed up for duets and improvisations. Yo-Yo Ma played the "Ave Maria" on the cello while Bobby McFerrin sang in the sweetest counterpoint the first prelude from Bach's Well-Tempered Clavier.

The main event was Dvorak's elegiac Cello Concerto. With Zander conducting, Yo-Yo Ma played one of the most soulful, singing performances I've ever heard. This heavenly music and music-making is not just consoling. I think it makes us feel a little less helpless. We can say to ourselves: if the human spirit is capable of such sweetness and generosity, such harmony, there's still a chance it might survive.

Boston Chamber Music Society, Brahms Quintets

August 15, 1991

There's some wonderful chamber music that we don't get to hear as often as we'd like because in order to perform it, a traditional string quartet ensemble would have to invite additional string, wind, or keyboard players. To deal with this problem, larger and more flexible groups like the Chamber Music Society of Lincoln Center and the Boston Chamber Music Society were formed. The Boston group, now in its tenth year, has about a dozen regulars, and while they haven't found the perfect configuration for every composer—Mozart, for instance, tends to elude them—their Brahms has been exceptional. So they were wise to devote the first two recordings of their projected 10-disc series to Brahms.

In the basic classical repertory from Bach to Bartok, Brahms may still be the most controversial composer. The cholesterol level may be too high for contemporary taste. There's a heaviness-to-sweetness ratio that some people may find unhealthy. But these performances are warm, flowing, and impassioned without the thick over-assertiveness that often ruins Brahms. Sometimes they even make Brahms sound quite modern. Two of Brahms's greatest chamber works, a trio and a quintet, center on the clarinet. The Boston Chamber Music Society's eloquent clarinetist is Thomas Hill. His partners in the Clarinet Trio are pianist Mihai Lee and cellist Ronald Thomas (who is the co-founder of the group). Thomas, along with the elegant violinists Arturo Delmoni and Lynn Chang, and that vigorous viola virtuoso Marcus Thompson join Hill in the Clarinet Quintet.

The second Boston Chamber Music Society disc includes the Piano Trio in B major and the C-minor Piano Quartet. The Trio, Opus 8, is one of Brahms's earliest works, and it retains its youthful quality even though Brahms thoroughly revised it thirty-five years later. The pianist here is Christopher O'Riley, who is one of the most exciting and satisfying younger performers on the circuit. The Trio gains in size and dynamism from O'Riley's presence.

Brahms's tragic C-minor Quartet probably began as his expression of sorrow over the death of his friend Robert Schumann and his own hopeless love for Clara Schumann. If this sounds like a 1940s movie, you're right. It was *Song of Love*, starring Katherine Hepburn, Paul Henried, and Robert Walker as Brahms. But it wasn't as moving as this performance of the Quartet. The performers are Arturo Delmoni, Marcus Thompson, Ronald Thomas, and Mihai Lee. They're all playing at their extraordinary best, and Northeastern Records has recorded them superbly. The next recording by the Boston Chamber Music Society will be trios by Tchaikovsky and Shostakovich— I look forward to it.

Josephine Barstow, *Opera Finales*

April 16, 1992

The world premiere of Puccini's *Turandot* took place at La Scala in 1926, nearly a year and a half after the composer's death. Toscanini conducted. It was already a highly charged evening. Mussolini had refused to attend the premiere because Toscanini had refused to play the fascist anthem, "Giovinezza." Just before the final scene of the opera, right after "Nessun dorma" and the death of the servant girl Liu, Toscanini put down his baton and announced to the audience that this was the point where Puccini had died. He then stepped down from the podium. Puccini's inability to complete *Turandot* certainly caused a lot of trouble, considering how little music he actually had left to write. Toscanini was in charge, and the young composer Franco Alfano was not his first choice to complete the opera. Toscanini evidently made Alfano expand his original ending, and then Toscanini himself abridged it. It's this shortened version that gets performed.

The plot of *Turandot* concerns a Chinese ice-princess who doesn't want to marry. She agrees, however, to marry the man who can answer her three riddles. Whoever tries and fails, though, pays with his head. When a mysterious prince answers the riddles, Turandot is horrified. The prince offers to put his life in her hands if she can discover his name. Finally, he tells her his name and she realizes that she's in love with him. It's the love duet, which uses earlier themes from the opera, that Puccini didn't finish, and even with a great actress like Maria Callas, the ending has always seemed an anti-climax.

But Alfano's original ending is four minutes longer than Toscanini's abbreviated version, and it's really much more psychologically convincing. It fleshes out Turandot's reactions, gives her a little more time to accept her fate, to admit that she's fallen in love. And now we can actually compare the moment of Turandot's first kiss on the wonderful old Callas recording with the same passage in Alfano's original version, on a new recording with the British soprano Josephine Barstow, the Italian tenor Lando Bartolini, and John Mauceri conducting the Scottish Opera Orchestra and Chorus.

Barstow is an intensely theatrical singer. She and Mauceri help convince us that this is the better ending. Of course, no one knows what Puccini himself might actually have written. This London compact disc also includes the great finales from Richard Strauss's *Salome*, Luigi Cherubini's *Medea*, and, best of all, Leos Janacek's *The Makropoulos Case*. Barstow is quite terrifying as the 337-year-old Elina Makropoulos, who finally has to face her death.

Giulio Cesare

April 26, 1993

Peter Sellars's production of Handel's *Julius Caesar* may be the best thing he's ever done. It's one of Handel's greatest works: an endless flow of melody, comedy, heroic spectacle, and poignant interior drama. Sellars updates the story of Julius Caesar's encounter with the young Cleopatra, the assassination of Pompey, and Roman imperialism in the Middle East. His contemporary images are sometimes savagely satirical. Caesar is Reaganized. Cleopatra is a bathing beauty whose brains aren't all in her bikini. Pompey's young son Sesto is a kind of preppy Hamlet who turns radical revolutionary when he has to avenge his father's death. These work because the ironies in the opera itself seem very modern. Handel's awareness of the tragic cost of political life looms behind all the jokes. Sellars assembled one of the finest casts I've ever seen in an opera production, and with Craig Smith's impassioned and dramatically paced conducting, the five hours fly by. PBS made a big mistake not to air it on television.

The dazzling soprano Susan Larson, a Sellars regular, is Cleopatra. Wearing a low-cut gold lamé, gown, she seduces Caesar by descending from the rafters like a Ziegfeld girl sitting on the hook of a giant building crane. Who is Caesar not to be ravished by her? Caesar is magnificently sung and powerfully acted by the extraordinary countertenor Jeffrey Gall. Early music star Drew Minter gives the most vivid performance of his career as the magenta-haired, sexually ambivalent punk-rocker Ptolemy. And mezzo-soprano Lorraine Hunt, in the male role of Sesto, is hair-raising in his ferocious determination to destroy his father's killers.

One of the great moments of 18th-century opera is the duet she sings with contralto Mary Westbrook-Geha, who plays the matronly but equally vengeful Cornelia, Pompey's widow and Sesto's mother. They've been dragged off as political prisoners. Their achingly beautiful goodbyes blend in mutual lament. This scene is magnificent. Sellars has the two singers weave in and around each other in a haunting choreography of pain.

His camerawork, however, doesn't always show off his staging to best advantage. His relentless close-ups and cross-cutting never establish the location of a scene, and the camera doesn't always flow with the music. Still, the more you watch, the more what you see makes sense on its own terms. At the end, when Caesar and Cleopatra are giving their first public press conference together, TV seems the most appropriate medium. And when all the characters, including the ones who've been killed, re-emerge to join in the final chorus of joy, the effect may be even more shattering on a TV screen than it was in the theater.

Krenek

November 29, 1993

When the Nazis came to power, they banned some of the most progressive music as "Entartete"— "degenerate." Careers were cut short; many musicians were exterminated in the holocaust. London Records has just started a new series called ENTARTETE music. The first issue was the most popular opera of Weimar Germany, Ernst Krenek 's jazz opera, *Jonny spielt auf*, which can be translated as something like "Johnny Strikes Up" or "Johnny Plays On." It was both an innovative and scandalous work. On stage there were a car, a train, a radio, and a telephone; the plot included an interracial affair; and the orchestra had a saxophone. The public went wild. By 1930, it had more than 70 productions, and the Nazis had a fit.

Jonny spielt auf is actually a very peculiar work. It's both highly symbolic, like a late Ibsen play, but it's also the 1927 ancestor of those low-budget rock 'n roll movies, except here it's jazz that has to be defended from the squares. The title character, Jonny, is an amoral black jazz violinist. He steals an Amati violin from a famous but obnoxious virtuoso which complicates an already complicated romance between a composer and a soprano. The composer is obviously Krenek's satirical portrait of his own earlier, more conservative self, a man who would rather escape to a glacier than face the real world. When he finally turns away from that symbolic glacier, he wins the love and respect of the soprano. At the end, they take the train to America, the very train that the angry violin virtuoso falls under—right on stage. But the real triumph is the Music of the Future. The final tableau was one of the most famous images of its time—Jonny fiddling on top of a gigantic globe of the world.

Unlike some less fortunate composers, Krenek migrated to America and died here a couple of years ago at the age of 90. *Jonny spielt auf* survived the Nazis. It was even performed at the Met. But it doesn't survive its own dated material. The nose-thumbing use of jazz, minstrel-show, and popular dance music is still delightful. But its more serious side, especially a 12-minute monologue sung by the composer, alone on his glacier, is pretty tedious. Krenek's greatest importance may be his influence on Kurt Weill's *Threepenny Opera*, which was produced a year later. But *Jonny spielt auf* is a cultural landmark and it's good to have a complete recording. The cast, conductor Lothar Zagrosek, and the Leipzig Gewandhaus Orchestra are good, especially Krister St. Hill as Jonny. There's also a single disc of excerpts reissued by Vanguard—with such familiar opera stars as Evelyn Lear as the soprano, Thomas Stewart as the violinist, and Lucia Popp as Jonny's girlfriend. The performance is, on the whole, livelier and more theatrical, but it's missing some of Krenek's jazziest music.

Leon Fleisher

February 23, 1994

Listening to Leon Fleisher's new solo recital disk, you're immediately struck by how unusual it is. Fleisher's playing is unusually brilliant, and unusually musical. The selections themselves are unusual: little-known 19th- and 20th-century piano pieces in a wide variety of styles. Most unusual of all is that the pieces are all written to be played only with the left hand. Fleisher is probably the greatest pianist this country has ever produced. He's also the most famous living virtuoso of piano music for the left-hand. Nearly thirty years ago, at the height of his career, he developed Repetitive Stress Syndrome in his right hand and essentially had to stop performing the standard repertoire. He has continued to play concertos for the left hand—he's also become a distinguished conductor. But this is his first solo album in nearly three decades, and it's a stunning achievement.

The disk begins with a familiar sound. The themes are from Bach's Chromatic Fantasy and the Liszt Sonata. But the piece is actually by the Austro-Hungarian composer Jeno Takacs—his Toccata and Fugue, written in 1951. Practically every piece on the album is influenced by Bach counterpoint or Lisztian Romanticism—or both. The real treasure is a moving, serious-minded, and harmonically adventurous transcription by Brahms of Bach's monumental Chaconne from the D-minor Partita for solo violin. Brahms felt he could capture on the piano the difficulty and daring of the music by concentrating it all in the left hand. By coincidence, he sent it to his friend Clara Schumann at a time, late in her career, when her right arm was suffering from tendinitis.

Everything else on Leon Fleisher's album is from the 20th-century. Robert Saxton's *Chacony* was written in 1988 for Fleisher himself. The other composers include Scriabin, Saint-Saens, and Vladimir Horowitz's teacher, Felix Blumenfeld, who was paralyzed on one side. The album ends spectacularly with pianist-composer Leopold Godowski's 12-minute *Symphonic Metamorphoses of the "Schatz-Walzer"* (from Johann Strauss's *Gypsy Baron*). I'm sure I'm not the first person to say it, but this album proves once again that Leon Fleisher has more music in his left hand than some pianists have in their entire bodies.

Angela Gheorghio and Roberto Alagna

September 3, 1996

They're young, they're beautiful, and they're in love. They're also opera singers. This sensational couple is Rumanian soprano Angela Gheorghiu and Sicilian-French tenor Roberto Alagna. They got married on April 26, between performances at the Met. It's been a long time since a soprano and a tenor were publicly in love with each other just as their careers were taking off. Gheorghiu and Alagna met in 1992 in their Covent Garden debuts as the young lovers in *La Boheme*. They practically spent their honeymoon onstage. The day after they were married they appeared together at the Met both in *Boheme* and on the televised 6-hour James Levine 25th-anniversary gala, singing the enchanting "Cherry Duet" from Mascagni's *L'Amico Fritz*. They were adorable—loving and tenderly attentive. This duet is also one of the highlights of their new disc, though they're not as charming as another married couple, Pia Tassinari and Ferruccio Tagliavini, whom the composer himself chose for his famous recording half-a-century ago. And conductor Richard Armstrong isn't as sensitive as either Mascagni or Levine. It's nevertheless an endearing souvenir of a happy moment for these appealing young singers.

Gheorghiu and Alagna's stories are already the stuff of myth. Alagna is 32, a Sicilian from Paris. Two years ago, his first wife died of a brain tumor, leaving him with a small daughter. He was probably not discovered, as is frequently reported, in a pizzeria. But he evidently really was inspired by Mario Lanza movies on TV and really did teach himself to sing by listening to records. His voice is clear and focused, with strong Italianate high notes and impressively crisp and natural diction, especially in French. But he can also sound dry, and though he's said to be a good stage actor, on disc he tends to let everything sound the same. In a witty Offenbach aria, his high notes go into a disconnected overdrive, and it's hard to tell the aria was meant to be funny.

Gheorghiu is 30, and went to the conservatory in Bucharest. She was also married before, to someone the columnists call a "plumbing engineer." Her voice is warm, fluid, and flexible, though her intonation can get a little edgy. She looks like a ballerina, with long dark hair and fragile doe-eyes—perfect for Verdi and Puccini's consumptive heroines. Her recording and video of *La Traviata* have been getting consistently better reviews than Alagna's solo album. Her new solo album is also a little disappointing. Still, it's as a team that Alagna and Gheorghiu have captured our imaginations. In the "Tonight" duet from *West Side Story*, their English is a little shaky but they're better matched than Kiri te Kanawa and Jose Carreras on Bernstein's own recording. They're touching and ardent in the "Garden Scene" from *Faust* and, despite a sluggish tempo, ecstatic in the love duet between Dido and Aeneas—also in French—from Berlioz's *The Trojans*.

It'll be fun to see what happens to Gheorghiu and Alagna. So far, they seem to be handling the hype with good grace. Everyone wants them to succeed. And if they do, it'll be better than fun.

[PS. Gheorghiu and Alagna separated in 2009 and announced they were back together in 2011.]

David Helfgott

March 7, 1997

Last Tuesday night, pianist David Helfgott, whose painful personal history and apparent triumph over mental illness are depicted in the Oscar-nominated movie *Shine*, launched his 18-concert North-American "Celebration of Life" tour in Boston's Symphony Hall. I confess, I was curious. I didn't care much for *Shine* (which I found coldly manipulative), and I'm not a fan of either the soundtrack CD or David Helfgott's live recording of the Rach 3 (as characters in the film keep calling Rachmaninoff's Third Piano Concerto to prove they're musicians). Still, something in me wanted to be present for Helfgott's first appearance in this country. But I'm sorry I went. I can't remember being so thoroughly depressed by a public performance.

The press-ticket situation ought to have been a tipoff. Music critics were offered no complimentary tickets. "Everyone is welcome to share the joy of David's celebration," the publicity director of the national tour told me, but they "didn't need press" for sold-out concerts. This also suggests a desire on the part of Helfgott's handlers to avoid serious critical evaluation. And now that I've shared David's joy, I can't blame them. Neither the movie nor the CDs (which are now Billboard's No. 1 Classical and Crossover Classical albums) prepared me for the pathetic incompetence of Helfgott's playing.

Helfgott himself is an endearing figure. He came bounding onto the stage wearing a white "puffy" shirt with ruffled cuffs (like the one on *Seinfeld* that Jerry gets trapped into wearing for an appearance on the *Today* show). He trotted to the center of the stage to greet the applause, then immediately sat down and began to play a brief program that lasted only an hour and a half, including the intermission. The selections by Mendelssohn, Chopin, Liszt, and Beethoven were challenging but pretty safe.

Helfgott is like a talented amateur who can handle most of the notes. But he has no focus, no concentration, and little musical understanding. His sense of rhythm is erratic. The faster he plays, the fewer notes he hits. The slower he plays, the more the musical line dissolves into a muffled muddle. What was most surprising to hear in person was his lack of any real projection, or color, or personal "touch." No color, no poetry. Except when he suddenly played very loud, the notes were actually hard to hear. Like Glenn Gould, or Pablo Casals, he groans, growls, or mutters along with the music. But the quieter the playing, the louder the vocals.

People giggled; couples elbowed each other. He got more giggles in a Chopin Ballade, when he kept scratching his side with his right hand, simian-fashion (when he wasn't waving his right arm about as if he were conducting). This Ballade had so little momentum, the audience thought it was over and interrupted with applause. He jumped up, bowed, then played the rest as if he were starting a new piece. The other misplaced applause came after the first movement of Beethoven's *Waldstein* Sonata, but this was a more excusable mistake since the only way anyone who wasn't familiar with classical music could have known it had more than one movement was to buy a $15 souvenir program book.

The people behind me were calling this event a great human celebration. Certainly Helfgott seemed to be having a ball, grinning and leaping up from his chair to get his ovations, shaking hands with front-row well-wishers. I think he had no sense of how badly he'd played. But was this a triumph over an infirmity or merely cashing in on it? During intermission, a friend came up to me relieved to find someone who shared his dismay. "It makes me queasy," he remarked, "this isn't a concert, it's a freak show."

CLASSICS FOR DUMMIES

April 2, 1997

My mother was the first person on her block to get a telephone, a radio, and a car. But I didn't follow so easily in her adventurous footsteps. I was once convinced that computers meant the end of good writing. Now I couldn't live without one. Same with e-mail. When was it I was sneering at CD-ROMs? Who needs pictures to listen to music? What does it mean to listen "interactively"? And frankly, given my track record, I was nervous just about the process of installing the discs on my computer. But I'm head-over-heels over EMI's series of *Classics for Dummies*.

The installation turned out to be pretty simple, and though you can treat these CD-ROMs as ordinary compact discs and just listen to them, the "interactive" stuff is great fun. You can read a fairly snappy biography of each composer. You can click on certain outlined words and see pictures of parents, home town, or a famous concert hall. You can hear a piece of music and read a detailed but comprehensible play-by-play of what's going on every second, as you watch the seconds ticking off in a corner of the screen. And each disc has one short piece for which you can look at a score and actually choose which instrument you want to hear. You can even play conductor and change the tempo. Eventually you'll even be able to change the instrumentation.

This *Classics for Dummies* series derives from the bestselling books that explain in ordinary language such esoteric subjects as the internet, personal finance, golf, and wine. Each of the 24 CD-ROMs now available is devoted to a single composer, and the information is helpful—though there are some factual errors and typos which I'm told are already being corrected. Some of the writing is a little condescending. Does anyone really need to be warned—and I quote from the Beethoven disc—"not to slip at the title of the third symphony"—that "it's Eroica not Erotica"? But I haven't found much of that lowest common denominator.

There's about an hour of music on each disc, so we get only single movements or short pieces (the Wagner disc includes only overtures and brief orchestral selections). But the choices are astute. Most of the performers, from the rich catalog of Angel records, are pretty classy: violinists Nathan Milstein and Joseph Suk, pianists Claudio Arrau and Annie Fischer. Carlo Maria Giulini conducts Beethoven and Verdi, Simon Rattle conducts Prokofiev and Stravinsky, Klaus Tennstedt conducts Mahler. If we don't get the complete Mozart Clarinet Concerto, at least we get the sublime slow movement, and in my favorite performance, by Jack Brymer with Sir Thomas Beecham and the Royal Philharmonic.

Not every performance has that special vitality, but nothing I've heard betrays the score. The choice of composers is pretty conservative. There are none born in this century, and no women. That may change. EMI is donating entire sets of these CD-ROMs along with some seed money to a major national organization of music teachers, to help get classical music back into the schools. That might be just what it takes to get a new generation interested, and the marketers at EMI are no dummies.

Kurt Weill, *Die Bürgschaft*

June 7, 2000

Kurt Weill's political and moral fable *Die Bürgschaft* (*The Bond*, or *The Pledge*), was first performed in Berlin in 1932, just before the Nazi takeover, which is one of the reasons it wasn't performed in Germany again until more than a decade after World War II. It was also Weill's major break with his collaborator Bertolt Brecht, with whom he'd worked on eight previous pieces, including *Threepenny Opera* and *The Rise and Fall of the City of Mahagonny*, a partnership that produced among countless memorable numbers, "Mack the Knife," "Surabaya Johnny," "The Alabama Song," and "The Bilbao Song." His new librettist was Caspar Neher, Brecht and Weill's brilliant set designer. Neher's story owes a lot to Brecht's plays, though the tone is less satirical than appalled and saddened at the way money and power undermine the pledge, the social bond, the human instinct for kindness, public or personal.

Ultimately, Neher's plot goes back to a parable in the Talmud in which kindness and generosity prevail over self-interest. But "It's not people who change," the chorus keeps reminding us, "it's the circumstances that change people." The particular circumstance of this opera is the invasion of an ominous Great Power. In the end, the kind man who once pledged to cover his friend's debt coldly refuses to protect him from a murderous mob. This grim fable foreshadows not only the Nazis but also the corporate greed of the 1990s. Yet if the tone is different from Brecht's glittering cynicism, the music remains unmistakably Weill's, though from the very first notes, he achieves a new level of urgency and momentum. Weill's orchestration, especially his use of winds, reaches new expressive heights. The composer Ernst Bloch said this music had "a touch of a Jewish Verdi to it."

Weill uses small and large choruses in an extraordinary variety of ways. Each individual number fits into a larger design with cinematic fluidity. *Die Bürgschaft* combines the simple narrative of folk opera with the solemn choral pronouncements of oratorio.

The performance, conducted by Julius Rudel and recorded at last year's Spoleto Festival USA, in Charleston, is by turns hard-driving and lyrical, and shot through with nervous energy. It's too bad Weill didn't live to see a revival of this ambitious work. It may never be as popular as *The Threepenny Opera*, but anyone who loves Weill's music will cherish it.

Dresden Music Festival

July 6, 2000

One of the most moving places I've ever been to was Dresden—the civilian city in Eastern Germany that the Allies firebombed in 1945 (maybe most Americans know about this from Kurt Vonnegut's *Slaughterhouse 5*). I spent a day there on a summer vacation trip in 1966. I was a graduate student. I wanted to go to Dresden because the museum there had two paintings by Vermeer—my favorite painter, very few of whose works survive. In those days, to get into East Germany, even for a day, you had to go through a lot of red tape—pun very-much-intended. It was a bureaucratic nightmare. But it was worth the effort. The museum was exceptional, with its great Vermeers, Rembrandts, Titians, and the famous Raphael Sistine Madonna, with its mischievous cherubs leaning on their elbows and eying the Madonna and Baby Jesus floating on a cloud.

Dresden had been one of the cultural capitals of Europe—the German Paris—with its grand palaces, onion-topped church spires, and elegant promenade overlooking an elbow of the Elbe River. It was the home of one of the oldest and greatest orchestras in Europe. Great composers lived and worked there, from Heinrich Schütz, Beethoven and Carl Maria von Weber, Schumann and Wagner, to Richard and Johann Strauss. Bach tried to get a job there. In 1966, the city was still in ruins. You could look right through the skeletal steeples at the ugly apartment houses going up in the distance. The Zwinger, the magnificent palace which housed the old master paintings and the famous collection of Dresden porcelain, had miraculously escaped devastation, though the courtyard was still piled with rubble. The whole city was one of the most heartbreakingly beautiful ruins I'd ever seen.

So last month, when I got a call from the German National Tourist Office inviting me to join a group of media people for a five-day junket to cover the Dresden Music Festival, I was more than just happy to get a free trip and hear some interesting performances. Dresden was a city I already cared about—I wanted to see how it was doing.

East Germany, as we know, even since the re-unification, is not exactly thriving. The population of Dresden has been declining. Jobs are scarce. Families break up because someone gets an offer from Hamburg or Hanover that can't be refused. I was told, though, that the Jewish population was on the rise—that there are now some 500 Jews living in Dresden and a new synagogue is under construction.

There are at least two other sources of hope for this city. The historical buildings are being lovingly restored—or, where restoration isn't possible, completely rebuilt. "This is one of our new old buildings," our guide said, pointing out the beautiful hotel, once a royal palace, where our group was going to have dinner. There are still signs of the devastation, but the magnificence of the historical district is slowly coming alive again.

The other success is the Dresden Music Festival itself. It was actually started by the Communist government, in 1978. One of the first buildings the Communists reconstructed was the spectacular 19th-century Semper Opera House, which was still gutted when I was there in 1966. Now the two-and-a-half-week festival attracts more than 100,000 tourists from all over the world. Six or seven events go on simultaneously throughout the city. Walking through the city center, I heard a local high school chorus singing Negro spirituals on the steps leading up to the terrace overlooking the river.

This year, the Festival's theme was Baroque and Jazz. We saw a fascinating but hard-to-follow high-tech production of Handel's opera *Xerxes* and a concert performance by the Dresden Philharmonic of Richard Strauss's mythological opera *Daphne*, which had its world premiere in Dresden. The conductor was Christ of Prick, who conducts in English-speaking countries under the name "Perick." Let's say he rose superbly to the occasion. One of the best concerts took place in a 400-year-old church, the Annenkirche, with glowing acoustics.

The performers were the Baroque Orchestra of Freiburg, maybe the most accomplished historical-instrument ensemble I've ever heard, and the astounding young German counter-tenor Andreas Scholl, already a very big star in Europe.

Chick Corea played a morning concert at the opera house that the sell-out crowd ate up, though between his unvarying up-tempo cheeriness and my jet lag, I snoozed through it. The liveliest concert took place in the courtyard of the Zwinger Palace, under a rich midnight-blue sky, with the lit-up towers of the city rising above the palace walls. The lead performers were the rhythmically indefatigable 72-year-old Cuban singer Ibrahim Ferrer and 82-year-old pianist Ruben Gonzalez, the stars of *The Buena Vista Social Club*. 4,500 people clapped and sang along for three hours and by the end everyone was standing up and dancing in place. Even the girl reading a letter by a window in one of the Vermeer paintings across the courtyard must have looked out for a moment with an expression of sheer joy.

Samuel Barber

October 10, 2000

As the nephew of the famous Metropolitan opera contralto Louise Homer and the life-partner of the opera composer Gian Carlo Menotti, it was inevitable that the American composer Samuel Barber would turn to opera. His first opera, the romantic melodrama *Vanessa*, had its world premiere in 1958 at the Metropolitan Opera and won the Pulitzer Prize. The plot is a little corny but the music still holds up. The Met later commissioned from him a grand opera, *Antony and Cleopatra*, for the opening of its new house at Lincoln Center in 1966, but it was a bomb of atomic proportions and Barber's reputation never quite emerged from under that mushroom cloud.

In the last few years, though, there's been a neo-Romantic revival. Audiences tired of atonality want to hear tunes they can remember. And Barber had a genuine gift for melody. His Violin Concerto and his setting of James Agee's *Knoxville: Summer of 1915* for soprano and orchestra have remained standard repertory items, and his moving Adagio for Strings, which was originally the slow movement of his string quartet, is so famous people know it without even knowing who wrote it. Even a revised version of *Antony and Cleopatra* has been revived.

My favorite of Barber's three operas is a little gem, a 10-minute, four-character opera called *A Hand of Bridge* that he composed in 1959, the year after *Vanessa*, and like *Vanessa*, it has a libretto by Gian Carlo Menotti. In it, we hear the inner thoughts of two married couples as they are playing their nightly bridge game. Geraldine is desperate about the impending death of her mother—the only person who has ever loved her. Her husband, David, frustrated by his subservient white-collar job, has sado-masochistic fantasies about "20 naked girls" and "20 naked boys," and "drinking scented wine from cups of Steuben glass." Their friend Sally escapes from the boredom of her marriage by shopping, and is currently obsessed with a "hat of peacock feathers," while her husband Bill daydreams about his affair with a woman named Cymbeline, in one of Barber's most seductive lyric tunes.

This isn't psychological profundity but it's a vivid picture of 1950s middle-class anxieties. And the verbal, melodic, and rhythmic juxtapositions, the skillful interweaving of the characters' internal thoughts with the card game they're playing, are delicious. On the original recording, first released in 1960 and just reissued, Geraldine is sung by Patricia Neway, who created the leading roles in several of Menotti's best operas but whose larger fame came from singing "Climb Every Mountain" in the original cast of *The Sound of Music*. The plummy-voiced Sally is Eunice Alberts, legendary conductor Serge Koussevitzky's favorite contralto. Tenor William Lewis and baritone Philip Maero are also excellent as the two husbands. This album, *Music of Samuel Barber*, also includes several early choral and orchestral pieces, as well as the famous Adagio for Strings, in a performance led by the well-known cellist/conductor Antonio Janigro. In all their hands, some of the best music of the 1950s is still alive and well.

Alcina

December 7, 2000

In opera, so many factors have to go absolutely right—singing, conducting, stage direction, scenery—it's almost by definition doomed to failure. So when an inspired production comes along, you have to be especially grateful. That was the case with Canadian director Robert Carsen's version of Handel's *Alcina*, which was first presented in Paris and which I was lucky to catch in Chicago last year. Alcina is a sorceress, a latter-day Circe, who enchants men and transforms them into animals. The twist in Handel's opera is that Alcina falls in love with one of her victims, the knight Ruggiero. But Ruggiero has a fiancée, Bradamante, who doesn't give up. She follows him, disguised as a man, to Alcina's bower of bliss, where Morgana, Alcina's attendant, falls in love with her at first sight, thinking she's a man.

In one of director Carsen's most inspired scenes, Morgana sings a love song to Bradamante's jacket, which is hanging on a chair. Morgana kneels on the chair and wraps the empty sleeves of the jacket around her. She even slaps a sleeve when it tries to touch her improperly. The phenomenal French soprano Natalie Dessay sings Morgana.

Handel operas disappeared for more than a century and a half after their first successes. The 19th century, with its insistence on realism, couldn't handle Handel's plots about magic and sorcery. But the post-Freudian 20th-century found in these implausible stories, as in mythology itself, profound patterns of all-too-human behavior. The winding corridors of Alcina's palace, like the woods in Shakespeare's *A Midsummer Night's Dream*, are like the interior of the human heart—though

Alcina's sacrifice of her power over others when she falls in love is darker and more painful than Shakespeare's comic transformations. At the beginning of the production, soprano Renee Fleming as Alcina rules every inch of her domain. When she loses her magic power, the elegant but blank white walls of Tobias Hoheisel's haunting set close slowly and relentlessly in on her. And in perfect time to the music. Handel's aching sympathy clearly went not to the virtuous lovers but to the defeated sorceress.

The 19th century didn't know what to make of the music either. In Handel's long, formal, three-part arias, singers have to repeat the entire opening section. Audiences used to find this repetition merely repetitious. But as the young director Peter Sellars demonstrated in his memorable Handel productions, the repetitions can actually reveal the deepest insights. The repeated music underlines the increasing futility of Alcina's desperate incantations. Of course, no recording can capture the full range of a complete production. But early-music conductor William Christie, his period orchestra, Les Arts Florrisants, and the magnificent all-star cast perform this ravishing music as if it were actually about something powerful, urgent, and mysterious. And now you don't have to go to Paris or Chicago to hear that.

Ida Haendel

May 30, 2002

On the documentary *The Art of Violin*, the Polish violinist Ida Haendel plays a Brahms Hungarian Dance in 1956. She was probably in her early twenties. American audiences haven't had a chance to get to know her extraordinary playing as well as audiences in Europe or Latin America. Lucky for me, for the past ten years she's been playing regularly with the Boston Symphony. Her Sibelius Violin Concerto with Sir Simon Rattle was one of the concerto performances against which I measure all others. Sibelius and Benjamin Britten, and her teacher, George Enescu, were among the composers who loved how she played their work. She was just back in Boston, playing Bruch's G-minor Concerto, under the direction of Ilan Volkov, who is about half a century her junior. The Adagio was a love song of throbbing concentration, softer and slower than it's usually played. Haendel's violin is like a silken thread—indrawn, intimate, one long held breath, and aware of the tears underlying every human emotion.

For years her recordings have been hard to find here, but that's changing. VAI has issued a memorable video of Haendel playing the Brahms Violin Concerto and Sarasate's Carmen Fantasy. There's not a wasted motion—none of the usual violinistic writhing or hair tossing. Every gesture serves the music. Her most recent recording is a two-CD set of works for violin and piano—on one disc scintillating pieces by Szymanowski, Bartok, and Enescu, with pianist Vladimir Ashkenazy; on the other, her Decca recordings from the 1940s. Some of the repertoire overlaps, so you can hear performances of Bartok's colorful and exuberant Rumanian Folkdances recorded almost fifty years apart. For all her hair-raising virtuosity, Haendel seems never to have been interested in mere self-display. We can hear Haendel in 1947, with pianist Ivor Newton, then in 1996 with Ashkenazy. I'm especially taken with the poignant Hebrew Melody—the only known recording of her sister Alice at the piano.

Haendel must be one of the most articulate musicians around. She speaks seven languages fluently, including English, Russian, and Polish, and has published an autobiography. On a documentary she herself narrates, she says that were it not for her being a violinist, she and her family would have stayed in Poland— "and been murdered like all the Jewish people there. But by some divine decree," she says, "it was a salvation for all of us—my immediate family and myself." Ida Haendel's life really depended on her playing, and she still plays the violin as if it were her salvation.

Christmas Records

December 22, 2000

Christmas can be the season to be jolly but it can also be a time for serious contemplation and meditation. The greatest composer of spiritual inquiry is Johann Sebastian Bach. And Bach's deepest investigations into the meaning of Christmas probably lie in the cantatas he wrote for the holy services of that period. Cantatas are relatively short works for individual voices, chorus, and orchestra. Like poems, they explore a theme through a series of interrelated images divided into sections, like stanzas. These images might come from the Bible or from homilies or prayers.

Conductor Craig Smith and Emmanuel Music, the orchestra and chorus of Boston's Emmanuel Church, are among the world's leading Bach experts. For the past thirty years, they've been performing complete cycles of Bach's more than 200 sacred cantatas as part of the service each Sunday. One reason the Bach cantatas are less familiar than other Bach works may be that so many performances of them have a kind of monolithic uniformity. What distinguished Smith's approach at Emmanuel is his deep awareness of their underlying spiritual conflicts. He moves through Bach's shifting moods with extraordinary sensitivity, so that each cantata becomes a powerful drama. Four of these Christmas-season cantatas are on Emmanuel's first Bach recording. They range from the military splendor of winds and brasses depicting war with the devil to Bach's tender lullabies for the baby Jesus.

Numerous Emmanuel musicians have gone out into the world and begun major careers yet many of them still love the sense of community at Emmanuel and return there often. You can hear this intimacy reflected in an exquisite freedom of phrasing. And these musicians don't seem to have lost their idealism, their spiritual center. If they are so convincing about Bach wrestling with spiritual questions, maybe it's because they themselves continue to wrestle with the same questions.

Marin Alsop

January 9, 2006

The ominous opening of Brahms's First Symphony might be a fitting soundtrack for some of the dark clouds that hung over Marin Alsop's career this year. The Baltimore Symphony Orchestra board announced that the American conductor was going to be their new music director, making her the first woman to run a major American symphony orchestra. But some of the Baltimore players wanted to try out other conductors before a final decision was reached. The nay-sayers were disregarded but not before they made their dissatisfaction public—not a good beginning for a collaboration. Shortly after this controversy, Alsop was awarded a MacArthur Foundation Grant, the so-called "genius" grant, and the Baltimore brouhaha seemed to evaporate.

I'm glad, because I've admired the power and lean, clean musicality of her performances. This year alone, Naxos Records has released four new CDs: two Brahms discs with the magnificent London Symphony Orchestra, a disc of Kurt Weill's two symphonies, with Alsop's current orchestra, the Bournemouth Symphony, and a disc devoted to concert music by Leonard Bernstein. I didn't think the world needed more recordings of Brahms symphonies—there are only four of them and every major (and minor) conductor has recorded them. Yet listening to Alsop, I'm glad these exist. She brings both the heroic, complexly dramatic First and the sunnier, more relaxed Second vividly to life. Alsop doesn't confuse leanness with thinness. Both works get powerful, compelling, surprisingly fresh performances. It's as if Alsop herself is discovering these overfamiliar works for the first time.

Alsop has been a strong advocate of 20th-century music. Kurt Weill's concert music isn't as well known as his theater music, but his Second Symphony, completed in Paris in 1934, unlike the Brahms symphonies, isn't played as often as it should be. It swings between Weill's dark mixture of smoochy melody and edgy irony.

Weill's early First Symphony, from 1921, isn't as individual or polished a work as the Second and completely disappeared until 1956. Alsop leads it with conviction. Her new Bernstein disc includes three lively, tuneful pieces composed by her mentor between 1946 and 1980. Bernstein's own favorite was his 1954 *Serenade*, an exploration of love inspired by Plato's *Symposium*.

These recordings—and maybe even the controversy—suggest that Alsop is a significant new voice in classical music. It sounds as if Baltimore audiences are in for a treat.

Sarah Caldwell

March 30, 2006

For some twenty years, in the 1960s and '70s, the most exciting opera productions in this country were happening in Boston. The person responsible for them was Sarah Caldwell, who died at the age of 82 on March 23.

It's extraordinary to go to a theater and feel that what you're about to experience might be something you'll remember with pleasure the rest of your life. That's how I felt about Sarah Caldwell's productions for her Opera Company of Boston, the company she founded in 1958 and which closed shop in 1990. Not every production fulfilled that promise—some of them could be pretty dismal. But all of them were ambitious and noble ventures. And some of them made such an impression on me, decades later I can still relive them in my mind's eye. Take Schoenberg's *Moses and Aaron*, for example, which Caldwell presented in 1966—its American premiere, years before the Metropolitan Opera got around to it. It's a challenging, difficult work. But when the curtain went up on Caldwell's production, we saw two figures standing back-to-back in a spotlight. This simple but profound image alerted us to what the opera was about: that Moses and Aaron were opposite sides of the same person: the tongue-tied visionary and the easy talker who could communicate his brother's vision. Sarah Caldwell herself was a visionary who could also communicate her vision of opera as total theater.

It wasn't easy for her. For several years, she didn't even have a theater. But she could turn unpromising venues into theatrical gold. One of her best productions took place in a 19th-century brick building originally built to house a huge mural of the Battle of Gettysburg. It had a spectacular glass dome in the center. For her production of Gustav Charpentier's opera *Louise*, Caldwell transformed Boston's old Cyclorama into Montmartre, with jugglers, acrobats, and street vendors crowding the aisles. At the climax, a simple spotlight focused on a rotating mirror ball, high up under the dome, suddenly turned the whole theater into a gigantic whirling carousel we were all riding!

Caldwell worked with many major stars, but her reigning prima donna was Beverly Sills. One of Caldwell's American premieres was a dazzling production of an 18th-century opera by Rameau, *Hippolyte et Aricie*, in which Sills had to sing brilliant high notes, trills, and roulades. No one knew she could sing that kind of music. Or that her co-star could—an unknown young Spanish tenor named Placido Domingo. Sills later appeared at the New York City Opera as Cleopatra in Handel's *Julius Caesar*, singing a similar style of music—and that performance made her a superstar. But Caldwell was there first. VAI has now released four live recordings of Caldwell productions, including Sills, as Juliet, and the heartbreaking Tatiana Troyanos, as Romeo, in Bellini's *The Capulets and the Montague*s — maybe the best of Sills's legendary series of bel canto performances.

Caldwell worked with such important singers as Joan Sutherland and Marilyn Horne, Shirley Verrett, Jon Vickers, Renata Tebaldi, Phyllis Curtin, George London and Boris Christoff, Victoria de los Angeles and Regine Crespin. Sutherland and Horne appeared together in phenomenal duets from Rossini's *Semiramide*—the first time they did these roles in a staged production.

Caldwell also wanted to conduct. She became the first woman to conduct at the Metropolitan Opera, and the second to lead the New York Philharmonic. She made the cover of

Time magazine. But conducting distracted her from what she did incomparably: "total theater." Her greatest achievement was an adventurous repertory that mixed modern and unusual operas with the more familiar. She produced a dozen US premieres and such significant musical events as the first American performances of Mussorgsky's *Boris Godunov* in the composer's own orchestration, Verdi's *Don Carlo* in its original French version, and the original versions, very different from the ones we know, of such popular works as Puccini's *Madame Butterfly* and Gounod's *Faust*.

Finally, to its shame, Boston couldn't support Caldwell's company. She had bought an old movie theater and turned it into an Opera House. But it needed too many expensive repairs. She finally had to sell it. And her health problems were getting increasingly severe. Those of us who loved her work always kept hoping she'd make a comeback. The news of her death on March 23rd dashed those hopes.

Ruby Elzy

June 29, 2007

The story of Ruby Elzy is a powerful example of how talent can overcome seemingly insurmountable odds. One of four children, she was born, her biographer David Weaver tells us, in abject poverty in a small town in Mississippi. Her father abandoned the family when Ruby was 5. But she could sing. A visiting professor, astounded by her voice, helped her get into college. Then she got a fellowship to Juilliard. In 1933, she appeared opposite Paul Robeson in the movie version of Eugene O'Neill's *The Emperor Jones*. When George Gershwin heard her sing, he cast her in the major role of Serena in his new opera, *Porgy and Bess*. She made her Broadway debut in this role in 1935, at the age of 27, and sang the part more than 800 times, on Broadway and on tour. Her future success was all but guaranteed.

She had an extraordinary soprano voice—both pure and searing. She was good looking and she could act. Serena is the woman whose husband is murdered by the villain Crown, and Elzy's rendition of "My Man's Gone Now" electrified the audience. She never made a commercial recording of it, but three of her performances have survived, two of them from radio broadcasts. Before Porgy opened, Gershwin took five of the leading players into a recording studio to conduct parts of the opera with an orchestra. On this rehearsal recording, made on August 19, 1935, Gershwin himself introduces and conducts Ruby Elzy in "My Man's Gone Now."

All three of Elzy's surviving performances of "My Man's Gone Now" are on a remarkable new disc compiled by David Weaver that includes all 20 of her known recordings, the majority of which are spirituals.

In 1941, Ruby Elzy appeared in another film, *Birth of the Blues*, with Bing Crosby and Mary Martin. She had already made her recital debut at New York's Town Hall and been invited by Eleanor Roosevelt to sing at the White House. Her repertoire also included art songs and arias, the most ambitious of which is probably "Elsa's Dream" from Wagner's opera *Lohengrin*, in a stunning performance from 1937.

In the 1930s and '40s, it would have been impossible for an African-American singer, however extraordinary, to sing Wagner's lily-white heroine in a fully-staged opera production. But in 1943, Elzy was preparing the role of Verdi's Ethiopian princess Aïda, when she had to have surgery. It was supposed to be a relatively minor operation, but she died in a Detroit hospital at the age of 35. Since her death, she's been largely overlooked, except for Gershwin mavens. But thanks to her biographer-turned-record-producer David Weaver, no one who hears this recording could possibly forget her.

Pop Kulcha

Eskin's Rags

August 26, 1987

Someone says "ragtime" in a word-association game and you're sure to answer Scott Joplin, or Irving Berlin, or maybe E.L. Doctorow. We tend to think of this irresistibly syncopated music as primarily male-originated and male oriented—saloon or brothel music that finally went respectable. But pianist Virginia Eskin's new record on Northeastern, *Pickles and Peppers*, has a surprise for us. This is an album of piano rags written by women. Most of them were composed during the heyday of ragtime, between the Gay—or Naughty—Nineties and World War I, and most of them are more technically complex than the rags we're more familiar with. There are also two intriguing contemporary rags by Judith Lang Zaimont.

The informative liner notes by Carolyn A. Lindemann point out that playing the piano at the turn of the century was primarily woman's work. And that when young middle-class women heard piano rags played in the local five-and-dimes by sheet-music sales clerks, they bought the music, brought it home, and even began to compose. Ragtime was becoming domestic though not completely domesticated. On Eskin's record, we find such kitchen and cupboard titles as "Red Peppers," "Pickles and Peppers," and "Chicken Chowder," the "Dusty Rag," and the "Dish Rag." But then again, there's also "The Thriller!" (with an exclamation point) by May Aufderheide and Charlotte Blake's "That Poker Rag." One of my favorites is Julia Lee Niebergall's "Horseshoe Rag," published in 1911.

There were probably more women ragtime composers than we'll ever know, since many of those who felt the drive to publish had to publish under assumed names or signed the sheet music only with their initials. Most of these rags were written by gifted young women who were compelled to give up their musical ambitions in order to raise a family. Some of the composers included here remained so obscure it's been impossible to learn anything about them at all.

Eskin, long an advocate of women composers, is a particularly effective advocate for these pieces. Her witty rhythmic changes, her impressive variety of touch—now boisterous and clangy, now slyly delicate—are the signs of a classical virtuoso, but most other "serious" musicians don't play with such freshness, such rightness of style when they turn to popular music. *Pickles and Peppers is* a serious recording—it's the history of popular culture, it's social history, it's the history of yet one more overlooked contribution to the arts by women. There's plenty here to think about. But because the material itself is so engaging, it's also one of the most delightful records released this year. If you don't want to think, you can just sit back and enjoy.

Kiri Sings Gershwin

September 9, 1987

Angel Records, which has given us some of the greatest opera recordings ever made—the Flagstad *Tristan*, the Schwarzkopf *Rosenkavalier*, the Callas *Carmen*—has just issued one of the most grotesque records by an opera singer I've ever heard: *Kiri Sings Gershwin*. Of course, there's always a problem when opera singers attempt popular music. Very few of them have ever been able to lighten up, to sound natural or free enough to bring it off. Kiri Te Kanawa, long before she sang at Princess Di's wedding or became a Dame, made some passable records of show tunes in her native New Zealand. Lately she has turned to show music again, like the complete *West Side Story* conducted by Leonard Bernstein, which has met with extraordinary but to me inexplicable popular success. She may have one of the most beautiful soprano voices in the world, but popular music only compounds the problems she already has with opera. Her syrupy tone and stiff sense of rhythm, her too-studied diction, and her inability to point words without coy overstatement (when she points them at all) completely sink America's most buoyant composer, George Gershwin. Sometimes she sounds as if she hadn't the slightest idea what she was singing about, other times as if she were singing to four-year-olds. And her affectation of an American accent only exaggerates her distance from the idiom (a distance much further than New Zealand). There's barely an easy, spontaneous, or joyous note on this whole Gershwin album. Listen, for example, to the characteristically charmless, almost desperate version of "But Not for Me."

I wish we could just dismiss this whole misguided effort,

but there's some valuable material here. Conductor John McGlinn, with the New Princess Theater Orchestra, uses the newly rediscovered original orchestrations, and we get to hear most of the original lyrics, too. There's even the first recording of a long-lost song, the sweetly syncopated "Meadow Serenade" written for *Strike Up the Band*, which exists today only because Gershwin's friend, composer Kay Swift, was able to transcribe it from memory (it's Dame Kiri's best moment). The arrangements of "The Man I Love," "I Got Rhythm," "Embraceable You," and "Nice Work If You Can Get It" refreshingly convey the real Broadway and Hollywood of the '20s and '30s.

But McGlinn doesn't understand Dame Kiri's voice. In his effort to recapture the lighter, jazzier style of the period, his faster pace and insistent bounciness—even in the ballads—only seem to rush her, which isn't a very stylish thing for any conductor to do.

Fortunately, Angel has also issued a purely instrumental record of McGlinn doing Gershwin overtures and sound-track music, again in original orchestrations, and it's a delight, especially "Stiff Upper Lip," the funhouse music from the 1937 film *A Damsel in Distress*, in which Fred Astaire danced with his second and third best partners, George Burns and Gracie Allen.

Jonathan and Darlene Edwards

October 7, 1987

The title of this new CD on the Corinthian label, *Jonathan and Darlene's Greatest Hits*, is misleading. It sounds like a pop album. But Jonathan and Darlene Edwards are more than pop musicians—much more. In fact, they are, and have been for many years, at the forefront of the American musical avant-garde. Jonathan's daredevil rhythmic syncopations are equaled only by Darlene's uncanny sense of pitch. Her staggering microtonalities couldn't be reproduced even through electronic manipulation (quarter tones are nothing compared to the kaleidoscopic shadings she can squeeze between two notes); and though some opera singers have come close, none has ever matched her ability to sing in so many different keys at once. John Cage's aleatoric, or chance, music can't approach the Edwards's unpredictable tempo changes, polyrhythms, and devastating tonal clashes. What's deceptive is that Jonathan and Darlene use popular songs as the basis for their technical experiments. But their work far surpasses what Stravinsky did with popular tunes in *Petrushka*. They take "Take the 'A' Train" further than the Kronos Quartet ever dreamed of taking Jimi Hendrix.

Since Jonathan and Darlene never make personal appearances, recordings are the only way we can get to know their work. Cynics even question whether their entire enterprise is some sort of elaborate hoax. There's even a rumor that they are really pop vocalist Jo Stafford and her husband, bandleader Paul Weston. But how could pop musicians bring off anything so technically daring, so far ahead of what even the furthest out electronic composers are attempting? Sadly, they are not taken as seriously as they should be by the new-music establishment. Perhaps it's their wickedly satiric sense of humor, their very derision of the trendy and avant-garde, that makes them objects of suspicion (their first album, for example, had a picture of two left hands hovering over a piano keyboard). Perhaps they have simply aroused jealousy with their popular success (their second album, *Jonathan & Darlene Edwards in Paris*, won a Grammy). But it's hard to think of two more profoundly serious and dedicated artists.

Their five brilliant LPs and the new CD make it extremely hard to choose only one selection. How about "I Love Paris," with its subtle mimetic effects and musical allusions?

Jonathan and Darlene Edwards's astonishing treatment of Cole Porter makes Schoenberg's atonality or Stockhausen's synthesizer sound like "Twinkle Twinkle Little Star." As with most searching and iconoclastic creative geniuses, only the tireless efforts of open-minded critics and time itself will ultimately confirm their immeasurable and irrevocable contribution to contemporary culture.

Gershwin, *Of Thee I Sing* and *Let 'Em Eat Cake*

December 23, 1987

Maybe the best George Gershwin recordings to be released this year, the fiftieth anniversary of his death, are the reconstructions of the two satirical musicals he wrote with his brother Ira in the early '30s, *Of Thee I Sing* and *Let 'Em Eat Cake*. *Of Thee I Sing* was a big hit—the longest running book-musical of the entire decade. It had three hit tunes—the title song, "Love is Sweeping the Country," and "Who Cares?" It was even the first musical comedy to win a Pulitzer Prize. *Let 'Em Eat Cake* is a sequel with many of the same characters. But it's much darker in tone, and it was a flop. These recordings, conducted by Michael Tilson Thomas and starring Maureen McGovern, a rather charmless Larry Kert, and the irresistible Jack Gilford as Vice-President Throttlebottom, mark the first attempt to record complete (or almost complete), stylistically authentic Gershwin musicals. Most of the original orchestrations for *Of Thee I Sing* were lost in a storeroom until 1984. *Let 'Em Eat Cake* required more extensive restoration, since none of the original orchestrations have ever been found.

Of Thee I Sing satirizes American presidential elections. John P. Wintergreen gets elected by running on a platform of love, and nearly gets impeached because he marries the wrong—but really, of course, the right—first lady. His political skin is saved when his wife announces her impending motherhood in a song called "Posterity Is Just Around the Corner." The musical numbers mix a Gilbert & Sullivan lunacy (like the political satire of the Marx Brothers in *Duck Soup*, two years later) with pure Broadway. The title song catches some of that cheeky spirit, especially in the little phrase that comes at the end of the recurrent fanfare: "*Of Thee I Sing*, baby."

Let 'Em Eat Cake, two years deeper into the Depression, adds a new ingredient, the *Threepenny* cynicism of Kurt Weill. In the late '20s and early '30s, political satire in the form of musical comedy was an international phenomenon. We shouldn't forget how much Weill owed to Gershwin. Today, at least on these recordings, *Let 'Em Eat Cake* is the more exhilarating and daring score. It bursts out of the musical comedy mold that *Of Thee I Sing* was only beginning to push against. The plot deals with the revolutionary overthrow of the American government by the "blue-shirts." Ira Gershwin called it "a satire on Practically Everything." Even the one love song that became a standard, "Mine," concerns the self-centeredness of the romantic couple. Kruger, the revolutionary, expresses some of the negativism that probably cost *Let 'Em Eat Cake* its audience in 1933. Ira Gershwin's reference to Boris Thomashefsky, the founder of the Yiddish Theater in America, is especially pointed here. Thomashefsky was conductor Michael Tilson Thomas's grandfather.

Into the Woods

April 13, 1988

Stephen Sondheim is practically the only contemporary Broadway composer whose musical and literary ambitions go beyond the stock Broadway formulas for success. His adventurousness has begun to pay off. He's won a Pulitzer Prize. His latest show, *Into the Woods*, seems to be one of his biggest hits. Like most of his other musicals, *Into the Woods* has an intriguing premise to match its intriguing title. It takes a handful of familiar fairy tales (some of them rather Grimm), updates them, and watches what happens when the characters interact. There's Jack (of bean and beanstalk fame), a Little Red Ridinghood who is surprisingly aroused by the wolf, and the Baker's Wife is so eager to be, as she says, in Cinderella's shoes that she has an affair with Prince Charming. Sondheim isn't the first composer to give fairy tales a modern slant. But his classy combination of tricky word-play and musical sophistication sounds like no one but Sondheim. As in Jack's mother's description of their old cow, or Prince Charming's facile seduction of the Baker's Wife.

I think the deepest source of Sondheim's musical energy is parody. In his very best shows, beginning with *A Funny Thing Happened on the Way to the Forum*, and including *Company*, *Follies*, *A Little Night Music*, and *Pacific Overtures*—his music takes off from pre-existing forms: vaudeville routines, '50s girl trios, Viennese waltzes (he's a veritable Broadway Brahms), even Kabuki. Yet in his very imitations, Sondheim is capable of exploring the most moving and complex feelings. As a Noel Coward character once said, "Extraordinary how potent cheap music is."

The problem with Sondheim recently may be that his musical sources aren't cheap enough. Since *Sweeney Todd*, his ambitiousness has gotten hard to separate from pretentiousness. The more operatic he gets, the further behind he leaves his tight forms, his sharp edge, and his originality. More and more Sondheim's new shows feel like variations on his own old ones. A nasty duet for two rival lovers in *Into the Woods* is an awful lot like the one in *A Little Night Music*. Cinderella is as afraid to make up her mind as Amy in *Company*. Relationships fall apart for almost exactly the same reasons they fall apart in other Sondheim shows: self-consciousness and self-delusion, what in *Follies* he called the "God-why-don't-you-love-me-oh-you-do-I'll-see-you-later Blues." Even the ambiguous endings have begun to seem predictable, calculated, and underlined.

Still, *Into the Woods* is probably Sondheim's best score since *Sweeney Todd*. The title song is a neat Disney parody. The juicy "No One Is Alone," is a cross between Rodgers & Hammerstein's "You'll Never Walk Alone" and "Being Alive," the just-this-side-of-sentimental conclusion of *Company*. It may be Sondheim's prettiest ballad since "Send in the Clowns." If the tunes aren't quite as memorable as they used to be, at least the accompaniments have a new chamber-music delicacy. The cast itself is fine, maybe a little anonymous, except for Bernadette Peters, who's terrific as "the witch from next door." She helps make "The Last Midnight" Sondheim's most enjoyably chilling post-nuclear existentialist waltz in several seasons.

Irving Berlin/Elizabeth Welch

May 11, 1988

"You're the top," Cole Porter wrote, "you're a Berlin ballad." Of all our great songwriters, Irving Berlin is probably the most popular, in subject as well as in appeal. Other composers may write more sophisticated music, or more classical; other writers write wittier and more emotionally complex lyrics. Yet no one has tapped the spirit of this century like Berlin. "White Christmas," his most famous song, doesn't just celebrate a holiday but captures what it felt like in 1942 for an American soldier to be away from home at the time when families usually gather together. "God bless America" is more truly an American national anthem than the official one. Other songwriters may have hated to get up in the morning, but imagine anyone besides Berlin making a great song out of it, perhaps the most human song ever written about military life. "There may be trouble ahead," Berlin wrote with political acuity in 1936. Nevertheless, he has Fred Astaire and Ginger Rogers, in one of their most ambitious numbers, decide to "face the music and dance." Some of his songs have a naive tendency to be cute, anti-intellectual, sentimentally optimistic or self-pitying. Songs like "You Can't Get a Man with a Gun," "A Pretty Girl Is Like a Melody," or "A Man Chases a Girl (Until She Catches Him)" are now part of pre-feminist history. But at his best, his directness and simplicity have an irresistible charm and power.

Of all the good records to be issued in Berlin's honor, my favorite is the new *Irving Berlin Songbook* by Elizabeth Welch. Welch made her first Broadway appearance in Blackbirds of 1928, the longest running all-Negro musical in Broadway history. Two years later, after the opening of Cole Porter's show *The*

New Yorkers, the producers got nervous about a white woman singing "Love for Sale," a song about a prostitute, and they replaced her with Welch. In 1933 she knocked London on its ear and stayed. She appeared in musicals, radio, and films, including several with Paul Robeson. And she's still remarkable. Welch was 79 when she made this album, and her voice and diction might be the envy of singers half her age. I love her easy elegance, the playfulness of her phrasing, and the tenderness of her smoky delivery.

One of the most moving songs on the Berlin album is "Supper Time," which he wrote for Ethel Waters in 1933. At first it seems a typical blues song about a woman abandoned by her man. But it's actually about a lynching—like Billie Holiday's "Strange Fruit." Welch's rendition keeps Ethel Waters's understatement but adds a few heart-wrenching undercurrents of her own.

What better tribute to a composer on his living centennial than for his music to be performed with such deep understanding and affection by a singer of a younger generation like Elizabeth Welch?

Lotte Lenya Sings Kurt Weill

August 3, 1988

August 31, 1988, marks the 60th anniversary of one of the great musical and theatrical works of the century—*Threepenny Opera* by Kurt Weill and Bertolt Brecht. CBS has performed a valuable service in reissuing on CD its classic recordings of two Kurt Weill masterpieces: *The Threepenny Opera* and *The Rise and Fall of the City of Mahagonny*, recordings that are both historically important and theatrically riveting. Both were originally supervised by Weill's widow, Lotte Lenya, and on them she also recreates her original roles. Lenya was an actress, not a trained singer, but her tremulous, gravelly, ironic voice is the perfect embodiment of the Romanticism-gone-sour that is at the heart of this music.

Lenya also made two LPs that CBS has converted to CD with more dismaying results. One was an album of Weill's Berlin theater songs—mostly collaborations with Bertolt Brecht—songs like "Mack the Knife," the "Alabama Song," the "Bilbao Song," and "Surabaya Johnny," songs that became pop hits for such singers as Bobby Darin, Louis Armstrong, the Doors, and Bette Midler. But who else could give them Lenya's unique edge?

Lenya also recorded an album of theater songs Weill wrote after he emigrated to America in 1935. His Broadway shows—*Lady in the Dark, One Touch of Venus*, or *Knickerbocker Holiday*, which "September Song" comes from—have remarkable numbers in them. Weill worked with distinguished lyricists: Ira Gershwin, playwright Maxwell Anderson, and comic poet Ogden Nash. Some of Nash's best verses are in his lyrics for Weill. But few of these numbers match Weill's breakthrough works of the late '20s. Lenya's world-weariness actually helps reduce some of the saccharine content. It's the Berlin album, though, that's especially high on my list of desert-island records. My original copy wore out long ago.

So now both these albums are available in a format that doesn't wear out, and that considerably improves the original engineering. But in order to fit both LPs onto one CD, four of the best German songs were left out. Numbers like the eerily graphic "Ballad of the Drowned Girl," a song about German revolutionary Rosa Luxemburg from Brecht's rarely-performed *Berlin Requiem*, and the hilariously harrowing "Sailor's Tango" from *Happy End*, in which a doomsday storm drowns the cigar-smoking, whiskey-guzzling sailors in a lovely sea of "blue—so blue."

But there's a more insidious omission. With no acknowledgement, the central sections of "Surabaya Johnny" and the "Bilbao Song" have been edited out—fully a third of each song is missing. The only trace of them is in the accompanying booklet that prints all the words. Besides being immoral, these abridgements butcher Weill's innovative structures. They leave out some of Lenya's most spine-tingling moments or else make others seem melodramatic because they haven't been properly prepared for. The original LPs are hard to find, but at least they're officially still available—and they remain more indispensable than ever.

Bernstein at 70

August 24, 1988

Hard to believe that on August 25 Leonard Bernstein is turning 70! His brash youthfulness has been enlivening the musical scene for so long, it's shocking to think of him as getting older. CBS records has been reissuing many Bernstein recordings on CD, but by far the most enjoyable is a compilation called *The Bernstein Songbook*. Little of Bernstein's youthful spirit ever got into his more solemn classical compositions. His symphonies are dreary and derivative. His recent opera, *A Quiet Place*, is an embarrassing soap opera. But Bernstein wrote some of the best musical comedies in Broadway history. This album celebrates his brilliant achievement with an anthology of some of his most memorable numbers culled from original-cast, soundtrack, and revival albums. There's even a live performance by Frederica von Stade at the Kennedy Center in January 1977—honoring the Carter inauguration with a selection from one of Bernstein's biggest flops, *1600 Pennsylvania Avenue*.

The unmistakable Bernstein voice and rhythm was all there in 1944, in the very opening to his very first show, *On the Town*. Bernstein himself conducts. It's hard not to hear a portrait of Lenny in the song "Carried Away," sung here by the team who were not only in the original cast of *On the Town* but also wrote the book and lyrics: Betty Comden and Adolph Green. There are irresistible numbers from the TV sound track of *Wonderful Town* with Rosalind Russell in one of her greatest triumphs, and from the original cast recording of *Candide* (the best version), with Barbara Cook in her show-stopping satiric aria, "Glitter and Be Gay." There are two superb excerpts from a 1973 recording of *Trouble in Tahiti*, Bernstein's first opera, and "Simple

Song," the prettiest number from his controversial *Mass*, composed for the opening of the Kennedy Center in 1971.

The Bernstein Songbook has a few odd mistakes. One of the most ambitious ensemble numbers to find its way into a Broadway musical is the "Tonight Quintet," from Bernstein's biggest hit, *West Side Story*. It proves that the popular theater didn't necessarily restrict Bernstein's fertile imagination. But though the "quintet" is listed on the CD, what we get is only the more conventional duet version. Someone at CBS can't count. The CD attributes "Somewhere" to Carol Lawrence when it's actually sung by Reri Grist. No question, though—the original cast of *West Side Story* is still definitive.

One of Bernstein's most charming enterprises was the music and lyrics to four songs for a production of *Peter Pan* in 1950, starring Jean Arthur and Boris Karloff. The original cast album has been out of print for years, but the new Songbook has two numbers, including Karloff as the menacing Captain Hook singing the "Plank Song." It's not surprising that Leonard Bernstein would write music for a play about a boy who never grows old.

Mary Martin and Ethel Merman

September 7, 1988

Through reruns, TV series from the '50s and '60s have won new followings. Cable and local stations have given *Burns & Allen*; *Car 54, Where Are You?*; *Perry Mason*; and *Your Show of Shows* new leases on life. But the one-shot live-TV specials are almost never rebroadcast. In many cases that's probably no great loss. The so-called "spectaculars" were often spectacular duds. But at least one show remains cherished in some people's memories—the *Ford 50th Anniversary Show*, a two-hour variety program broadcast on June 15, 1953 and, as far as I know, never repeated.

The highlight of that program was a 12-minute duet—a medley of songs sung by two of the greatest musical-comedy stars of all time—Ethel Merman and Mary Martin—maybe the only time they ever performed together in public. It was staged and conceived by choreographer Jerome Robbins, and put together with a wit and cleverness and affection that you don't often associate with television. Immediately after the telecast, Decca records put out a little 10-inch LP of the duet, but it wasn't in print long.

I've seen tantalizing snippets of the medley on documentaries, but now Lyric Distribution has put out a budget price video-tape of the entire program. The duet certainly holds up. Merman and Martin are at the top of their form, and they obviously loved working together. Merman's brashness and Martin's sweet sensitivity are miraculously complementary, and we even get a taste of Martin's brashness and Merman's sensitivity. The medley begins with a couple of the standards they themselves introduced—Merman's "There's No Business Like Show

Business" from *Annie Get Your Gun* and Martin's "Wonderful Guy" from *South Pacific*. Then they greet each other ("Hi Ethel!" "Hi Mary!") and the medley takes off. I love Merman vamping the camera with her saucer eyes in "The Sheik of Araby." This segues into a comical series of "I" songs: "I'm in the Mood for Love," "I Love a Parade," "I'd Climb the Highest Mountain," "I'm Sitting on Top of the World," "I've Got a Feelin' Your Foolin'." They tease each other, and one-up each other, and their voices blend as if they were made for each other. They sing rings around "Tea for Two." They end, together, with a reprise of "There's No Business Like Show Business" that's surprisingly moving. Maybe there really is no business like it.

The rest of the show has its moments too, especially the stirring renditions of "He's Got the Whole World in His Hands" and a verse from "The Battle Hymn of the Republic" by the magnificent Marion Anderson. Co-hosts Oscar Hammerstein and Edward R. Murrow and sponsor Henry Ford pontificate ponderously but it's oddly moving to hear that at least some people in the '50s were actually worried about the past and the future.

She Loves Me

September 21, 1988

I never saw *She Loves Me*, but a few years after it closed I picked up a copy of the original cast album at a cut-out sale, and I immediately fell in love with it. It was the show that songwriters Sheldon Harnick and Jerry Bock finished four years after their Pulitzer Prize winning *Fiorello!* and just before their biggest hit, *Fiddler on the Roof*. It was produced by hitmaker Hal Prince, the first musical which he also chose to direct. Starring in it were some of the most appealing and original young Broadway personalities: Barbara Cook, Daniel Massey, Barbara Baxley, and Jack Cassidy, along with the veteran Hollywood actor Ludwig Donath.

Films of Broadway shows, and films made into Broadway shows, rarely are as good as the originals. *She Loves Me* is based on an endearing movie, Ernst Lubitsch's touching 1940 comedy *The Shop Around the Corner*, starring James Stewart and Margret Sullavan as two bickering shop clerks in pre-war Budapest who haven't yet discovered that the secret romantic correspondence they are conducting is with each other. But the ingratiating Broadway cast is good enough to make all their characters their own; invidious comparisons are irrelevant.

The success of the score is partly a result of the way the show was put together. Instead of the usual method of creating a libretto—injecting musical numbers into a scenario—*She Loves Me* actually started with a full script, a play by Joe Masteroff based on both the Lubitsch film script and the 1937 play by Miklos Laszlo that the movie was based on. So the musical numbers are uncommonly well-integrated. The tunes and lyrics are always at the service of character and atmosphere.

Perhaps you can appreciate the witty subtleties of the score even better on a recording than in a theater. In a delightful number called "Sounds While Selling," the voices of clerks and customers blend in a comic collage of sales talk.

Even the overture has a combination of humor and affection—the Lubitsch touch.

The CD was lovingly produced by Polydor's Larry Lash, who includes interviews he conducted with members of the original show and evocative color photographs of the original production. There's even a note indicating that you might program your CD player to repeat the brief "Thank you, madam" chorus which reappears in the show—but not on the album—every time a character makes a sale. With its Eastern-European setting and music-box tunes, its lilting waltzes and tangos, *She Loves Me* has the texture and refinement of a classic operetta.

A friend of mine has a saying that goes, "When all else fails, try quality." *She Loves Me* began with quality. It wasn't the greatest commercial success, but it didn't fail, either—it did everything it wanted to. In its quiet way, it's a landmark musical. And this CD ensures that it won't be forgotten.

Bulgarian folk music

November 2, 1988

Probably no one was more surprised than Nonesuch Records that one of its best sellers for 1988 was an album of Bulgarian music in its Explorer series. For years that much-applauded series filled a major recording gap in ethnic music, but I don't think it's ever produced an album that hit the charts. *La Mystère de la Voix Bulgares* by the Bulgarian State Radio and Television Female Vocal Choir was already a hot item in England before it was released here. To coincide with its American tour a second album has just been issued.

Volume Two consists of material that was recorded in Bulgaria as recently as last year and as long ago as 1957, as in the duet, "The Fox Has Lost His Cubs." Nearly half of the cuts were done in the '70s, and some of them with groups and soloists other than the now famous Female Choir. Though this second collection is also strikingly beautiful, it's at somewhat of a disadvantage for not having been released first. Part of the success of Volume One was that it was such a revelation. It introduced a lot of western ears to those dissonant eastern European harmonies in pitch-perfect seconds and sevenths, and those extraordinary vibratoless women's voices—part nasal, part chest voice. You could imagine the wavering tunes of a harvest song, a wedding song, a love song, or a lament carrying across an open field. That album also established the peculiar genre of folk music not merely transcribed but artistically arranged and carefully rehearsed by a very impressive professional choir. There are even original compositions. These are concert not field recordings.

So Volume Two really has to rely more heavily on the material itself for its surprises, and though that material remains wonderfully evocative I'm not sure how much it adds to what we've already heard. Partly because that first volume was nothing if not wide-ranging. One tune could sound as if it were made for Carmen Miranda, another as if the Chordettes had heard the Female Choir harmonizing before they recorded "Mr. Sandman" (or were members of the Choir fans of the Chordettes?). Maybe I'd be a lot more receptive to Volume Two if I knew more specifically what each song was about. I'm not fluent in Bulgarian and neither volume includes translations—only titles such as "Young Childless Wife," "I'm Going to Buy You Some White Silk," "Confession," or a song, simply called "Teasing." On second thought, maybe we really don't need to know more than the title, after all.

As before, the performances are astonishing—delivered with a powerful vocal and emotional intensity. When those vibratoless voices break out into the shakes, it's as if the earth itself is trembling under all of us. In the most moving song on the second volume, the lament "Young Childless Wife," Radka Aleksova is the heart-rending soloist.

Show Boat

December 21, 1988

Everybody knows *Show Boat*. Songs like "Ol' Man River," "Bill," "Make Believe," "Can't Help Lovin' Dat Man," "Why Do I Love You?" flow in the collective American bloodstream. But this new album is unprecedented in its completeness. It not only has the entire original score but even all the numbers that were either cut out or added in later productions. And they're all placed in the context of a powerful and brilliantly constructed music drama. *Show Boat* was produced in 1927, and it's probably the first "serious" musical in Broadway history. It's not just romantic entertainment—it also deals with our heritage of racial prejudice and with the changes in American culture between the late 1880s and 1927. Its self-conscious sense of theatricality, its "show-within-a-show" plot, provides the perfect backdrop for the deceptions and self-deceptions of the main characters—all of them actors on the show boat: Julie LaVerne, the star who conceals her mixed blood in order to pass for white; Magnolia Hawks and Gaylord Ravenal, the lovers who would rather "make believe" than face their real difficulties. Even Ellie, the comedienne, admits that "Life Upon the Wicked Stage" ain't nothin' like what her fans expect. *Show Boat* celebrates "theater" but also evaluates it, especially by measuring it against natural feeling, and—in "Ol' Man River"—the force of nature itself.

One thing that strikes me about the complete score of *Show Boat* is its complex and sophisticated structure. Take the extraordinary overture, for example, recorded here in its original version for the first time. The opening theme anticipates one of the most touching moments in the show, not a song but a little verse that Julie sings, her premonition of disaster. It's the same theme we hear when young Magnolia is offstage practicing the piano. The tune runs like an operatic motif through the whole show. The next theme in the Overture is "Can't Help Lovin' Dat Man," which is not only one of Jerome Kern's best loved ballads, it's also central to the plot—a song that only black people are supposed to know. Why should a star like Julie LaVerne know it? This theme is followed by music from the powerful choral lament sung by the black workers as they polish the showboat auditorium—"Misry's Comin' Aroun'"—a number that was actually cut out of *Show Boat* after its first tryout performance. This is its first recording.

    The original orchestrations, complete with banjo, are terrific. John McGlinn conducts the London Sinfonietta with verve and the right period flavor. The cast is uniformly excellent, but as Julie, the role created by Helen Morgan, soprano Teresa Stratas stands out: her wrenching performance can already be included among the legendary ones.

Anything Goes

January 3, 1989

Anything Goes was Cole Porter's biggest hit of the '30s, the fourth longest-running musical of that decade. The irrepressible score included such instant classics as "I Get a Kick Out of You," "You're the Top," "Blow, Gabriel, Blow," and of course, "Anything Goes." The original stars were William Gaxton and pudgy, befuddled Victor Moore, who'd just been teamed in two Gershwin political satires, *Of Thee I Sing* and *Let 'Em Eat Cake*. And as Reno Sweeney, the lady-evangelist-turned-nightclub singer, Ethel Merman created one of her landmark roles. *Anything Goes* has had numerous revivals. But in each of them songs were deleted, rewritten, sometimes vulgarly rearranged, or replaced by more famous ones from other Porter shows. The 1987 Lincoln Center production with Patti LuPone had a completely revised book. Now John McGlinn, who directed last year's wonderful recording of *Show Boat*, with all its original music, has done it again for *Anything Goes*. Even the dance numbers are intact.

In the '30s, when a musical closed, the instrumental arrangements were often lost or destroyed. But McGlinn had invaluable help in reconstructing *Anything Goes*. One of the original arrangers, Hans Spialek, was still alive, and he had a photographic memory. He died shortly before the project was completed, at the age of 89. The inventive orchestrations, by Spialek and Robert Russell Bennett, included parts for three trumpets, English horn, bass oboe, and cellist. Under McGlinn's direction, the London Symphony plays them with panache. Like *Show Boat*, McGlinn's *Anything Goes* includes numbers that were cut from the original show. Merman wouldn't sing the raunchy "Kate the Great" because her mother was going to be in the audience. Catherine the Great, Porter suggests, made more than history.

Veteran actor Jack Gilford is a delightful Moonface Martin, Public Enemy No. 13, and opera star Frederica von Stade, who was Magnolia in *Show Boat*, sings the stuck-up debutante Hope Harcourt superbly. But Kim Criswell as Reno and Cris Groenendaal as Billy Crocker, who gets thrown into the brig for not being Public Enemy No. 1, are disappointingly bland. A high-power performer like Patti LuPone can, for a moment, make you forget Merman. But Criswell is so generic, even her brashness seems to have been learned by rote.

So many dull performances of classical music on original instruments prove that authenticity is not enough. Complete fidelity to American musical comedy classics has to mean finding personalities comparable if not identical to the original stars, and that's the big hole in this otherwise admirable new recording. By the way, can anyone identify Drumstick Lipstick? In "You're the Top," it rhymes with "Irish Svipstick " (the way Fanny Brice, with a Yiddish accent, might say "Irish Sweepstakes"). It's the only item in the song the annotator can't explain.

Leroy Anderson

February 8, 1989

Listening to these delightful CDs of Leroy Anderson recordings (*The Leroy Anderson Collection*) made between 1952 and 1962, I've been trying to figure out what name to give the form of music he wrote. Mendelssohn wrote songs without words—isn't that Anderson's musical genre? If Schubert wrote "Musical Moments" for the piano, could we call Anderson's three-minute pieces symphonic miniatures? Is he not taken seriously because he was so popular or because his pieces were so short? Or because his primary outlet was the Pops? Or was he just never ambitious enough?

Anderson was a music major at Harvard in the late '20s. In 1936, he started writing for Arthur Fiedler and the Boston Pops. I have to confess, and this is a dangerous admission to make if you live in Boston, that I'm not a fan of the Pops. I hate the way good popular music is homogenized into phony, quasi-symphonic arrangements for which they were never intended (and Anderson wrote his share of these). But his original music for Pops was different, part of an authentic tradition of Americana, the band concert—one of the original ancestors of Pops. In the early '30s, Anderson had led the Harvard Band, and his use of brass instruments descends directly from Herbert L. Clarke and John Philip Sousa, as in his familiar "Bugler's Holiday."

Anderson used all sorts of popular forms, from waltzes to jazz. In 1951, "Blue Tango" became the first instrumental to reach number one on Your Hit Parade. He himself played piano and organ (he was a church organist), double bass, trombone, tuba, and accordion. He loved colorful instruments, like sleigh bells and pennywhistle, and even added a few to the repertory, like sandpaper, an alarm clock, and, of course, a typewriter.

Anderson's most ambitious undertaking was probably his Broadway show about silent movies called *Goldilocks*, with a book by Jean and Walter Kerr. It wasn't a hit, but it acquired a devoted posthumous following, especially for pieces like the "Pyramid Dance," music for the making of a silent-movie epic.

This collection has its share of facile and sentimental numbers. Anderson's tunes never pierce the heart the way those of the great American songwriters can. But the ability to entertain, the "talent to amuse," as Noel Coward once wrote about his own talent, shouldn't be too easily dismissed. His best numbers have a bright wit and charm. In their small way, they're memorable. Leroy Anderson reminds me of the ending of one of my favorite poems by William Carlos Williams, "The Pink Locust": "I am not, / I know, / in the galaxy of poets / a rose / but who, among the rest, / will deny me / my place."

Smithsonian American Musical Theater Collection

April 19, 1989

It was probably commerce, not a sense of history, that created the first original cast recordings. Now we can hear the fruits of those enterprises on this glorious set of American theater music. The Smithsonian has gathered some of the most memorable songs of the century, most of them sung by their original performers. There are history lessons—the origins of musical comedy in operetta, minstrel shows, social satire, and Tin Pan Alley—and lessons in stylistic authenticity. You'll hear legendary performers like Lillian Russell and George M. Cohan in their only commercial recordings, and forgotten stars like Edith Day, on her enchanting 1920 recording of "Alice Blue Gown"; 18-year-old Wynn Murray, who stopped her very first show, Rodgers & Hart's *Babes in Arms*, singing " Johnny One-Note"; and Adele Astaire, Fred's irresistible sister, who joins her brother in a couple of irresistible numbers, with George Gershwin himself at the piano.

I can think of few great stars who aren't here. You can hear Al Jolson, Eddie Cantor, Paul Robeson, Helen Morgan, Bill "Bojangles" Robinson, Danny Kaye, Ethel Waters, Ethel Merman, and Mary Martin in the freshness of their early success. And performers like Alfred Drake, John Raitt (who's Bonnie's father), Carol Channing, Rosalind Russell, Barbara Cook, Judy Holliday, Rex Harrison, Barbra Streisand, and Richard Burton in their most memorable musical roles. Practically every major songwriter or songwriting team from Victor Herbert to Stephen Sondheim is represented. There are also numbers from neglected shows like *The Golden Apple* by Jerome Morross and

John Latouche, in which Kaye Ballard is a turn-of-the-century American Helen of Troy seducing a traveling salesman named Paris on a "Lazy Afternoon."

There are fascinating surprises. Clifton Webb, Hollywood's classiest villain and the original Mr. Belvedere, was the suave song-and-dance man who in 1933 made the first recording of "Easter Parade." In 1940, Mary Martin sang "My Heart Belongs to Daddy" with a sly sexuality that's a whole other story from her later, more wholesome image. Ethel Merman's original 1934 recording of Cole Porter's "I Get a Kick Out of You," from *Anything Goes*, has a delicacy of phrasing that belies the cliché that she was only a brassy belter.

Did musicals after the war lose their buoyant sophistication, their inspired lunacy, their touching innocence? Did their seriousness get bloated? their sentimentality too calculated? With so much rare archival material at its disposal, maybe Smithsonian shouldn't have included so many shows whose original cast albums are currently available. Yet it's fascinating to hear the more recent songs in their historical or generic context. The Smithsonian collection makes a compelling case that the best American theater songs can match any of the world's great vocal music pleasure for pleasure.

Bernard Herrmann

May 3, 1989

Background music in the movies is supposed to affect your mood—heighten the suspense, make you feel romantic, give you the creeps, or underline how silly or cute someone is behaving. But you're not exactly supposed to listen to it. It's not there to call attention to itself. Maybe that's why when a serious composer produces an inflated, soupy, melodramatic score derivative of Rachmaninoff or Tchaikovsky or Bartok and Ligeti we can dismiss it as "movie music." But there's no question that some extremely talented composers have done some impressive work for film: Alex North, Dimitri Tiomkin, Max Steiner, more recently John Williams and Ennio Morricone, and the composer of music for many of Alfred Hitchcock's American films, Bernard Herrmann.

Herrmann, unlike many of his contemporary movie composers, was not born in Europe but in New York City, in 1911. He died in 1975. He attended NYU and Juilliard, and besides his movie scores his best known composition is his opera *Wuthering Heights*. He also wrote ballets and a cantata called *Moby Dick*. His first Hitchcock film was the minor comedy, *The Trouble with Harry*, in 1956, and Herrmann's charming New England atmosphere might very well be the best thing about that movie. He went on to do *The Man Who Knew Too Much, The Wrong Man, Vertigo* (one of the great scores), *North by Northwest, Psycho,* and *Marnie*. Herrmann also wrote the music for such remarkably diverse films as *Citizen Kane* and *The Magnificent Ambersons* (for Orson Welles), *Jane Eyre, The Snows of Kilimanjaro, King of the Kyber Rifles,* and Truffaut's *Fahrenheit 451*. In 1941 he won his only Oscar for *The Devil and Daniel Webster*. On a recent album of *Alfred Hitchcock's Film Music* we hear the suites from *Psycho* and *North by Northwest*.

Herrmann himself conducts the suite from *Psycho*, and the minute you hear the exciting opening notes you not only remember the film, you remember hearing the music too. A good score can linger in your mind even if you're not fully conscious of it. And the music also stands on its own. I want to hear the recording over and over again—without necessarily wanting to see the movie. I love those driving rhythms, rhythms of escape (I guess I can't quite forget the story), the way they alternate with that sweeping melody in the strings.

In *North by Northwest*, I was surprised at the flamenco rhythms, the castanets and tambourines. I certainly don't remember this dazzling Spanish orchestration from the movie—is it the whirling dance of international intrigue?

Herrmann's most distinctive writing is for strings—which can be extremely compact and intense yet forward moving at the same time. I hear the influence of Ravel, Stravinsky and Bartok, and even Mahler. But I also very much hear Herrmann's own sensibility, his delicacy and taste. Both his love themes and his suspense music are refined, subtly melodic, never drippy or melodramatic. And the suites are beautifully put together. The repeated themes are like an obsessive rondo—maybe even more powerful alone than when they are reflecting the obsessions of particular characters in certain movies.

D'Oyly Carte Gilbert & Sullivan

May 10, 1989

After Richard D'Oyly Carte produced Gilbert & Sullivan's *Trial by Jury* in 1875, he decided to start a company that would put on every new work by this celebrated team. Twelve full length operettas followed, and they've all been performed regularly ever since, not only by D'Oyly Carte's company in England but by professional and amateur groups all over the world, even in America. I was in my Junior High School production of *The Mikado* (I played Ko-Ko, the Lord High Executioner of Titipu) and I've been in love with G&S ever since. The Gilbert & Sullivan craze in this country began over a century ago. In fact, *The Pirates of Penzance* had its world premiere not in London but in New York, on New Year's Eve, 1879. The first complete D'Oyly Carte recordings started to appear before 1920. Some of the performers on them began their careers under the supervision of Gilbert & Sullivan themselves—performers like the great comedian Sir Henry Lytton, who spent fifty years with the company. He's on the 1927 recording of *The Gondoliers* (just reissued by Arabesque), singing the patter song of the Duke of Plaza-Toro, the celebrated hero who led his regiment from behind.

G&S performances have certainly declined from their early brilliance. The music-making on these old recordings is tighter and livelier. The tempos have an astonishing speed and buoyancy. The diction itself is breathtaking. Just listen to George Baker, as the lovesick and sleepless Lord Chancellor in *Iolanthe*. Baker kept recording the major G&S comic roles until he was nearly 78, but was never in D'Oyly Carte's company nor ever appeared in a professional G&S production.

The timing is as dazzling as the satire is timeless. Corruption, cowardice, pretension, and self-love are among the objects of Gilbert's droll humor and tingling barbs. One number in The Mikado goes: "A should die in misery,/That is, assuming I am B." In *Princess Ida*, Gilbert even parodied himself. Sullivan's music tackles—and explodes—the clichés of 19th-century opera and music hall. But it's also exhilarating in itself, irresistibly pretty, and even deeply touching, as in *Iolanthe*, where love can be a matter of life and death and some human feelings are taken with surprising seriousness, even by fairies.

There was Nellie Briarcliffe as the doomed Iolanthe. Other notable performers include the delicious Winifred Lawson, Bertha Lewis, and Martyn Green, the most famous Gilbert & Sullivan star of the century, as Ko-Ko, Green's first complete recording in a leading role. An added treat on the new CDs of *Gondoliers* and *Iolanthe* are selections even more historic than the complete operas themselves—some of the earliest G&S recordings ever made, including one made in 1902 of the Mikado explaining his humane system of justice. It's sung by Richard Temple, who in 1885 actually created the role of that philanthropic potentate.

Crossover

March 28, 1990

A recent CBS album called *Anything Goes: Stephane Grappelli and Yo-Yo Ma play (mostly) Cole Porter* raises again that nagging issue—the difficulty of cultural exchange between the worlds of pop and classical music. How few opera singers there are, for instance, who can sing pop songs without condescension or without making them sound bloated. And how few pop musicians can bring off a classical piece. Barbra Streisand once recorded an album of classical art songs, but instead of bringing new energy to these lieder, she tried so hard to be proper, the songs ended up sounding merely square. MCA has recently reissued on compact disc an old Decca album of the late Jascha Heifetz playing popular selections from Stephen Foster to Kurt Weill. After a luscious violin arrangement of "White Christmas" the tables are turned and Heifetz accompanies Bing Crosby in a couple of concert songs. Crosby over sentimentalizes the Lullaby from Benjamin Godard's *Jocelyn*, but I think his laid back crooning actually generates an odd intensity in Hermann Lohr's Gypsy song, "Where My Caravan Has Rested."

Sometimes the crossover is inspired. Think of the piccolo trumpet solo by George Mason of the New Philharmonia Orchestra on the Beatles' "Penny Lane." Paul McCartney had heard Mason playing Bach's 2nd Brandenburg Concerto on a BBC TV show and decided it was just what his song needed. The trumpet solo was the last thing he added. Mason sounds like a cornetist in an old-time band concert. He conveys both a celebratory dazzle and a deep nostalgia for more innocent days.

One of my favorite mixtures of classical and pop is the appearance of the Hollywood String Quartet on one of Frank

Sinatra's best albums, *Close to You*, which was recorded in 1956. Despite its name, the Hollywood String Quartet may be the greatest chamber ensemble produced in America. Its first violinist, Felix Slatkin, and cellist, Eleanor Aller, are the parents of Leonard Slatkin, the conductor of the St. Louis Symphony. In Nelson Riddle's sensitive arrangements, the Quartet reflects the earthy sweetness of Sinatra's youthful voice and the touching intimacy of his phrasing. Robin and Rainger's "With Every Breath I Take" takes on an emotional complexity chamber musicians and lieder singers should envy.

I wonder what Sinatra could have done with Schubert? Yo-Yo Ma's Schubert is already legendary. But on his Cole Porter album with Grapelli it's remarkable how much character he can get his cello to inject into the fairly conventional jazz arrangements. Ma is a musical chameleon. His jazz playing seems as completely convincing as his classical—teasing, but elegant, never trivializing. To Yo-Yo Ma, fun can be a serious business and still remain fun. That's probably why his playing is so easy to love.

Mary Martin Sings - Richard Rodgers Plays

August 8, 1990

The Broadway musical has been in something of a Renaissance—I don't mean particularly on Broadway itself, but on recordings. Great old scores are being revived with their delightful and stylish original orchestrations. My one disappointment has been with the singers, most of whom seem awfully bland compared to the lively personalities of the great stars for whom the songs were first written. One of the greatest of them is Mary Martin, the wide-eyed girl from Weatherford, Texas, who floored Broadway in 1938 by innocently singing Cole Porter's "My Heart Belongs to Daddy" wearing a fur jacket and nothing else. But after Rodgers and Hammerstein's *South Pacific*, her image was fixed as the clean-cut girl-next-door. Boy-next-door, if you count *Peter Pan*. Or nun-next-door if you count her biggest hit, Rodgers and Hammerstein's *The Sound of Music*. She was always charming, but her material became awfully sanitized. When Mary Martin and Richard Rodgers got together in 1957 for a recording session of Rodgers tunes, they chose only songs that had not been written for her, like "Some Enchanted Evening," the big song in *South Pacific* she never got to sing. In fact, most of the songs they recorded are by Rodgers and his earlier and greater partner, Lorenz Hart. It's good to have Mary Martin singing lyrics that call for some of the slyness and wryness that first made her a star. Like Rodgers and Hart's wicked "To Keep My Love Alive," which they wrote for the revival of *A Connecticut Yankee* in 1943. It was Hart's last lyric. He died a week after the show opened.

Mary Martin never sounded like anyone else. She obviously has a trained voice, but its humanizing flaws—the occasional little creak or croak—make it instantly recognizable. Her diction is flawless—sometimes even a little too manicured. But she never preens. A few weeks ago, I heard a Broadway Evening at the Boston Pops, and the singing cipher who did "Night and Day" was so full of himself, a friend of mine remarked that he should have changed the words to "Night and day, I am the one." Mary Martin gives herself to the song. Her phrasing makes you believe she knows the implications of every word. She seems to be living one of the best Broadway songs ever written, Rodgers and Hart's "It Never Entered My Mind," from their 1940 musical, *Higher and Higher.*

This album includes some fascinating rarities, like "Moon of My Delight," from *Chee-Chee*, a show—so help me—about a man who doesn't want to become a eunuch. It was Rodgers and Hart's biggest flop. The orchestrations on this album by Robert Russell Bennett are all rather on the syrupy side. Some of the verses are even in the wrong place. And yet the recording was made with the composer himself at the piano. So much for authenticity. Richard Rodgers was clearly not one of the keyboard geniuses of the Great White Way, but his brief and clunky accompaniments for a performer so close to his heart make a touching souvenir.

Decca Original Cast Albums

November 28, 1990

Oklahoma! may be the best loved original cast Broadway show album of all time. It was first issued on 78s by Decca in the 1940s. Later, a second volume appeared containing three numbers that weren't on the original set. Now, for the first time, everything recorded by the original New York cast is on a single album. I love original cast recordings, with the famous songs in their intended contexts, and sung by the performers who introduced them. I even love hearing the songs that didn't become hits—like this oddly sour number from *Oklahoma!*, "Lonely Room." It's sung by Alfred Drake, probably the most vibrant leading man in the history of Broadway musicals.

Among the Decca albums that have finally appeared on CD are three shows by Rodgers and Hammerstein: their first two collaborations, *Oklahoma!* and the equally folksy but more ambitious *Carousel*, and *The King and I*, starring Gertrude Lawrence at the end of her great career and Yul Brynner at the beginning of his. Rodgers and Hammerstein are often praised for changing the course of American musicals. Supposedly for the first time, songs were completely integrated into a plot, and symbolic ballets revealed the inner life of the characters. But today *Oklahoma!* sounds more like old-fashioned operetta, much less adventurous than the shows Rodgers and Hammerstein each did earlier with other partners—like *Show Boat*, *On Your Toes*, or *Pal Joey*. *Oklahoma!* and *Carousel* were already reflecting middle-American sentimentality and family values that were replacing the urbane sex and satire that sparked the shows and films of the 1930s. Hammerstein's ersatz homespun can get awfully corny, even preachy. But there's still Rodgers' endless flow of melody and the vivid performances by people like Alfred Drake and Celeste Holm in *Oklahoma!*, and, in *Carousel*, John Raitt (who's now better known as Bonnie Raitt's father) and the touching Jan Clayton (who played the mother in TV's Lassie series).

One of Rodgers and Hammerstein's most successful collaborations is a show they produced but didn't write: *Annie Get Your Gun*, which was the biggest hit ever for both its songwriter, Irving Berlin, and its star, Ethel Merman. Who could forget the irrepressible Merman as Annie Oakley one-upping sharpshooter Ray Middleton? Oddly, on the album, Merman doesn't actually sing "There's No Business Like Show Business," the song that became her personal anthem.

Decca also issued Leonard Bernstein's delectably funny and unpretentious vehicle for Rosalind Russell, *Wonderful Town*. Three of Bernstein's four best shows were about New York City, and *Wonderful Town* is surely his most wackily sophisticated musically, as when Russell and Edie Adams do the "Wrong-Note Rag."

MCA has done well by these shows. The sound has been digitally remastered, and while some recent scholarship might have been more informative, the original liner notes and covers are a sweetly nostalgic touch.

Fernwood 2-Night

January 1, 1991

After a hard night at the concert hall, I like to stretch out in front of the TV to watch an old movie or re-runs of old comedy shows. Recently, my favorite has been *Fernwood 2-Night*. In the late '70s, when Jimmy Carter was still president and Ronald Reagan was revving up his assault on Liberalism and on the White House, Mr. Television wasn't Uncle Miltie but Norman Lear. He's the producer of such hit sitcoms as *All in the Family, The Jeffersons, Sanford and Son, Maude,* and *One Day at a Time*. These shows changed the face of TV humor by injecting situation comedy with trenchant social and political satire. The subjects were no longer Lucy wanting to break into show biz, but women's rights and gay liberation, racial prejudice, politics, and even television itself. My favorite of Lear's shows was *Mary Hartman, Mary Hartman*. It was a wild soap opera parody with Louise Lasser as an Ohio housewife beleaguered by a mass murderer, her husband's impotence, and the waxy yellow buildup on her linoleum.

Perhaps the quintessential Norman Lear shows were the remarkable spin-offs of *Mary Hartman, Fernwood 2-Night* and its sequel, *America 2-Night*, his send-ups of late-night TV talk shows. "Tonight!," the announcer begins after the theme music, "Almost live and nearly from Hollywood, it's *America 2-Night*, 30 minutes of big-time entertainment brought to you on the UBS network, from the Broadcasting Mall in Alta Coma, the unfinished furniture capital of the world."

The host is Barth Gimble, who, it's insinuated, is on the lam from Miami on some sort of morals charge involving a minor. Barth arrives in Fernwood, Ohio, after his wife-beating twin brother Garth has impaled himself on an aluminum Christmas tree. Martin Mull plays Barth (he also played Garth) with hilarious self-infatuation and contempt for the stupidity of others. And Fred Willard plays Barth's announcer, Jerry Hubard, with such wide-eyed naïveté that his appalling ignorance and bigotry—and awful puns—are actually an endearing counterpart to Barth's relentless snideness. Try to imagine Barth explaining Mount Rushmore to Jerry.

A talk show also has to have a band and Fernwood's is Happy Kyne and the Mirth Makers. Happy, who's played by composer Frank DeVol, is a singularly mirth-less drip who owns a fast food chain on the side ominously called the Bun 'n' Run. There are some regular guests, like Connie Bushman from the Pet Control Center, who wants animals to have a good time, too, so she develops a brothel for dogs. And there are one-shot visitors, like the enterprising Puerto Rican man who trains minority college graduates to become ethnic stereotypes, so they can hire themselves out to middle-class white neighborhoods that want to get their property taxes lowered.

I find *Fernwood 2-Night's* nightmare vision of America both exhilarating and extremely upsetting. Its satire of sex, greed, and prejudice seems even funnier—and more pointed—today than it was twelve years and two presidents ago.

The Original All-American Sousa!

May 1, 1991

Most serious classical music lovers probably don't have the same affection for marches as they do for other kinds of lighter music. Waltzes, for instance, also keep to one rhythm, but three-quarter time is more interesting than 4/4, and marches just don't have the same romantic appeal. Love is a more interesting and complex emotion than militant patriotism. But this new album of Sousa marches reveals a greater variety than marches are usually credited with. Of course, the album includes the famous ones like "Stars and Stripes Forever," "Semper Fidelis," and "The U.S. Field Artillery March" (better known as "The caissons go rolling along"). We're told in the informative historical notes that for the "Artillery March" Sousa used an Army tune composed just after the turn of the century by Edward L. Gruber. The performance by Keith Brion and the New Sousa Band keeps with Sousa's frequent practice of ending with pistol shots.

Sousa's marches weren't all intended for marching. Some were concert pieces, like the delightful Grand March "The Pride of Pittsburgh," which here gets its world premiere recording. It was written for the Pittsburgh Exposition in 1901 to honor two Pittsburgh composers: Stephen Foster and Ethelbert Nevin. Sousa quotes two of their tunes in witty counterpoint, Foster's "Come Where My Love Lies Dreaming" and Nevin's still familiar "Narcissus." There are also marches Sousa based on melodies from his operettas (he wrote 15). And there's one with a middle-eastern flavor called "Nobles of the Mystic Shrine," which was written as a tribute to his Masonic lodge.

Hundreds of recordings were made by the so-called Sousa Band, but the Victor Talking Machine Company released only six actually conducted by Sousa himself. Each was made immediately after the marches themselves were composed, between 1917 and 1923. All six are on this new Delos CD, such as Sousa's own 1923 recording of "Nobles of the Mystic Shrine". There's also a speech that Sousa made on a radio program sponsored by Bond Bread on November 6, 1929, his 75th birthday. He died two years later. John Philip Sousa's own buoyant live broadcast performance of "Stars and Stripes Forever" is of course a favorite. Sousa also wrote words about the American flag to his memorable tune: "Let despots remember the day / When our fathers with mighty endeavor / Proclaimed as they marched to the fray / That by their might / And by their right / It waves forever."

Tippecanoe and Tyler Too

September 30, 1992

Hearing a new recording of 19th-century American political music, it occurs to me that this country hasn't had a memorable new campaign song since Irving Berlin wrote "I Like Ike!" Up until this year, the Democrats have relied on "Happy Days Are Here Again" as their party anthem. That song was written for a 1930 movie musical called *Chasing Rainbows* and FDR appropriated it for his 1932 campaign. It's a significant political statement in itself that this year the Democrats exchanged "Happy Days Are Here Again" for Fleetwood Mac's "Don't Stop Thinkin' About Tomorrow." And what does it say about the Republicans that while Pat Buchanan and Pat Robertson were bashing gay lifestyles in Houston, the Republican convention theme song, "The Best of Times," was from *La Cage aux Folles*, a Broadway musical about the family values of a homosexual couple?

The new album is called *Tippecanoe and Tyler Too—Politics as Usual! in the 1800s*, and it's a thoroughly delightful piece of musical and political history. It begins with the campaign of Andrew Jackson, which brass player Jay Krush reminds us in his liner notes was the first time the American public really got to express its direct voice in a national election (before that, members of the Electoral College were chosen by state legislatures). The songs continue through the Civil War period and end with the election of Ulysses S. Grant and the American centennial. The title song is the 1840 campaign song of William Henry Harrison and John Tyler. It must surely have helped them defeat incumbent president Martin Van Buren.

I'm happy to report that some of these old songs are as

scurrilous as politics ever gets. One is called "Buck's Private Confession Publicly Revealed." It's from the 1856 election campaign and puts some nasty words about Democratic candidate James Buchanan into his own mouth. Fortunately, negative campaigning doesn't always work. Buchanan won—he was our only bachelor president. The marvelous folk singer Linda Russell is the satirical voice of Buchanan. Rudolph Palmer is the cheery fortepianist.

Maybe Buchanan won because his own campaign song was written by a great songwriter, Stephen Foster, who was Buchanan's brother's wife's brother. Some of the songs here are also about serious issues—abolition of slavery, universal suffrage, national unity—and they enrich this album. Along with the satirical and the celebratory, there are several dirges for presidents who died in office. The most moving, appropriately, is "President Lincoln's Funeral March," composed by T.M. Brown.

The singing by Linda Russell, tenors Patrick Romano and Frederick Urrey, and bass baritone John Ostendorf is thoroughly idiomatic, not at all operatic. The five members of the Chestnut Brass Company play their keyed bugles, cornopeans, ophicleides, and saxhorns with brilliant precision and energy. Maybe all that Bill Clinton or George Bush really needs now is a great campaign song.

Maybe not.

Cole Porter

October 8, 1992

A century after he was born in Peru, Indiana, on June 9, 1891, and more than half-a-century after his first song hits swept America, Cole Porter is still sung and still listened to. His music has never lost its insinuating appeal, his lyrics have lost none of their freshness or sharpness. All those topical lists, in songs like "You're the Top" and "Let's Do It," present the most vivid picture of their time. But I think it's that very specificity that makes them so universal. Which may be why they've survived so many different approaches. This recent collection is most extraordinary for its variety of performers and styles. Represented here are not only the worlds of the legitimate theater and film, the stars Porter wrote for, but also the great figures from the world of jazz and pop music who took over and helped spread the word. So we not only get Fred Astaire, Ethel Merman, Mary Martin, Gertrude Lawrence, and even James Stewart, who introduced "Easy to Love" in the 1936 film *Born to Dance*. But there's also Ella Fitzgerald, Billie Holiday, Louis Armstrong, Artie Shaw, Art Tatum, Benny Goodman, and the late Sylvia Syms. There are even a couple of awful but fascinating souped-up versions by opera singers. It's great that the producers allow us to hear some of the songs in radically different incarnations.

I'm especially glad that this set includes some of Porter's own favorite performers like jazz singer Lee Wiley, and cabaret star Mabel Mercer, who was one of the century's greatest interpreters of pop and theater lyrics. Porter is often dismissed—or admired—as a rich escapist. But I think underlying everything he wrote is an awareness of exactly what he wanted to escape from. Listen to his poetic autobiographical lament about the loneliness of wealth, "Down in the Depths (on the 90th Floor)." In its original—and definitive—1936 version by Ethel Merman it has an almost tragic grandeur. "When the only one you've wanted wants another, / What's the good of swank / Or cash in the bank galore?"

Listening to these songs from the 1930s, I'm impressed by how contemporary Porter's celebrations of diversity and irreverence and his Depression cynicism seem right now. What could be more timely than these lines he himself sings from "Anything Goes": "Just think of those shocks you got / and those knocks you got / and those blues you got / from those news you got / and those pains you got / if any brains you got / from those little radios."

Was Porter predicting the Walkman back in 1934?

Elvis Costello

February 24, 1993

Elvis Costello said he learned to read and write down music when he began working on his new album, *The Juliet Letters*. He collaborated with a highly respected classical group, the Brodsky String Quartet. But is this a new and original concept or just a pretentious imitation of the classics?

Back in the 1950s, a Frank Sinatra album called *Close to You* created a sensation because the songs were accompanied by one of America's greatest chamber groups, the Hollywood String Quartet. It remains one of Sinatra's warmest and most elegant albums. Or think of the Beatles. A string octet helped darken and deepen the mood of "Eleanor Rigby." And in "Penny Lane," David Mason of the Philharmonia Orchestra played a brilliant piccolo-trumpet obbligato. It sounded like a fanfare out of Handel and energized the song in surprising ways. More recently, the Kronos String Quartet played an arrangement of Jimi Hendrix that showed how classical strings could be just as gutsy as more traditional rock instruments.

But Elvis Costello's *The Juliet Letters* is on a whole different level of ambition. It's not merely a series of songs with a classical-style accompaniment, but a real song cycle—not a single continuous story but a series of evocative, thematically connected songs in many different moods—art songs—the sort of thing Schubert and Schumann did, not something you'd associate with pop music.

The song that's at the heart of the album is "I thought I'd write to Juliet." It's based on a letter that Elvis Costello received during the Gulf War. The cycle consists of a series of imaginary letters. Costello says he was inspired by something he had read about real people writing letters to Juliet Capulet in Verona. His co-writers and composers are the Brodsky String Quartet, who are especially admired for their performances of Dimitri Shostakovich's beautiful but bleak string quartets.

I really like the tension between the sound of the strings and the rough sound of Elvis Costello's expressive but distinctly unclassical voice. He sings with passion and irony, something Barbra Streisand seemed afraid to do when she recorded her album of classical art songs. The Brodskys' accompaniments are rich and varied, and of course wonderfully played.

I wish some of the songs had more melodic profile. They're more recitative than aria. Some of them sound as if they were ground out by committee—a committee heavily influenced by Kurt Weill. But I'm finally impressed by the consistent intelligence and the pervasive sense of melancholy. I find *The Juliet Letters* a lot more moving than, say, Paul McCartney's *Liverpool Oratorio*, which felt more like liverwurst—more an imitation of classical music than a real intersection between classical and pop. I wish more pop artists had Elvis Costello's guts to really revitalize classical forms and open up such daring new possibilities.

Barbra Streisand, *Back to Broadway*

November 4, 1993

Barbra Streisand got her start on Broadway, and that's where she became a star. So I'm happy that she's gone, as the title of her new album says, *Back to Broadway*. She's in great voice, and among the dozen show tunes she's recorded here are some surprises, and some of the best things she's ever done. But the selections and arrangements are so erratic, you never know if the next cut is going to be a classic or a bomb. *Back to Broadway* runs the current gamut of Broadway styles, from the Rubick's-cube complexity of Stephen Sondheim to Andrew Lloyd Webber at his most treacly. The two worst songs on the album are from Webber's new musical version of *Sunset Boulevard*, which hasn't yet opened on Broadway. In Billy Wilder's film, *Norma Desmond*, the faded silent screen star played by Gloria Swanson, says that in her day, stars "had faces." The problem with these songs is that they're utterly faceless. Webber is recycling his already generic material yet again.

In *Hello, Dolly!*, Dolly Levi says, "Some people paint; some sew, I meddle." Streisand's own meddling sometimes works miracles. One of the best things on the album is "*The Music of the Night*," from Webber's Phantom of the Opera. Streisand sings it with Michael Crawford, the original Phantom and Streisand's old co-star in *Hello, Dolly!* Their interlacing voices create more intricate and interesting patterns than anything Webber originally intended.

Some of Streisand's meddling, though, doesn't work. She overcomplicates the open-hearted romanticism of "Some Enchanted Evening." She turns Kurt Weill's subtle and insinuating "Speak Low" into a disco disaster. In the other duet on the album, two unrelated songs from West Side Story with Johnny Mathis, her intensity overpowers his soft-focus sound. The straighter she sings, the better, as in "The Man I Love," or "Luck Be a Lady," a song she was born for. But her unconvincing slow tempo drags down another song from *Guys and Dolls*, the more delicately conversational "I've Never Been in Love Before."

Then there's Stephen Sondheim. His verbal and rhythmic prestidigitation is right up Streisand's Shubert Alley. She actually got Sondheim to add new verses to "Children Will Listen," the song from *Into the Woods* that she sang at Bill Clinton's inaugural party. Although it loses some of the irony it had in the original show, it has a new political bite. Streisand personalizes everything she sings. But when she sings words she really believes, the ferocity of her conviction can be overwhelming.

Spike Jones

July 21, 1994

Have you ever thought that electronic music sounded like gunshots, sirens, or gurgles, gargles, burps, hiccups, and sneezes? Well Spike Jones and his City Slickers did it all first, and they did it without electronics.

Lindley Armstrong Jones began recording for RCA in the summer of 1941, and became one of America's most popular stars. He satirized every kind of music from hillbilly to Hawaiian, and contemporary subjects from Knock-Knock jokes to the Nazis. In "Der Fuehrer's Face," he gives Hitler a raspberry. Classical music is another favorite target. A highlight of the new Catalyst disc called *Spiked!* is a six-part send-up of the *Nutcracker Suite*. One of Jones's most popular recordings is his "musical depreciation" of Luigi Arditi's classic song "Il Bacio" (The Kiss). Ina Souez, the marvelous Donna Anna on the very first complete recording of Mozart's *Don Giovanni*, in 1936, proves she's also a good sport. Sopranos, beware of "Il Barkio."

Other familiar voices include those of Mel Blanc (alias Bugs Bunny) and the tongue-twisted Doodles Weaver, brother of NBC-TV President Sylvester "Pat" Weaver and uncle of Sigourney Weaver. No style goes undeconstructed; no pretension goes unpunctured. Also few ethnic stereotypes or human impairments are ignored. Some of these 50-year-old jokes are not what you would call politically correct. But the comedy keeps its bite because the timing of the City Slickers is so sharp and their playing so brilliant. Many of the dated references are explained to a new generation in the richly detailed notes (with great photos) on Rhino Records' 2-disc *Spike Jones Anthology*.

No less distinguished a Jones fan than novelist Thomas Pynchon contributes a thoughtful essay for the Catalyst disc. If I count correctly, only five cuts overlap, which means both sets are indispensable to anyone who loves music and likes to laugh.

Passion

November 14, 1994

Stephen Sondheim is our greatest living songwriter. By injecting serious, sometimes even painful content into tired old formulas, he both transforms the formula and makes the formula part of what the song is about. In his show *Follies*, for example, there's a torch song called "Losing My Mind," which was introduced by the late Dorothy Collins. It's about the corrosive, self-destructive power of a passion that isn't returned. The character really is losing her mind. That it's sung as a torch song, rather than, say, as an operatic mad scene, heightens the irony. "Losing My Mind" becomes a song about the very nature of torch songs. More recently, Sondheim's has attempted a more operatic style. To me that style often seems pretentious and unmemorable—not as good as the best opera and a betrayal of Sondheim's own greatest talent. Snippets I heard from his latest show, *Passion*, made me think it was just more of the same. Driving down to New York from Boston to see it, I started listening to the new original-cast album. I couldn't stop. Now I think it's the fulfillment of Sondheim's recent musical experiments. It's the tightest of all his scores—as worked out as a Mahler symphony, an intricate network of musical and verbal themes that become more haunting each time they reappear. And in this rich musical tapestry, Sondheim has embedded some of his purest and most heartfelt songs, not least of all the extraordinary Donna Murphy singing "Loving You."

Murphy plays the infirm and ugly Fosca (which is Italian for dark or shadowy). She falls passionately in love with the handsome young Captain, Giorgio, played by Jere Shea, who is already passionately in love with the beautiful Clara (which means clear or bright). Murphy's expressive speaking voice is as musical as her singing voice, ranging from a Streisand-like soaring at the top to a smoldering Lauren Bacall growl at the bottom. She makes her first entrance down a long flight of stairs behind a scrim—a dark, shadowy figure hunched-over like a praying mantis. She's an object lesson for actors on how posture can project character. Murphy's stage presence is electric. Marin Mazzie makes a moving, complex Clara—not just another pretty face. And Adrianne Lobel's shifty, evocative set is practically another character. But in some ways the album is even better than the production. The two-hour show is nearly half music, and almost all of it is on the album, including most of the music that accompanies spoken dialogue. So we get the complete story but without the unaccompanied dialogue. The album proves that most of that extra dialogue is unnecessary. Even the most important moment in the plot—when Giorgio discovers he's really in love with Fosca—is actually more convincing on the record because Sondheim's bleak but beautiful music reveals more about human feeling than words alone can say.

Oscar-winning Songs

March 24, 1995

In 1934, seven years after the first Oscars, the Motion Picture Academy started to recognize the best song from a film. The first winner was "The Continental," which Fred Astaire and Ginger Rogers danced in *The Gay Divorcee*. Rhino Records has just issued a five-CD set of all the prize-winning songs of the last sixty years.

Bob Hope made his Hollywood feature film debut in *The Big Broadcast of 1938*. One of the high points was a duet he sang with the endearing Shirley Ross, who played one of his ex-wives. "Thanks for the Memory," of course, became Hope's theme song. But it's useful to remember that in the movie, the song was a response to a particular context. "Thanks for the Memory" is surely the most touching and civilized song ever written about a divorce.

Nine other songs were nominated for an Oscar in 1938, including such eventual standards as Irving Berlin's "Change Partners" and "Jeepers Creepers" by Harry Warren and Johnny Mercer. Berlin would later get the Oscar for "White Christmas." Warren had already won for "Lullaby of Broadway," and Johnny Mercer would go on to win four Oscars (a record he shares with three other songwriters). Jerome Kern, Dorothy Fields, Harold Arlen, Rodgers and Hammerstein, Frank Loesser, Lerner and Loewe, and Stephen Sondheim all won Oscars, but neither Cole Porter nor George and Ira Gershwin ever did. John Lennon and Paul McCartney never even got nominated. In 1937, one of the Gershwins' greatest songs, "They Can't Take That Away from Me," lost out to a Hawaiian number called "Sweet Leilani," sung in the film *Waikiki Wedding* by the phenomenally popular Bing Crosby—one of four Crosby hits to receive Oscars. Harold Arlen and Ira Gershwin's "The Man That Got Away," from the 1954 Judy Garland version of *A Star Is Born*, is my nomination for one of the greatest musical numbers in film history. But it lost to the pretty but innocuous "Three Coins in the Fountain," which was the first Oscar-winning song written for a movie's title credits—and one of three winners associated with Frank Sinatra. As Fats Waller said, "One never knows, do one?"

About half the winners are conventional love songs like "The Way You Look Tonight" or "All the Way." But there are just as many catchy novelties like "On the Atcheson, Topeka, and the Santa Fe" or "Zippedee-Doo-Dah" (one of six winners from Disney films). I especially like the songs that play a part in the dramatic or emotional situation of a film, like "Over the Rainbow," "Baby, It's Cold Outside," or "Que Sera Sera" (the only Oscar-winning song from an Alfred Hitchcock movie). Tex Ritter's great title ballad for "High Noon" is a distillation of the film's archetypal conflicts. It's one of the main reasons people took this Western so seriously.

In recent years, the competition has been pretty feeble, though there are happy surprises, like Stevie Wonder's "I Just Called to Say I Love You" or Bruce Springsteen's powerful AIDS anthem, "Streets of Philadelphia." You can hear all 60 Oscar-winners on the new Rhino set, many but not all of them recorded by their original performers or composers. Unfortunately, because of licensing problems, we get no Sinatra, Shore, Streisand, or Springsteen. Richie Havens recorded a good cover version of "Streets of Philadelphia" especially for this set. An 80-page booklet full of interviews and fascinating information helps distract from what's missing. After all, popular songs can reveal as much about their times as headlines.

"And this year, the winner is . . ."

Germaine Montero

April 3, 1995

In the 1960s, it was a refreshing change from the voice of Judy Collins to hear the earthy, uncompromising, sometimes even grating voice of Germaine Montero. An actress of extraordinary expressivity, variety, and bite, Montero was a Parisian who went to Spain in her early '20s and worked closely with the great Spanish poet and playwright Federico García Lorca. After Lorca's assassination by the fascists in 1936 (when he was 37), Montero returned to Paris, where she appeared in famous productions of Lorca's *Blood Wedding* and Brecht's *Mother Courage*. She also became a cabaret star. One of my college teachers turned me on to two of Montero's LPs: *Canciones de España*, which has just been reissued, and a haunting, hair-raising album of Lorca's poems and songs (which I hope will also be reissued). During the Spanish Civil War, some of these folk songs had been transformed into satiric political ballads. For example, "Los Quatro Muleros" ("The Four Mule Drivers")—a song of sexual desire—became "Los Quatro Generales." Montero sings the original version as if she knows perfectly well its other implications.

There are songs of love—requited and otherwise, comic and desperate, some in the voices of women, some in men's voices; also lullabies, religious songs, and songs of civic boosterism. One song—transcribed by Lorca himself—tells of a virtuous wife who would rather have her husband, in his coarse gray cape, than the Commander who is trying to seduce her with his fancy one.

These recordings were made in 1959 and 1960. The arrangements by conductor Salvador Bacarisse are colorful but retain the slightly dated theatrical flavor of a time when folk music was just being rediscovered. For me, they have their own nostalgic charm. Montero is also a creature of her time. But her power and conviction still ring true after more than thirty years. I don't love this album in exactly the same way I loved it when I was in college. But I still love it.

Kurt Weill, *From Berlin to Broadway*

March 19, 1996

A new two-disc set of historical Kurt Weill recordings is not only thorough but it also makes available some of the rarest material, including, for example, a recording of playwright Bertolt Brecht singing "Mack the Knife," the most famous song from his most famous collaboration with Weill, *The Threepenny Opera*. He recorded it in May 1929, less than a year after the opening, and his conductor here, Theo Mackeben, conducted the world premiere. This recording is featured on Pearl Records' first major historical retrospective of the theater music of Kurt Weill—as the title of the album says—*From Berlin to Broadway*.

These are the very first recordings not only of *Threepenny Opera*, *The Rise and Fall of the City of Mahagonny*, and *Happy End*, but also music from Weill's Broadway hits. There's *Knickerbocker Holiday*, with Walter Huston as Peter Stuyvesant. Supersophisticate Gertrude Lawrence stars in *Lady in the Dark*, the first Broadway musical about psychoanalysis, which was also the musical that turned a young featured comedian named Danny Kaye into a star.

For the first time a single set of discs allows us to hear the continuities and discontinuities that were part of Weill's transition from being a European composer who imitated American jazz to an American composer who clung to European traditions of operetta. It's hard to tell if the music to the ballet "Venus in Ozone Heights" is by the world-weary Berlin cynic or the sentimental Broadway optimist.

It's actually Maurice Abravanel conducting "Venus in Ozone Heights," the ballet music from *One Touch of Venus*, star ring Mary Martin as a Roman statue who comes to life and wreaks havoc. All the selections are marvelous. There's the ferocious first recording of the *Threepenny Opera Suite* by one of Weill's biggest champions, the great conductor Otto Klemperer. Ernst Busch, the actor who first sang "The Ballad of Mack the Knife," never recorded it, but he later appeared in the opera *The Silver Sea*, and we have the two powerful songs he recorded from that. We get not only Walter Huston's famous recording of "September Song," but also the flip side, a song about Venus and Mars called "The Scars," with surprisingly raw lyrics by Maxwell Anderson.

Of course there are also nearly—though not quite—all of Lotte Lenya's original recordings, dating back to her earliest versions of "Pirate Jenny," "The Bilbao Song," and "Surabaya Johnny." But the great discoveries are the six recordings of Weill songs that Lenya made in the early 1940s accompanied at the piano by her husband, Kurt Weill himself. These are their only documented performances together—and they're unforgettable.

Ira Gershwin at 100

March 5, 1997

December 6, 1996, marked the 100th birthday of the "other" Gershwin, George's older brother and closest collaborator Ira, who died in 1983. That night, Carnegie Hall presented a gala tribute to him, and on March 7, on Great Performances, most PBS stations across the country will be telecasting a 90-minute video of that concert.

Some of this country's best poets are the song lyricists whose lively language, fresh imagery, and what Ira Gershwin called "fascinating rhythm" capture aspects of American life that more strictly literary poets don't often deal with—from personal relationships to politics. "Who cares what banks fail in Yonkers," Ira wrote during the Depression, "Long as you've got the kiss that conquers?" "Of thee I sing, baby," begins the cheeky title song of the 1931 political satire for which Ira became the first lyricist to win the Pulitzer Prize. In the preeminent American opera, *Porgy and Bess*, he warns us: "It Ain't Necessarily So."

The witty contraction "'S Wonderful" swings into the verse with the exhilaration of colloquial American English at its most colorful—don't trust anyone who sings "It's wonderful." I wouldn't trust anyone who changes any of Ira's words. What foolish political correctness made Karen Akers, one of the most sensitive singers in the long lineup of stars and semi-stars at Carnegie Hall, change the line in "But Not for Me" from "It all began so well,/but what an end./This is the time a fell-/er needs a friend" to the clunky "this is the time/a person needs a friend." Didn't she hear the rhyme of "well" and "fella"? Didn't she get the irony of Ira's gender bending?

This Ira Gershwin Gala is one of those formula enterprises—you know, the over-orchestrated overture, the generic announcer who introduces the movie-star co-hosts as "Mister" Michael York and "Miss" Angie Dickinson, the production numbers with ballet dancing that has nothing to do with the songs, and the hosts reading from a script that has barely enough facts to be informative and barely enough anecdotes to be entertaining.

At Carnegie Hall I saw some marvelous Gershwin home movies, but many of them have been edited out of the TV version, along with Michael York's recitation of Gershwin lyrics, and the late composer Burton Lane's reminiscences of his collaboration with Ira. Lane died only a few weeks afterwards—it's too bad all that's left of him in the TV version is his effervescent accompaniment to the smarmy preening of Michael Feinstein, one of those singers who gives the term "song stylist" such a bad name.

Lane's presence, though, is an important reminder that after George Gershwin's untimely death, his brother worked brilliantly with other composers, like Jerome Kern, Harold Arlen, Vincent Youmans, Kurt Weill, even Aaron Copland! Of course, the main purpose of the show is to hear Gershwin's lyrics, and we get a nice balance between great standards like "The Man That Got Away" and obscure novelty numbers like "Just Another Rhumba," which Jon Lovitz delivers with deadpan charm. The performer who most lived up to the material is Rosemary Clooney, who lived next door to the Gershwins, and may be our greatest living interpreter of classic popular songs. She sings a couple of the best ones ever written, including "Love Is Here to Stay," the opening verse to which George Gershwin didn't live to write. Clooney tells us that it's the only music ever composed by Ira himself.

Porgy and Bess

September 8, 1998

This year is George Gershwin's 100th anniversary. Although there hasn't been a major new Gershwin recording, there have been some interesting releases of music from Gershwin's most ambitious work. After *Porgy and Bess* opened in 1935, it took sixteen years to get a complete recording. In 1951, Columbia Records' Goddard Lieberson, who would become responsible for his company's extraordinary series of Broadway original cast albums, produced it with care and originality. It was one of the first opera recordings to use sound effects—like rolling dice or the sounds of a fight—and established an approach still going today. This album has the strongest cast of any complete version. New York City Opera baritone Laurence Winters, who had a bigger career in Germany than in this country, is vocally shining and characterizes the crippled but optimistic Porgy with profound honesty. He matches Todd Duncan, the original Porgy, by not trying to imitate him. This recording restores the powerful "Buzzard Song," which Gershwin cut before the New York opening. Winters gives it the eloquent intensity of a great Schubert song.

Avon Long, as Sportin' Life, the cynical, seductive drug pusher, is equally impressive—the smoothest talking and smoothest singing Sportin' Life on record—all snake oil and venom. Who could resist?

To ensure authenticity, Columbia included five members of the original *Porgy and Bess* company, including Helen Dowdy, the Strawberry Woman—and the best one you've ever heard.

There have been some Gershwin discoveries since 1951, and you can hear some of these on a new album of *Porgy* excerpts with Erich Kunzel and the Cincinnati Pops. Gershwin's original version of the opening scene of act three is an elegiac Requiem trio for Bess, Serena, and Maria. This is followed by Bess and Serena's lullaby "Lonely Boy," which Gershwin dropped during the Boston tryout in exchange for Bess's reprise of "Summertime," which Anne Brown, the original Bess, otherwise wouldn't have gotten to sing.

Kunzel also gives us a fascinating bit of musical history—the first recording of the original version of Gershwin's first opera—the one-act *Blue Monday: Opera a la Afro-American*, which was performed—once—on Broadway by white singers in blackface. Later it was retitled *135th Street* and reorchestrated. But the cut I'm sure everyone will keep coming back to is "It Ain't Necessarily So," sung by the performer who was allegedly the model for Sportin' Life: Cab Calloway. It was his very last recording, made in 1993, the year before he died. He was 86 years old, and he's amazing!

Follies

January 1, 1999

The Ziegfeld Follies were among the most frivolous Broadway extravaganzas of the 1920s and '30s. Every big star played the Follies, but the central Follies image is of statuesque show girls in revealing costumes and mile-high headpieces descending steep flights of steps. Remember Lucille Ball's parody on *I Love Lucy?* It's also the subject of one of Stephen Sondheim's most extraordinary musicals, and one of his bleakest. It's the perfect New Year's Eve disc, especially if you're already depressed. I saw the original production with someone I was breaking up with and I've no doubt it helped precipitate the painful end of the relationship.

It was a very expensive show and lost money, even after 500 performances. But its stature has remained secure—in spite of the fact that up until now the complete score has never been recorded. Now, on a new 2-CD set, even the songs dropped in the particularly trying tryout period are included, and they're some of Sondheim's best. The central song in *Follies* is "I'm Still Here," the ultimate survivor anthem, written for—and evidently about—B-movie star Yvonne De Carlo. Before it was written, though, De Carlo's show-stopper was a raunchy comedy number called "Can That Boy Fox-trot." Anne Miller sings it on the new recording.

The plot of *Follies* is simple—and complicated. At a reunion of Follies girls in an about-to-be-demolished theater, decades after the last Follies, two friends and their stage-door-Johnnie husbands reconnect. They're all convinced they married the wrong person and are living in misery, resigned—or unresigned—to their choices. In the second act, something thrilling happens. The gutted theater suddenly fills with opulent scenery, and the anguish of each of these characters is transformed into a Follies production number. Like Hamlet's play-within-a-play, Sondheim's show-within-the-show reveals a deeper truth. Sally, who married Buddy, has never gotten over her obsession with Phyllis's husband Ben. The reunion forces her to confront her desperation. The curtain parts, she emerges into a spotlight, in a sequined gown, and sings Sondheim's greatest torch song, "Losing My Mind," which is just what she's doing. On the new album, Donna McKechnie, who got her first big break in Sondheim's *Company*, doesn't have the aching innocence of Dorothy Collins in the original cast, but she has an intensity of her own.

Sondheim fills *Follies* with an amazing variety of musical styles, or parodies of them, from Romberg operetta to Gershwin and Porter ballads. Yet Sondheim's parodies are often the songs most completely his own. They're the nightmare funhouse mirror that reflects both the follies of our lives as well as the folly of Sondheim's profession, the absurdity—and the giddy joy—of musical comedy itself. Sondheim is our greatest post-modern composer. And nowhere is his self-conscious self-examination more unflinching. The cast includes Tony Roberts and Laurence Guittard, who are marvelous as the two unhappy husbands, and in cameo roles Kaye Ballard, Liliane Montevecchi, and Phyllis Newman. But the real star of this album is Stephen Sondheim himself.

Threepenny Opera

December 12, 2000

One of the most famous Original Cast albums is not from a Broadway show but an Off-Broadway show: the legendary 1954 Theatre de Lys production of Kurt Weill's *Threepenny Opera*, which starred his widow, the legendary Lotte Lenya, and became the longest running musical of its time. When I was finally old enough to see it, that off-Broadway production had already been running more than six years. None of the original cast members—Lotte Lenya, Jo Sullivan, Bea Arthur, John Astin, Charlotte Rae—was still in the show. But I loved it anyway. And I can't think of a better way to wrap up the Kurt Weill centennial year, the 100th anniversary of his birth and the 50th anniversary of his death, than with the new reissue of the original cast album. The appearance here of Lotte Lenya, as Jenny Diver (the role she created in the original Berlin production in 1928), automatically gives this recording major historical significance.

I also love the performance of the "Barbara Song" sung on this recording by Beatrice Arthur, decades before *Maud* and *Golden Girls*. Her expressive baritone is perfect for the role of Lucy Brown, the jailkeeper's daughter who once tried to save herself for the perfect man but who all-too-easily loses her upright perpendicularity to the charms of Mack the Knife. I met Bea Arthur once backstage at Boston's Symphony Hall, where she was taping a Pops concert. I told her how much I admired this recording, and she was touched that someone remembered it. She said she still considered this production, especially working with Lenya, the best thing she ever did.

The most controversial aspect of this *Threepenny Opera* was the adaptation by composer Marc Blitzstein, who shortened it, simplified Weill's original orchestration, and supplied his own English translation. Many Weill aficionados condemn the way Blitzstein cleaned up Bertolt Brecht's nastier lyrics. In fact, those lyrics were expurgated only for the album because someone from the record company showed up at the recording session with a list of objectionable phrases, which Blitzstein changed on the spot in order to save the recording. The original "Mack the Knife" was far more degenerate than in the lyrics we know. Still, no one has yet come up with a more memorable—or singable—English version. So it's wonderful that the new CD closes with a performance of "Mack the Knife" with Lotte Lenya exuberantly accompanied by Marc Blitzstein, from an unknown TV interview show just before the opening, and only recently discovered in Lenya's personal archive.

Three Mo' Tenors

August 6, 2001

African-American women singers didn't have it easy getting into opera. Marian Anderson broke the color-barrier at the Met only in 1955. Since then, there's been a steady stream of superstars, from Leontyne Price to Shirley Verrett to Jessye Norman. Black male singers have had an even harder time. Paul Robeson never appeared in an opera. And though things are changing, they're changing slowly. The telecast and CD of *Three Mo' Tenors* attempts to remedy that situation, though the versatility of the three stars gets more emphasis than actual opera singing—and frankly, only one of them excels in opera. The tenors are Rodrick Dixon, Victor Trent Cook, who was nominated for a Tony Award in *Smokey Joe's Café*, and the marvelous veteran, Thomas Young, a singer with a voice of piercing focus, a face of haunting complexity, an incomparably sophisticated sense of style, and a gray pony tail. He's so admired by contemporary composers like John Adams and Anthony Davis that numerous roles have been written for him—sometimes even more than one in the same opera. He was chilling, for example, as both Black-Muslim spiritual leader Elijah Muhammad and a seductive hustler named Street in Davis's *Life and Times of Malcolm X*.

Three Mo' Tenors mixes opera with Broadway, sizzling jazz, blues, soul (the tenors do a terrific send-up of Gladys Knight and the Pips), gospel, and spirituals. Crammed into an hour, the TV version doesn't have quite the free-spirited exuberance that got the small but wildly enthusiastic audience singing and clapping along when the tenors kicked off their tour in Boston. Some of the very best numbers, like Young's wryly poignant, freshly reimagined "Send in the Clowns," are missing from both the telecast and the CD. Still, it's an entertaining, relatively ungimmicky hour. Even watching the rehearsed participation of the audience at New York's Hammerstein Ballroom is fun, though it's not as much fun as actually being there.

While opera gets short shrift, the shadow of one of the original Three Tenors, Luciano Pavarotti, looms especially large in the programming here, beginning with the inevitable three-tenors version of "La donna'é mobile," Verdi's most famous tenor aria.

There's also Pavarotti's theme song, Puccini's "Nessun dorma," which Young sings with an unshowy seriousness, and the aria with the nine high Cs from Donizetti's *Daughter of the Regiment*, the one that first brought Pavarotti to international attention. Rodrick Dixon sings it accurately but not without effort; he's no serious competition for the master. His strong voice is well-suited for Broadway, though. The one show song left in the telecast is the high-minded but sentimental anthem "Make Them Hear You," from *Ragtime*, which Dixon appeared in.

Victor Trent Cook, more a countertenor than a tenor, is most at home singing in a jazzy falsetto. His rendition of the spiritual "Were You There" is too over-the-top to feel genuine, but his live-wire, zoot-suited, hip-swiveling impersonation of Cab Calloway in "Minnie the Moocher" is a show-stopper.

On stage, *Three Mo' Tenors* was primarily (and rightly) a showcase for Thomas Young's phenomenal versatility. He's the real artist; on TV he's more like one of the guys. There's still a glimpse of his wide range, though, which encompasses, along with opera, "America the Beautiful," astonishing scat, and his own arrangement of Annie Ross and Wardell Gray's deranged "Twisted."

Three Mo' Tenors is the brainchild of Marion J. Caffey, who starred as Jelly Roll Morton on Broadway. His official bio says he is now (quote) "completely dedicated to conception, writing and directing." I hope his future "conceptions" include lots more Thomas Young.

Gosford Park

February 28, 2002

One of the most poignant scenes in *Gosford Park* comes after an indiscreet outburst by one of the servants, played by Emily Watson, shakes the precarious stability of the country estate. The lady of the house, Kristin Scott Thomas, asks a handsome celebrity played by Jeremy Northam, to distract the other guests from the embarrassment by singing. The guests are pleased or relieved or bored, depending on their level of snobbishness, while the servants gather furtively in the corridors to listen, or even dance, thrilled at their proximity to a famous star. Northam's character is Ivor Novello, who is the one real person in this fictional plot—and another element in Altman's complex mosaic of dichotomies: master or servant, winner or loser, considerate or thoughtless, imaginary or real. Novello was a matinee idol, a popular British movie and stage personality, who, like Noel Coward, also wrote plays and songs. In one memorable exchange, the dowager Countess, played with delectable snideness by Maggie Smith, makes a show of her contempt for celebrity:

"Tell me, how much longer are you going to go on making films?"

"I suppose that rather depends on how much longer the public wants to see me."

"It must be hard to know when to throw in the towel. What a pity, about that last one of yours—what, what was it called? *The Dodger.*"

"*The Lodger.*"

"*The Lodger.* It must be so disappointing when something just . . . it *flops* like that."

"Yes it is . . . Rather disappointing."

The Lodger was actually a film landmark, Alfred Hitchcock's very first thriller, and Ivor Novello gives a memorable performance as the moody loner who may or may not be Jack the Ripper. Contrary to Maggie Smith's insinuation, it was actually a hit. "How do you manage to put up with these people?" his friend the Hollywood producer (Bob Balaban) asks Novello. "You forget I earn my living by impersonating them," Novello replies. In *Gosford Park*, Novello's songs express the romantic longings neither the servants nor the aristocrats can ever realize. Every lyric seems to provide a wry commentary on the action. Altman gives even Novello's sentimentality an ironic edge.

After his great World War I anthem "Keep the Home Fires Burning," my favorite Novello song is a droll novelty number called "And Her Mother Came Too!" In the film, you don't get to hear the punch line because the plot is taking a sudden turn. But on the soundtrack album, Jeremy Northam sings it all—and in impeccable style.

The album also gives us a couple of rather strange songs by soundtrack composer Patrick Doyle with words by Robert Altman—one not used in the film, the other barely noticeable in Altman's labyrinth of episodes. His cutting back and forth between the aristocrats and the servants, one room and another, is like Gosford Park itself, the vast country house—a labyrinth of shadowy corridors; Mary, Maggie Smith's young maid, winningly played by Kelly Macdonald, repeatedly gets lost trying to find her room. She's also the character who unwinds the mystery. In the dim light, those corridors seem like a prison, an image out of a Piranesi etching—which I think is just Altman's point: who isn't trapped by the barriers of money and class? Patrick Doyle's evocative score dovetails elegantly with Novello's tunes and subtly reinforces that sense of labyrinth, spinning out its thread of repeating musical motifs, alluring and ominous, as it follows the characters—and leads us—through those winding corridors of house and plot.

Jerome Moross Centennial

August 22, 2003

Jerome Moross was a prodigy—a disciple of Aaron Copland, Charles Ives, and Henry Cowell, a high school friend of the legendary film composer Bernard Herrmann, and an assistant to George Gershwin. He was part of a movement of composers who were breaking away from European traditions and bringing American idioms—folk music, ragtime, blues, fox trots and one-steps—to theatre, ballet, opera, the concert hall, and film. He was nominated for an Academy Award for what many people consider the best music ever composed for a movie-western—William Wyler's *The Big Country*, starring Gregory Peck and Burl Ives (who won a best-supporting-actor Oscar).

The first time I saw Jerome Moross's name was on my original cast album of *The Golden Apple*, an experimental Off-Broadway musical that won the New York Drama Critics Award as best musical of the 1953-54 season, and the first show to go from Off-Broadway to Broadway. It was a daring enterprise—really an opera but disguised as a musical comedy, with no spoken dialogue. It had a huge influence, especially on Leonard Bernstein. *The Golden Apple* moved Greek myth from Mount Olympus in Greece to Mount Olympus in Washington State, just after the Spanish-American War. Kaye Ballard played an American Helen of Troy, and introduced a song that has become a standard for night-club and cabaret singers, the seductive "Lazy Afternoon."

The lyrics to "Lazy Afternoon" are by John Latouche, who collaborated with Moross on another ingenious work, four short dance-operas called *Ballet Ballads*. Moross also uses American mythology brilliantly in his 1945 ballet score Frankie and Johnny, which transforms the theme of that raunchy old song in highly dramatic and surprising ways.

Moross's first work in Hollywood was orchestrating scores by other composers—for example, Aaron Copland's theme music for the movie version of *Our Town*. Later, he got to do his own original scores. Besides *The Big Country*, some of his better known films are *The Adventures of Huckleberry Finn, Five Finger Exercise, Rachel, Rachel* (Paul Newman's first directorial stint), and Otto Preminger's *The Cardinal*. His most famous composition was probably the theme music for the popular '50s TV western *Wagon Train*. But Moross was also a classical musician of distinction. The premiere of his First Symphony was conducted by no less a musical eminence than Sir Thomas Beecham. The New Grove Dictionary of Music applauds his "lyrical warmth," his individuality, and the way his music combines "spontaneous popular appeal and strength of musical purpose." Jerome Moross refused to get stuck in a single groove. He wrote music that both the most and least sophisticated listeners could enjoy. He deserves—and rewards—serious attention. He shouldn't be forgotten.

Forgotten Broadway numbers

December 31, 2003

When I was a kid growing up in New York, I fell in love with Broadway. If a show looked good on paper, my family would get tickets before it opened. Every now and then we'd get stuck with a clinker. One show, *Seventh Heaven*, which was inspired by a famous silent movie, had a pretty score by Hollywood's Victor Young and a cast that included Gloria DeHaven, Ricardo Montalban, and a remarkable young dancer named Chita Rivera, two years before *West Side Story* made her a star. But it got such bad reviews, it closed after only 44 performances. The cast album disappeared almost as quickly. It's been a collector's item. But it's just been reissued on CD, and there are some delightful numbers, like "Camille, Collette, Fifi," in which three Parisian hookers express their philosophy. One of them is Chita Rivera.

A show with even greater potential was *Fade Out—Fade In*. An affectionate satire of Hollywood in the '30s, it starred Carol Burnett and had music by Jules Styne with book and lyrics by Betty Comden and Adolf Green, famous for another Hollywood satire: *Singin' in the Rain*. During the run, Burnett was injured in a taxi accident and started missing performances. Then she signed up for a TV show. *Fade Out—Fade In* actually closed, then re-opened when Burnett was legally forced to return. But it never recovered its lost momentum. The long-out-of-print cast recording, also starring Jack Cassidy, has finally been issued on CD. One song is a particular gem—"You Mustn't Be Discouraged," with Burnett and dancer Tiger Haynes imitating a nauseatingly optimistic number by Shirley Temple and Bill "Bojangles" Robinson.

Both *Seventh Heaven* and *Fade Out—Fade In* are part of Decca's marvelous series of reissued cast albums. One new disc includes three musicals from the World War II era. Irving Berlin's *This Is the Army*, from 1942, features Berlin himself singing a song that he resurrected from a musical he wrote during World War I, "Oh, How I Hate to Get Up in the Morning."

In 1946, Harold Rome wrote a musical about the transition to civilian life called *Call Me Mister*. The number I can't get enough of features the delectable Betty Garrett lamenting the recent craze for Latin American dances, "South America, Take It Away." Another album has two shows with lyrics by the great Dorothy Fields. The highlight is "The Fireman's Bride," a surprisingly naughty number from *Up in Central Park*, with music by Sigmund Romberg. It's sung by Celeste Holm, who wasn't in the original cast, though the song seems written especially for her.

I really love listening to these old shows. Even the worst of them, with their combination of show-biz savvy and corny innocence, are a kind of unconscious history, revealing something about the time they were written. And then, if we're lucky, there's the one, cherishable song that transcends all the foolishness that surrounds it.

My Fair Lady on DVD

February 24, 2004

My Fair Lady, one of Broadway's most successful musicals, went on to become one of the Hollywood's most successful movies: in 1964 it won eight Oscars, including the awards for Best Actor, Best Director, and Best Picture. Warner Brothers has just put out a new two-disc special edition DVD, in a gorgeous new high-definition transfer, to celebrate the 40th-anniversary of the film's original release. The most interesting added material on this set is an unusually honest hour-long documentary about the making of the movie, narrated by Jeremy Brett, the actor who played the role of Freddie. It's hard to imagine a less controversial film than *My Fair Lady*, and yet there's a continuing controversy about the casting of the title role. On Broadway, Eliza Doolittle, the Cockney flower-seller whom linguistics Professor Henry Higgins transforms into an elegant lady, was played by a young Englishwoman who had only one previous Broadway credit. I'm referring, of course, to Julie Andrews. She not only had a lovely silvery voice, but she also brought a certain wistful poignance to the role that no one else has ever quite matched. On a DVD of musical-comedy clips from *The Ed Sullivan Show*, called *Best of Broadway Musicals*, you can see how magical she was singing and dancing "Wouldn't It Be Loverly" with members of the Broadway cast.

Two of the show's leading players—Rex Harrison and Stanley Holloway—repeated their roles in the film, but as usual, Hollywood chose a more established star for the title role—Audrey Hepburn, who was also wonderful, especially in the later scenes of her transformation. But she wasn't considered a singer, so the Hollywood pros did what they usually did with movie stars who couldn't sing: they brought in someone else to dub her singing voice. That uncredited singer was soprano Marni Nixon, who also dubbed the singing voices of Deborah Kerr in *The King and I* and Natalie Wood in *West Side Story*. According to Jeremy Brett, in the documentary, Hepburn was desperate to do her own singing (as was Brett himself, whose singing voice was dubbed for "On the Street Where You Live"). Two songs—"Wouldn't It Be Loverly" and "Show Me"—were actually filmed with Hepburn lip-synching to her own recorded voice. Later, her vocal tracks were replaced by Marni Nixon's. These outtakes of Audrey Hepburn's own singing have been found and are included on the DVD. You can see on her face the expressions you hear in her voice, a voice that gave these songs a dimension of character missing from the final version of the film. Marni Nixon's pleasant but generic singing erases Hepburn's inimitable and irresistible vocal personality.

Audrey Hepburn was one of the few people connected with *My Fair Lady* who wasn't even nominated for an Academy Award. Maybe because she didn't do her own singing. And that year, the Best Actress Oscar went to the star of *Mary Poppins*—Julie Andrews.

Alloy Orchestra

March 16, 2004

A few weeks ago I was part of a sold-out crowd having the time of its life at a silent movie—a screening of Buster Keaton's Civil War comedy, *The General*. Part of the attraction was the live accompaniment, perfectly synchronized, by the amazing Alloy Orchestra, a group that both composes and performs its own music. This "orchestra" is actually a trio—Terry Donahue on "junk percussion" and accordion, Roger C. Miller on synthesizer, and Ken Winokur playing percussion and clarinet. They provide atmosphere—comic, romantic, or ominous—and especially changes of mood. They also provide sound effects—a train whistle, a birdcall, a marching band, a rifle shot. They can reinforce a sight gag or underline the punch line of a joke. Ba-da-boom! Some of the Alloy's film scores are minutely worked out, months in the making; some are more improvised, with only a week or so of preparation. On DVD, you can hear them accompanying films as varied as Serge Eisenstein's very first film, *Strike*; Dziga Vertov's astonishing experimental 1925 documentary, *The Man with the Movie Camera*; and that fascinating prehistoric granddaddy of *King Kong* and *Jurassic Park*—*The Lost World*. I also love what they do with the marvelous short comedies of Fatty Arbuckle and Buster Keaton (the versions on the Kino label), as in the music that accompanies the scene in Coney Island in which Arbuckle puts on a woman's bathing costume because his own clothes have gotten soaked.

Two of the Alloy Orchestra's best scores are for Buster Keaton's masterpieces *The General* and *Steamboat Bill, Jr. The General* is one of the most complexly ironic treatment of American heroism in film. The title is the name of the train run by the Keaton character, Johnnie Gray, a Confederate army rejectee. He's good at his job—not only competent, but imaginative. Yet he's also a klutz, who can be most successful when he's most inept. At one point, he pulls his sword out of its sheath and the blade comes loose and flies into the air. But when it lands, it kills his most dangerous enemy. Without diminishing the comedy, the music is also truly heroic, evoking the grandeur and tragedy of the Civil War in what was the closest Keaton came to producing an epic. The merging of the two main themes—the riveting "train" music and the visceral "war" music—is chilling.

One of the great Keaton moments comes in *Steamboat Bill, Jr.* A cyclone is ravaging the town. Keaton is standing in front of a house when the whole front wall collapses on him. Miraculously, he's standing directly under an open window. Keaton was legendary for doing his own stunts—the wall could have killed him if it landed only inches to the left or right. In some screenings, though, that 2-ton wall doesn't look very heavy—maybe because the film speed is a little off. If the wall comes down just the slightest bit too fast, or too slow, it seems weightless. On the new DVD from Image, the projection speed has been corrected. And the Alloy Orchestra provides just the subtlest little drum thud when the falling wall hits the ground. I've never seen a version in which the weight of the wall—the danger to Keaton—is so completely realized.

Most silent movie music just fills the void. Some of it even gets in the way. But the Alloy Orchestra really helps us see what we're watching. And often the music—whether driving or fanciful—is actually worth listening to on its own.

Abbott & Costello

May 4, 2004

Bud Abbott and Lou Costello's best routines involved a kind of verbal music. In their classic ode to misunderstanding, "Who's on First?", the names of baseball players are as intricately interwoven as a Bach fugue.

This routine was already so famous, Abbott and Costello did part of it in their very first film, *One Night in the Tropics*, a 1940 romantic comedy in which they didn't yet get top billing.

But the musical use of language isn't the only music in their films. *One Night in the Tropics* actually has songs by Jerome Kern and Dorothy Fields, who wrote "A Fine Romance" and "The Way You Look Tonight" for Fred Astaire and Ginger Rogers in *Swing Time*, and also a song by Kern and Oscar Hammerstein. "Remind Me" is one of my favorite obscure Kern songs, sung in the film by Peggy Moran. I had no idea was written for an Abbott & Costello comedy.

The musicians who turned up most often in Abbott and Costello movies were the Andrews Sisters. Patty, Maxene, and LaVerne Andrews were icons of the 1940s—three sisters with instantly recognizable harmonies and a slippery sense of rhythm. They introduced "Boogie Woogie Bugle Boy," one of their biggest hits, in the Abbott & Costello army satire, *Buck Privates*, before Bette Midler was even born. The movie trailer calls them "songsational."

The military was certainly on America's mind before we entered the war. The selective service act was newly in place, and among Abbott and Costello's biggest hits were comedies about military life. Even the Andrews Sisters' dance steps were often like a flipped out military drill. And some of their most popular songs, like their revival of Harry von Tilzer's "I'll Be with You in Apple-Blossom Time," which they also sang in *Buck Privates*, were about distant travel and separation.

The most surprising song in an Abbott & Costello movie was not by the Andrews Sisters, but by Ella Fitzgerald, in her first feature film—a western spoof from 1942 called *Ride 'Em Cowboy*. The song itself—"A Tisket, A Tasket," her first number one record—has nothing much to do with the plot. I love Ella Fitzgerald from any period, but some of my favorite recordings of hers are among her earliest. Before she became a dignified jazz artist, "The First Lady of Song," she had a kind of pouty little-girl cheekiness that I find irresistible.

Maybe because most Americans shared the same feelings about the world, it was a good time for comedy and popular music. When I was a kid watching Abbott and Costello movies on television, I resented the intrusion of music that interfered with the jokes and slowed down the story. Now I can't wait to listen to the great and even the not-so-great tunes that more vividly than history books capture the flavor of wartime America.

The Triplets of Belleville

June 1, 2004

Mozart's great *Mass in C-minor* is not anything you'd expect to hear in a popular movie—least of all an animated movie. But it's used to powerful effect in Sylvain Chomet's edgy, unsettlingly eccentric *The Triplets of Belleville*. In this scene, the young hero, a champion bicyclist, has been abducted from the Tour de France and his devoted grandmother and dog are following his kidnappers across the Atlantic on a paddle boat. It's an inspired choice to have Mozart's roiling music depict the rolling waves of a turbulent ocean. What's even more unusual is that Mozart's sacred music is heard in the same film as a vaudeville show depicting such celebrated Americans-in-Paris as Josephine Baker and Fred Astaire (who does a dance in which he is devoured by his own shoes). But the heart of *Triplets of Belleville* is the Academy Award-nominated song "Belleville Rendezvous," which recurs throughout the movie. It's sung by the eponymous sisters—Parisian vaudeville stars in the 1930s.

Chomet's teasing quasi-nonsense lyrics and Benoit Charest's syncopated, off-kilter minor-key tune capture the feeling of 1930s jazz and are impossible to get out of your head. Unlike the song that actually won the Oscar, "Into the West," from the third *Lord of the Rings* movie, which was sung at the Oscar ceremonies by Annie Lennox, who co-wrote it—a song I can't remember at all. I'm especially fond of a scene late in *The Triplets of Belleville* when the grandmother, in the New World, joins the aged triplets on stage. She accompanies them striking the spokes of a bicycle wheel like a steel drum, while the triplets crumple a newspaper for percussion, pluck the bars of a refrigerator shelf, and use a vacuum cleaner as their wind instrument.

Some unforgettable Oscar-winning songs have also come from cartoons: "When You Wish Upon a Star," from *Pinocchio*, and "Zip-a-dee-doo-dah" from Disney's *Song of the South*. But the Academy has a history of big mistakes. In 1937, it bypassed one of the greatest American songs ever written, George Gershwin's "They Can't Take That Away from Me," for a Bing Crosby Hawaiian number called "Sweet Leilani"—and not one Beatles song was ever even nominated. I'm sure "Belleville Rendez-vous" will stay with us longer than . . . What was the song that won this year's Oscar?

Around the World in 80 Days

June 8, 2004

I never read Jules Verne's novel *Around the World in 80 Days*, but I fell in love with the story when I saw the film. Watching it on television or on videotape, with its image diminished to fit the small screen, the film seemed diminished too. But on the dazzling new wide-screen DVD, I fell in love with it all over again. With its sensational new photographic process, Todd-AO, and the continuous spectacle that really fills the screen. With the witty script mostly by one of my favorite writers, S.J. Perelman. And with the exhilarating discovery every few minutes of yet another famous star perfectly cast in what producer Michael Todd christened a "cameo" role.

If, as Stanislavski said, there are no small parts, only small actors, in this movie, no part was too small, and all the actors were big. Marlene Dietrich and Frank Sinatra are denizens of a Barbary Coast saloon. Buster Keaton is the conductor of a train passing through Indian territory—a wonderful reminder of the silent comedy genius in his great film *The General*. Sir John Gielgud is a valet complaining to employment agent Noel Coward about the tortures he'd undergone in the service of the super-punctual Phileas Fogg—the hero of the story, played with wonderful aplomb and touching dignity by David Niven. Hermione Gingold and Glynis Johns are a pair of London hookers wagering on whether Fogg will win his bet to travel around the world in a mere 80 days. Beatrice Lillie is the maddening Salvation Army reformer who just at the last minute almost keeps Fogg from winning.

Young Shirley MacLaine, in one of her first starring roles, as the Indian princess Niven rescues from a human sacrifice, is almost unrecognizable—except for that unmistakable little-girl voice. And who could resist the charming and irrepressible Mexican star Cantinflas as Fogg's man-of-all-trades Passepartout. "I'm looking for my man," Niven tells Dietrich, when Cantinflas has wandered into that rowdy bar. "So am I," Dietrich winks back.

Around the World in 80 Days immediately became my favorite movie, but I could afford to see it only once, because of the special ticket prices for the limited seatings. But I played the best-selling Decca soundtrack LP over and over again. This "background music" may have been the first time I ever became conscious of a film score. The composer, Victor Young, was obviously having a field day. *Around the World in 80 Days* was part adventure, part travelogue. Every working film composer had to write genre music: folk-themes for Westerns, exotic modal music for exotic locales like India or Japan, music for bullfights, speeding trains and ocean voyages, English anthems and French music-hall tunes. But how many composers ever got to do them all in a single film? The wonderful main title music is a soaring waltz that seems perfect not only for a flight over the Alps in a balloon but also for falling in love. Words were added later, but the music is really better without them. One of my favorite musical passages was for the exhilarating train ride through India's countryside. I've never gotten it out of my head.

Victor Young was a great song composer. He wrote such memorable standards as "Sweet Sue," and the haunting jazz favorites "Ghost of a Chance" and "Stella by Starlight." And dozens of movie scores: for films as various as Douglas Sirk's sizzling melodrama *Written on the Wind* and Cecil B. DeMille's biblical epic *Samson and Delilah*; for Preston Sturges's scintillating *The Palm Beach Story*; and for two of Hollywood's most extraordinary Westerns, Nicholas Ray's deranged *Johnny Guitar* and George Stevens's poignant *Shane*. Young was nominated 22 times for Academy Awards, but he only won one: for *Around the World in 80 Days*—which, in a way, was like writing music for 22 different movies.

Around the World was both lucky and unlucky for some of its participants. Robert Newton walked away with some of his best reviews as Fogg's nemesis, the obsessed Inspector Fix, but it was his last role. It was Michael Todd's first movie, and he was already planning his next project, *Don Quixote*, when he was killed in a plane crash. At least he lived long enough to marry Elizabeth Taylor and to win a Best Picture Oscar. But sadly, Victor Young died before the Academy Awards ceremony.

Marx Brothers

July 5, 2004

Hollywood's greatest film about opera—the one that does the most justice to all the social pretensions and artistic absurdities surrounding the opera world—is the Marx Brothers' *A Night at the Opera*, one of their films in a new 5-DVD boxed set of their MGM movies. In it, Groucho plays Otis P. Driftwood, a conman who gets suckered by Chico into signing up an unknown young Italian tenor—played by Alan Jones, the pop-singer Jack Jones's father and a familiar leading man in musicals of the '30s and '40s. When the Marx Brothers moved from Paramount to MGM, romantic subplots became more important than in their more anarchic earlier films like *Animal Crackers* and *Duck Soup*. Jones is in love with a beautiful young soprano played by Kitty Carlisle, whom more people probably remember as a panelist on the TV game show *To Tell the Truth*. Both Jones and Carlisle are fine singers, so they lend the plot some plausibility. The film ends with a very strong performance of the famous "Miserere" scene from Verdi's *Il Trovatore*, in which Carlisle sings beneath Jones's prison window before the tragic denouement—which, of course, isn't in the film.

The most famous sequence in *A Night at the Opera* is the so-called stateroom scene, in which a huge streamer trunk and dozens of people—maids, waiters, repairmen, a manicurist, and stowaways Jones, Harpo, and Chico—all get squeezed into Groucho's cramped cabin. Marx Brothers movies always have an element of social satire. What opera fan wouldn't love the way Groucho, Chico, and Harpo deconstruct—at times quite literally—the behind-the-scenes machinations of the opera world, especially visible in the rivalry between Groucho and the veteran German character actor Sig Ruman over the affections and the pocketbook of the deliciously clueless dowager, Margaret Dumont, who thinks her social standing can be improved by investing in opera.

Music actually plays an important part in all Marx Brothers comedies. The plot of *The Big Store* involves funding a music school for inner-city kids. Chico was a self-taught pianist, and in *The Big Store* he plays Schubert and teaches the kids how to gun-down the piano keys just the way he does. In Harpo's very best harp-playing scene, he wears a Louis XIV costume and plays in a trio with images of himself in a double mirror. Tony Martin sings a remarkable song called "The Tenement Symphony," which was Hollywood's vision of the American melting pot, although in 1941 African-Americans were still excluded from it.

The great musical numbers, though, are all Groucho's. His best song is in one of their weaker films, *At the Circus*. As the lawyer J. Cheever Loophole, he sings about the unforgettable "Lydia, the Tattoo'd Lady." The Marx Brothers surrounded themselves with some very distinguished creative people. "Lydia" was written by no less a songwriting team than Harold Arlen and E.Y. Harburg, the same year they wrote the songs for *The Wizard of Oz*.

The earlier Marx Brothers movies are scandalously unavailable on DVD, though there's a wonderful documentary called *The Unknown Marx Brothers*.

Some of Groucho's most hilarious adlibs were on his TV quiz show, *You Bet Your Life*. The ones that were too racy for a network audience were cut from the show, but these outtakes were shown every year at his sponsor's corporate convention. Some of these are now included on a new three-DVD set called *You Bet Your Life: The Lost Episodes*, and they're among the funniest moments on any DVD.

Judy Garland

July 26, 2004

Although people weren't exactly aware of it at the time, Judy Garland's life story was taking place on screen. Audiences were watching her, identifying with her, as she was growing up, from *The Wizard of Oz*, with its great anthem of innocent longing, "Over the Rainbow," to *A Star Is Born*, fifteen years later, with its more grownup anthem of erotic disappointment, "The Man That Got Away"—both with music by Harold Arlen. In between, came the infinitely charming piece of nostalgia, Vincent Minelli's *Meet Me in St. Louis*, his love letter to Garland at the beginning of their personal relationship. Who could resist Minelli's loving Technicolor re-creation of turn-of-the-20th-century St. Louis—the color fully restored on the spectacular new DVD—or the memorable songs by Hugh Martin and Ralph Blane? But it's Garland who gives the film its third dimension, its emotional honesty and depth—whether in the exuberant "Trolley Song," or the wistful "The Boy Next Door," or in the achingly poignant "Have Yourself a Merry Little Christmas." Garland, more than almost any other singer, revealed both her extreme vulnerability and her determination not to be defeated by it—feelings a lot of people shared in 1944.

Along with *Meet Me in St. Louis*, Warner Brothers has also just released DVDs of four other early Garland films, each of which gives her at least one chance to shine. In *Ziegfeld Girl*, released in 1941, Hedy Lamarr, Lana Turner, and Garland play three aspiring Broadway showgirls. Garland is the youngest and the most experienced. The best thing in *Ziegfeld Girl* isn't a big production number, but an old song Garland sings at her audition for Ziegfeld: "I'm Always Chasing Rainbows."

For Me and My Gal is from 1942, but the era is World War I. It was Gene Kelly's film debut, after creating the title role in *Pal Joey* on Broadway. The movie is rather unpleasant. The Kelly character deliberately injures himself so he can't be drafted. But his very first number with Garland, the title song, is completely delightful.

The post-War *In the Good Old Summertime* is MGM's musical remake of Ernst Lubitsch's bittersweet comic romance, *The Shop Around the Corner*—the one about the two sparring co-workers who don't realize the love letters they're writing are to each other. Buster Keaton plays a featured role, and it's amazing to see these two mythic personalities on screen together. Still noticeably missing from the current catalogue of Garland DVDs are *Easter Parade*, the only film she made with Fred Astaire; her best film with Gene Kelly, *The Pirate*; and *Summer Stock*, in which she does her iconic "Get Happy" (another Arlen song).

Just out on DVD, though, is Garland's very last film, from 1963, the underrated *I Could Go on Singing*, a classy soap opera that also draws heavily on the Garland legend—the conflict between career and private life, a question of child custody, even her appearance at the London Palladium. Garland gives a masterful, nuanced performance as a complexly flawed celebrity—smart, witty, sophisticated, needy—maybe the closest she ever came to a true portrait of herself. "The real Judy," the trailer, not inaccurately, proclaims. The score is an eclectic mix of standards by Schwartz and Dietz and Kurt Weill and Ira Gershwin, with a disappointing title song by Harold Arlen and Yip Harburg and new material by her longtime music director Mort Lindsay. Garland sells them all in a powerful way. For all her personal and professional disappointments, a few years before her premature death, she was still embarking into very promising new territory.

Movie Themes

November 25, 2004

The most famous movie music ever written may be Max Steiner's sweeping, heroic theme for *Gone with the Wind*. Even if you didn't know the story—is there anyone who doesn't know the story?—you'd know that this was going to be a movie of high drama—passion and courage—and probably great length. The theme itself is probably too simple to be something a composer would develop into a symphony, but its succinctness is one the qualities that make it impossible to forget. What most people don't remember is that there's music that comes even before the famous theme—a two-and-a-half-minute Overture that suggests the happy, peaceful life on that old plantation before the Civil War. *Gone with the Wind* has just reappeared in a new 4-disc DVD set, with a gloriously restored print and a handful of special features, including the fascinating documentary that shows us the screen tests for the many actresses who wanted the role of the decade—Scarlett O'Hara.

The music for *Gone with the Wind* is very different from the opening music of a movie that isn't as known nearly as well, but one that I think is one of the real masterpieces of world cinema—Federico Fellini's early *I Vitelloni* (which means something like "The Young Bucks" and was misleadingly titled for its first American release in 1953 *The Young and the Passionate*). It's the story of five friends who are trapped in the small Italian seaside town where they grew up, trapped in their lives—suddenly becoming too old to act like kids but are not ready for real responsibility. They're, of course, sexually frustrated (this is, after all, a Fellini movie) and even a little insecure in their sexual identity. A couple of them have artistic ambitions but don't know how to develop their talent, or where to go with it. Even before the credits roll, we see this would-be rat pack lurching arm-in-arm down a deserted street after a night of drinking. The music is by Fellini's great musical collaborator, Nino Rota, and it captures Fellini's affection and personal nostalgia (one of the young bucks is surely himself) for these guys and their heartbreaking hopelessness.

Another recent release is Jean Renoir's *The Golden Coach*, filmed in ravishing, supersaturated color, and starring that great life force, Anna Magnani. It's about a troupe of 18th-century Commedia dell'Arte players who travel to South America, and it's one of Renoir's most marvelous explorations about how the boundary between art and real life often blurs—and the sacrifices artists are compelled to make for their art. Renoir chose the perfect composer: Vivaldi, who immediately takes us back to an earlier time, a time of bustling energy, festivity, and elegance with just a touch of the street.

I'd like to end with a little closing music—from a film that I forgot had any music at all: the great horror-film director Tod Browning's bizarre, scary, and poignant *Freaks*, a 1932 classic about the underside of life at a carnival side show, with a cast largely made up of real human oddities: microcephalics, Siamese twins, and people with no arms or legs. Browning shows us these so-called freaks are more human than some better-put-together specimens. Seeing the film again after many years, I was especially hit by the irony of the score—the way the few seconds of lighthearted circus music at the very end makes such a chilling commentary on all the horrors that have gone before.

In all these films, music adds another dimension, another emotional layer. We think of film as a visual medium, but it's impossible to imagine these extraordinary movies without the music that goes with them.

Thin Man Collection

August 18, 2005

I've often had the feeling about great chamber music that it was like listening to the animated give and take of dialogue. And sometimes, seeing a play or a terrific movie, the dialogue seemed like listening to chamber music. The epitome of that conversational elegance was the repartee between William Powell and Myrna Loy in the dozen or so movies they made together, especially their six *Thin Man* films, made between 1934 and 1947. They were the perfect team—both so intelligent and witty and teasingly sexy. Their timing never missed a beat. Loy said that her dialogue with Powell reflected the ease and spontaneity of their real-life conversations. Powell said they weren't actors, just two people in perfect harmony. Their deep underlying affection lights up the screen.

Powell and Loy had appeared together before in only one other movie, the entertaining *Manhattan Melodrama*, directed by W.S. ("Woody") Van Dyke. It was his idea to pair them in *The Thin Man* and he directed the first four *Thin Man* films before his early death. "One take Woody," as Van Dyke was called, even keeps the murder plots crisply crackling. He revealed a talent for comedy of a starlet whose earlier movies included such items as *What Price Beauty*, *New Morals for Old*, and *The Mask of Fu Manchu*, in which Loy played Boris Karloff's even more sinister daughter. Powell had already portrayed another detective, the elegant but wifeless Philo Vance, in such first-rate thrillers as *The Kennel Murder Case*. In the trailer for *The Thin Man*, included on the DVD, Powell, as Philo Vance, greets himself as Nick Charles. The first *Thin Man* movie skillfully adapts Dashiell Hammet's novel. It emphasizes the mystery—

Powell and Loy don't appear until 11 minutes into the film. In the films after that, they're on screen from the very beginning—they're what the audience wanted.

The Thin Man films also have delicious supporting performances. Imagine young James Stewart as a villain. Legendary acting teacher Stella Adler makes a vivid appearance as a shady lady pretending to be high-class, but letting her Park Avenue accent slip into the gutter. There are juicy turns by Gloria Grahame and Marjorie Main, malevolent Joseph Calleia, nasty Sheldon Leonard, and Teddy Hart, songwriter Larry Hart's brother, playing a fast-talking lawyer. There are memorable comic scenes, like the one in *Shadow of the Thin Man*, when Powell tries in vain to resist an Italian waiter strong-arming everyone into ordering sea-bass; or the scene when Nick and Nora are stopped for speeding by a star struck cop on the Oakland Bay Bridge; or Nick taking Nora to a wrestling match; or the birthday party for Nick Jr. thrown by a most colorful array of low-lifes. All six films are dazzlingly written—the first four, using lots of Hammett's original dialogue, by Frances Goodrich and Albert Hackett, the husband and wife team who later won a Pulitzer Prize for their play *The Diary of Anne Frank*. Always the dialogue crackles, especially dealing with the subtle negotiations in marriage.

One footnote. The thin man isn't Nick Charles but the chief suspect (or as the stars pronounce the word in 1934, susPECT). By the fifth film, *The Thin Man Goes Home*, everyone seems to have forgotten the title's origin. *The Complete Thin Man* DVD set includes a bonus disc with a documentary on Powell and a better one on Loy; the lively radio version they did in 1936, hosted by Woody Van Dyke; and a fascinatingly awful episode about a suspicious beatnik from the 1958 *Thin Man* TV series with Peter Lawford and Phyllis Kirk. There are also trailers, cartoons, and two Robert Benchley shorts, including the hilarious "How to Be a Detective." All movie lovers should congratulate Warner Brothers for the sparkle of the restored prints. But no question about the main reason to see and re-see these films: if movies show us how to live, no pair of movie stars were ever more compatible, more loving partners than William Powell and Myrna Loy.

Unfaithfully Yours

August 2, 2005

Many films use classical music to heighten the emotion of a given scene. But very few directors exploit the possibilities of that music as brilliantly as Preston Sturges did in his 1948 *Unfaithfully Yours*, which has just appeared on DVD. It's one of my favorite movie musicals though it's not a musical in the usual sense of characters suddenly bursting into song. It's a movie about making music, classical music, and it stars Rex Harrison as a famous British conductor, modeled on the great Sir Thomas Beecham, who has been led to believe that his adored and adoring wife, Linda Darnell, has been unfaithful to him. Most of the film takes place at Harrison's next concert, or rather, in Harrison's mind—and the music he's conducting determines the nature of his fantasies of revenge.

The first piece Harrison conducts is the Overture to Rossini's opera *Semiramide*. Its wild mood swings, from contemplative and stealthy to manic, are perfect for Harrison's complicated machinations. The camera slowly enters Harrison's head, right through his eye, and we watch him, as jealous as Othello, working out a cunning murder plot. He slashes Darnell's throat with a straight razor, and makes a recording in which he imitates her screaming so that her supposed lover will rush to her rescue and get caught, with his fingerprints on the razor. In the fantasy, everything works perfectly, and in perfect time to the music. At one point, Harrison puts on a record with a jazz arrangement of that exact moment in the *Semiramide* Overture.

During the solemn Overture to Wagner's *Tannhäuser*, Harrison imagines offering Darnell magnanimous forgiveness in a wonderful send-up of Wagner's gooey spirituality. And in

Tchaikovsky's impassioned *Francesca da Rimini*, Harrison envisions challenging his alleged rival to a game of Russian roulette. Later, when he actually tries to carry out his fantasies, of course everything goes hilariously wrong. Reality has no place for the exquisite perfection of art. Harrison's wrestling match with his recording machine is a sidesplitting image of the artistic temperament coming to grief with technology, and Alfred Newman's Looney Tunes scoring brilliantly deconstructs the familiar classics.

Sturges's script is a masterpiece of wit and wordplay. When an inquisitive columnist wants to know why Harrison conducts from a score—a reference to Arturo Toscanini famously conducting from memory—Harrison answers acidly: "It's because I can actually read music." I love the scene in which the detective, wonderful Edgar Kennedy, who played lots of detectives in his long film career, turns out to be one of Harrison's biggest fans.

Unfaithfully Yours is also surprisingly moving in its examination of the self-delusions of passion. It was not a hit in 1948, partly because black comedy wasn't a very familiar genre, and Sturges's style ranges from sophisticated parody to broad farce. The studio didn't know how to publicize the movie—they called it a murder mystery. No wonder audiences were confused. But we know better now. *Unfaithfully Yours* is Sturges's last masterpiece, maybe the last great comedy of the 1940s and one of the best films about music. Thirty six years later, this marvelous film was painfully remade as a vehicle for Dudley Moore. Please, don't under any circumstances confuse them.

Fred Astaire and Ginger Rogers

October 24, 2005

If one function of art is to give us a deeper insight into the nature of reality, isn't it ironic that some of the greatest art seems to be so artificial? The formulaic plots and brilliant dialogue of Jane Austen or Raymond Chandler. The perfection of a Vermeer painting or a Mozart opera. What could be less natural than when Fred Astaire and Ginger Rogers, in the marvelous films they made in the 1930s, suddenly erupt into dance? Yet what feels more right? Their songs are often about dancing, and like opera arias, the dances lift what their characters are feeling to a higher plane, even beyond words. What could be more expressive of giving in to love than Rogers's swooning backbends? What could express greater joy in life than Astaire's buoyant and dazzling footwork? Could anything represent a successful relationship better than the intricate grace of their partnership?

Their dances are a sort of courtship ritual, which also includes the fun of courtship, as in such goofy numbers as Irving Berlin's "I'm Putting All My Eggs in One Basket," or George and Ira Gershwin's slippery exploration of how language itself can affect a relationship, "Let's Call the Whole Thing Off" ("You say ee-ther and I say eye-ther"), a tricky number that actually takes place on roller skates.

Some of the Astaire/Rogers dances have a more serious cast—like Berlin's "Let's Face the Music and Dance," from *Follow the Fleet*, which both encourages us to escape from the Depression and the shadows of war and also reminds us of the bleak future we're trying to avoid. It's one of their few numbers in which they're not dancing as their own characters but their characters are playing other characters in the dance—like the play-within-a-play in *Hamlet*. Maybe their most moving dance—their darkest and most beautiful—is to the Jerome Kern/Dorothy Fields song "Never Gonna Dance," from *Swing Time*. If dancing represents the joy of their lives together, then their dance of parting must also be a farewell to dancing itself.

One thing that makes the artifice of the musical numbers work so well is that the dances are imbedded in silly comic plots that are already artificial. I'm actually very fond of these farcical situations of concealment and mistaken identity, partly because the teamwork of the supporting actors is so delightful. But these are also the perfect films for DVD, because if you're not in the mood for the story, it's easy to skip from one breathtaking musical number to the next. You can create your own orgy of great songs and dances.

The Nicholas Brothers

February 24, 2006

At the end of *The Pirate*, a 1948 MGM technicolor musical starring Judy Garland and Gene Kelly, there's a marvelous dance routine to Cole Porter's "Be a Clown." Kelly is joined by two black dancers, Harold and Fayard Nicholas, who leap and tumble over one another. Yet, what at first seems merely acrobatic is done with the grace and elegance, the musical invention and interaction, of the highest level of dancing. In January, Fayard Nicholas, the older of the two brothers, died at the age of 91. Harold Nicholas died in 2000, at 79. In *The Pirate*, they had nothing else to do earlier in the film. To its eternal shame, Hollywood did not allow African-American entertainers to appear as major characters in films with primarily white casts. They could play wise-cracking or dim-witted servants. Or they could go to Europe, like Josephine Baker, whose electrifying talent and beauty were more important there than her race (her three fascinating films have been released on DVD by Kino).

In this country, the only chance these performers had to do any real acting was in films with all-black casts, either in the low-budget subculture of so-called "race films," or in a handful of high-minded, big-budget Hollywood landmarks, made by white directors. A 1943 musical called *Stormy Weather*, just issued on DVD by Fox, is a flimsy excuse to string together some of the most remarkable song and dance numbers ever filmed. It's significant that on the three new DVDs from Warner—King Vidor's *Hallelujah*; Marc Connelly's movie version of his Pulitzer Prize winning play, *The Green Pastures*; and *Cabin in the Sky*, the first film directed by Vincente Minnelli—a written disclaimer reminds us that "these films are the product of their time," which serves as a warning not to forget our country's tradition of racism, even in the entertainment industry. Yet the best moments transcend these issues, like when the extraordinary Ethel Waters in *Cabin in the Sky* sings one of the great songs she introduced, Vernon Duke's "Taking a Chance on Love."

The Nicholas Brothers appeared in hardly more than a handful of feature films, and most of them are not readily available. Special bonus features on the new Warner Brothers DVDs, though, include some real rarities: three short films they made when they were still kids. They were amazing! In *Pie, Pie Blackbird*, from 1932, eleven-year-old Harold and eighteen-year-old Fayard do a tap-dance that's so hot, the blackbird pie, which opens up to reveal the great Eubie Blake and his orchestra, begins to sizzle and smoke. (Blackbird pie was a common feature of early racial stereotyping.)

Now two of the grown-up Nicholas Brothers's films are on DVD. Their big number in *Stormy Weather* was applauded by both Fred Astaire and George Balanchine. At the climax, the brothers play leapfrog down a flight of high steps, and land in a series of hair-raising splits, from which they rise in slow motion without using their hands to push themselves up. In *Orchestra Wives* (one of only two films featuring Glenn Miller and his orchestra) they sing "I Got a Gal in Kalamazoo" and do a dance in which Harold does a double spin in the air, lands in a split, then literally walks up the side of a column into a somersault and another split.

There are even fewer films in which either of the Nicholas Brothers played an actual character. The only one I've seen is Robert Townsend's 1991 *The Five Heartbeats*, about a group of black kids who form a singing group that makes it all the way to the top. Harold Nicholas plays a retired hoofer who helps them polish their dance movements, and ends up the group's mascot. It's a touching performance and it's great to see his character throw down his cane and do an eye-popping little routine. It also underlines all those wasted years when he and his brother should have been playing the leading roles.

Busby Berkeley

May 8, 2006

There's a striking photograph taken in 1920 by the avant-garde photographer Man Ray—a close-up of a woman's face, upside-down, with a cigarette in her mouth. It's both erotic and sinister. In 1920, it was still a novelty to see a woman smoking. Fifteen years later, director and choreographer Busby Berkeley used that very image in one of his greatest dance numbers, in *Gold Diggers of 1935*. As Wini Shaw starts to sing "The Lullaby of Broadway," the camera gets closer and closer to her face, then suddenly swings around and her head is upside down, just as in that Man Ray photo. Then the outline of her face morphs into an outline of Manhattan Island, with the cigarette sticking up like the Empire State Building. Berkeley takes us into the life of the city. A policeman is walking down a deserted street, casting a long shadow in front of him—as in one of Giorgio di Chirico's surrealist paintings.

Maybe with a name like Busby, Berkeley had a hard time being taken seriously, but for all their frivolity, his best films are also trenchant depictions of the Depression, especially show business—one of the few businesses that didn't collapse after the stock-market crash. Show people were desperate to put on shows. Berkeley's plots involve schemes to raise money, and having to face social snobbery and censorship. Berkeley always maintains a snappy pace, the dialogue crackles, the performers—Dick Powell, Joan Blondell, Ginger Rogers, Zasu Pitts, Ruby Keeler—are amusing, attractive, and appealing.

And there are terrific songs by Al Dubin and Harry Warren: "Lullaby of Broadway," "42nd Street," "I Only Have Eyes for You," "Shuffle Off to Buffalo," the song that compares love to drug addiction ("You're Getting to Be a Habit with Me"), the moving Depression anthem "Remember My Forgotten Man," and "We're in the Money" (with Ginger Rogers, dressed only in silver dollars and singing in pig-latin).

It's rarely acknowledged how closely Berkeley evolved from avant-garde art. His famous kaleidoscopic dances, shot from above, are right out of Marcel Duchamp's optical experiments. In "I Only Have Eyes for You," Ruby Keeler emerges through the iris of her own eye. Almost all the dances are production numbers in stage shows and night clubs. But they're so elaborate, they couldn't possibly take place on any stage but a vast sound stage. So they become the shows we imagine in our heads—our dream theater.

"Lullaby of Broadway" is actually quite scary. The phalanxes of dancers, all in black and white, are more like storm troopers than pleasure seekers, yet they're dwarfed by an ominously empty space. The heroine dances with them, but when she tries to escape, they push her off a balcony and she falls to her death. The camera pulls back to that earlier view of Manhattan, which then morphs back to Winifred Shaw's face as she finishes her song. This is a disturbing view of the desperation to find pleasure. Busby Berkeley has once again put us through much more than we bargained for in a film musical.

Betty Hutton

March 16, 2007

I loved Betty Hutton when I was a kid. Her uninhibited, overflowing exuberance probably made up for my own shyness. I thought she was wonderful as the silent movie serial star Pearl White in *The Perils of Pauline* and as the aerialist hopelessly in love with Charlton Heston in Cecil B. DeMille's *The Greatest Show on Earth*—I was sure it was her performance that got the film its best picture Oscar. She blew me away as sharpshooter Annie Oakley in the movie version of Irving Berlin's *Annie Get Your Gun*, though seeing it again recently she seems badly directed. She was called the Blonde Bombshell because she virtually exploded every time she appeared on screen. She was a good singer, too, and had a number of hit songs—mostly specialty numbers written for her like: "He Said Murder, He Said," "I'm a Square in the Social Circle," and Hoagy Carmichael's "Doctor, Lawyer, Indian Chief "; but she could also really deliver a slow ballad like Frank Loesser's too-little known "I Wish I Didn't Love You So" and Berlin's "They Say It's Wonderful."

She was right in considering her best movie Preston Sturges's brilliant rule-breaking wartime comedy, *The Miracle of Morgan's Creek*. She plays Trudy Kockenlocker, a small town girl who wants to do something for the boys in uniform. She goes out on a date with a soldier, gets married that night, and when she learns she's pregnant, can't remember who it was she married.

After Hutton left Hollywood, her career sputtered out, as did her four marriages. She became addicted to painkillers. Years later, she was discovered working as a cook and housekeeper in a Rhode Island rectory and credits the priest there with saving her life. She actually went back to school, got her degree, and even did some college teaching. She got her start as a band singer and on Broadway and occasionally returned to live theater. It must have been in the mid 1970s that I saw her in Cole Porter's *Anything Goes* at a dinner-theater called the Chateau De Ville, in a distant suburb of Boston. A couple of friends and I got tickets for the opening night. It wasn't much of a production and it was especially disappointing that she wasn't in very good voice.

But she actually stopped the show twice—literally! Once was when she inserted a medley of her greatest hits, which was fun. But the second time was more painful. She was trying to do a Fred Astaire bit in which she tapped a cane against the stage and caught it as it bounced up. But she missed it, so she tried it again. "I'm gonna do this until I get it right," she announced, and repeated the shtick seven or eight more times until she finally caught the cane. The evening was beginning to seem like a disaster, until at one point she sat down at the edge of the stage and, completely out of the context of the show, said she was dedicating the next song to her ex-husband. At a very slow tempo, she almost whispered the most moving version I've ever heard of "I Get a Kick Out of You." She ended in real tears. And as they say, there wasn't a dry eye in the house either.

After the show, my friends and I decided to go backstage. She was very welcoming and was actually eager to talk—about her career and the ex-husband who mismanaged it and undermined her confidence. The next day the run of *Anything Goes* was cancelled. It was a sad end. But that irrepressible personality is still there for us in her best numbers and in her marvelous comic performance in *Miracle of Morgan's Creek*, her one movie masterpiece.

Lubitsch musicals

February 6, 2008

Ernst Lubitsch came to America from Berlin, and his best films are the most sophisticated comedies made in Hollywood between 1929 and the early 1940s, even after the stultifying production code went into effect in 1934. *Trouble in Paradise* was about two jewel thieves who fall in love while picking each other's pockets. In *The Shop Around the Corner*, James Stewart and Margaret Sullavan are a couple of bickering clerks who don't know they are writing each other love letters. It's infinitely more delicate and humane than any of its remakes, like *You've Got Mail*. *To Be or Not to Be*, with Jack Benny as the leading Polish Hamlet, is the most daring political satire to appear during World War II. And there's Greta Garbo playing a Russian commissar who is seduced by Paris in *Ninotchka*, her first comedy. "Garbo laughs!" read the ads, and so did everyone else.

But Lubitsch's very first American films were pre-code musicals, and they already had "the Lubitsch touch"—airy trifles filled with naughty double entendres that were too charming and funny to be offensive. The stars were mainly Maurice Chevalier and the very young and glamorous Jeanette MacDonald, who was an expert comedienne before her famous syrupy screen partnership with tenor Nelson Eddy. These early Lubitsch films are operettas about mythical European kingdoms, with high-born but down-at-the-heels ladies yearning for both money and romance, or married couples faced with extramarital temptation. In *Monte Carlo*, MacDonald abandons at the altar a ridiculous but wealthy fiancée and falls in love with a duke posing as her hairdresser. It's silly, but delicious, and it has some very good songs, including "Beyond the Blue Horizon," its theme song.

One Hour with You is a remake of a Lubitsch silent film called *The Marriage Circle*. In it, MacDonald's best friend is making a play for Chevalier, MacDonald's reluctant though tempted husband, but MacDonald thinks he's interested in someone else, so to keep him away from the imaginary "other woman" she keeps throwing him together with her trusted friend. *The Smiling Lieutenant* has a more darkly emotional side that foreshadows Lubitsch's later, edgier films. Chevalier, as a randy officer, meets a fresh-faced young violinist played by Claudette Colbert. "So you play the piano?" she asks him, "Someday we may have a duet." He answers: "I love chamber music." Guess what happens after that bit of dialogue.

But when Chevalier, on duty, winks at Colbert, Miriam Hopkins, as a dowdy visiting princess, thinks he's flirting with her. An international scandal is avoided when Chevalier is forced to marry Hopkins, even though he's still in love with Colbert, and continues to sleep with her. When Colbert and Hopkins finally meet, Colbert feels so sorry for Hopkins, she teaches her how to dress—and undress—in style, sadly relinquishing her own hold on Chevalier.

Lubitsch's most dazzling musical—and the one with the best score—is *The Merry Widow*, also with MacDonald and Chevalier. That hasn't yet been released on DVD, though you can catch it every now and then on Turner Classic Movies. But if you enjoy ultra-sophisticated romantic fluff, skillful acting, deft writing, and buoyant direction, these earlier films are sheer pleasure.

Sinatra DVDs

July 10, 2008

A bunch of Frank Sinatra movies have just been released for the first time on DVD. They prove once again what an amazing singer he was. My special favorite is *It Happened in Brooklyn*, a musical comedy from 1947 in which Sinatra stars with comedian Jimmy Durante and leading MGM operatic soprano, pretty Kathryn Grayson. There's a delightful number in which Jimmy Durante is trying to help Sinatra get a job demonstrating pop songs in a music store. His advice is that "The Song's Gotta Come from the Heart." Sinatra catches on very quickly. Of course, Frank Sinatra already knows how to sing in the most meltingly heartfelt way. The score is mostly by Sammy Cahn and Jule Styne, and it includes one of Sinatra's loveliest early hits, "Time After Time."

Another number that's particularly dear to my heart is not by Cahn and Styne but by Mozart and his best librettist, Lorenzo da Ponte. It's the famous comic duet from *Don Giovanni*, "Là ci darem la mano." Don Giovanni is attempting to seduce the peasant girl Zerlina on the day of her wedding to the hapless Masetto. "There," Don Giovanni sings, pointing to his palace, "we'll hold hands—there's where you'll tell me 'Yes' and I'll change your fortune." Zerlina is reluctant and cautious. She feels sorry for Masetto. But even she can't resist the Don's promises. In *It Happened in Brooklyn*, this number takes place in an Italian restaurant. Grayson is a budding opera singer and Sinatra is trying to get her to sing for him. But she can't sing a duet alone and so he joins her. (Peter Lawford accompanies them on the piano.)

Too often when pop stars cross-over into classical music,

their attempt to be refined makes them stiff and they lose all the liveliness they have when they sing their own kind of music. But Sinatra is as comfortable with Mozart as with Jule Styne. His voice is so rich and warm he doesn't need to make it operatic. And he sings with such spontaneity and seductive intent, the way he sings pop music, he actually gets Grayson to loosen up and give one of her most delightful and teasing performances. Of course his voice wasn't big enough to carry without amplification in a large opera house, and opera singers are never encouraged to croon. But I wish more opera singers had Sinatra's uncanny phrasing, musical flexibility, and emotional directness. And I wish he sang more opera.

Gypsy: 50th Anniversary

June 10, 2009

Although *West Side Story* may be more directly related to Shakespeare, *Gypsy* might very well be at heart the most Shakespearean of all Broadway musicals. When I was in graduate school, some of my classmates concocted a musical version of *Hamlet*, putting new lyrics to the songs from *Gypsy*. Critic Frank Rich once said that *Gypsy* was the Broadway musical's answer to *King Lear*. I think the two greatest stage performances I ever saw were the great Shakespearean actor Paul Scofield's Lear and Ethel Merman as Rose Hovick, the ruthlessly ambitious mother of actress June Havoc and superstar stripper Gypsy Rose Lee. In the ferocity of her sense of betrayal by the daughter who achieves the success she wanted for herself, Merman rose to tragic heights. "Rose's Turn," her big final soliloquy, is the Broadway version of a real operatic mad scene. Good as Merman's successors may have been, none of them came anywhere near her in this number.

Gypsy's magnificently brash, quintessentially American vulgarity makes it one of Broadway's greatest show-biz musicals. The music was composed by Broadway pro Jule Styne, who's best known showstopper before *Gypsy* was probably "Diamonds Are a Girl's Best Friend," from *Gentlemen Prefer Blondes*. And his lyricist was a young Stephen Sondheim, fresh from writing the lyrics for *West Side Story*. How many people knew then that he could also write music? Though they never collaborated again, they were an ideal team: Styne's score was pure Broadway, by way of vaudeville and burlesque, memorable, yet unpretentious and never artsy; Sondheim's lyrics are by far his earthiest and most colloquial, yet they also have their own kind of Broadway wit and elegance—as in the intricate rhymes in "Together Wherever We Go" ("Wherever I go, I know, you go / Whatever the row I hoe, you hoe / And any IOU I owe, you owe / No we owe / Together").

To celebrate *Gypsy's* 50th anniversary, Sony has reissued the original cast album with some additional material. One highlight is what seems to be a demo of Merman singing the poignant song that in the show the lonely young Gypsy sings to her toy animals on her birthday. Anyone who thinks Merman was only a belter needs to hear this recording. New bonus tracks on the cast album also include an interview with Jule Styne, and a bizarre autobiographical number recorded by Gypsy Rose Lee herself shortly after *Gypsy* opened.

With the great Merman and the touching Jack Klugman as the man who loves her but can only take so much, *Gypsy* is one of the best original cast recordings ever made. More than most show albums, it lets us breathe the pungent atmosphere of the whole show. Of Broadway itself.

Porgy and Bess

September 13, 2011

George Gershwin called *Porgy and Bess* an "American folk opera." It was his most ambitious undertaking. And from the very beginning, it was a source of intense controversy. Could it be a true opera if it combined operatic arias, duets, and sung dialogue with vaudeville numbers like "I Got Plenty o' Nuthin'" and "It Ain't Necessarily So"? Are its characters the mythic archetypes Gershwin intended, or just stereotypes. Some of its own performers had their doubts. Yet *Porgy and Bess* was also a powerful tool for civil rights. When the first road company came to Washington, DC, in 1936, the cast, led by Todd Duncan, who played the crippled beggar Porgy, refused to perform unless the theater admitted black patrons and allowed them to sit anywhere. That's how Washington's National Theatre was integrated.

This summer at Tanglewood, the Boston Symphony Orchestra presented a powerful concert-opera version of *Porgy and Bess* based on the original 1935 New York production, for which Gershwin cut an hour of music during its Boston tryout. British composer and jazz pianist Bramwell Tovey was the incisive conductor. During the overture he leaped down from the podium and pounded a deliberately mistuned rinky-dink upright.

The Tanglewood Festival Chorus, with more than 100 voices, underlined the way *Porgy and Bess* is in a tradition of operas that show us entire communities—like *Boris Godunov* or *Carmen*. I wish only that the Boston Symphony had used the more complete score. The outstanding cast included Alfred Walker as a warm and deeply touching Porgy, Jermaine Smith as the seductive drug dealer Sportin' Life (complete with mid-air splits), and soprano Marquita Lister, as the widowed Serena. Her "My Man's Gone Now" makes a strong argument for an operatic Porgy.

At the other end of Massachusetts, in Cambridge, the American Repertory Theater (ART) has just staged a new *Porgy and Bess*, also in a shorter version, but one emphasizing musical-theater over opera. It's actually scheduled for a Broadway run. When ART's production team—director Diane Paulus, Pulitzer Prize-winning African-American playwright Suzan-Lori Parks, and musical-adaptor Deirdre L. Murray—announced that they were going to flesh out the original by changing dialogue, adding back stories, and having a new, more upbeat ending, and that the original orchestration was being rearranged for a small contemporary ensemble, Stephen Sondheim got so angry he wrote to the *New York Times* attacking what he called their willful ignorance and arrogance. Doesn't Gershwin's music, he argued, already flesh out these characters?

But after a series of previews, much of what outraged Sondheim has been abandoned. Had they actually listened to him? I was relieved but also disappointed that most of what was left was so conventional. And given ART's intention to play down the work's perceived racial problems, I was surprised how much of the acting and choreography seemed to play up minstrel-show stereotyping. I also wish treating *Porgy and Bess* as musical-theater didn't require coarse and unnecessary amplification that makes everything sound canned. The star, though, is charismatic Audra McDonald. Her soaring voice, closer to opera than to Broadway, endows Bess with both power and a heartbreaking vulnerability. No back-story necessary. Her poignant second-act reprise of the lullaby "Summertime," is one of the high points.

As Porgy, Norm Lewis, singing in a solid Broadway style, is strong and unusually embittered, putting excessive emphasis on Porgy's painful handicap. *In Living Color's* David Alan Grier is a stylish Sportin' Life. The conducting and scenes with extended spoken dialogue can afford more of Grier's expert timing and show-biz pizzazz. My biggest disappointment is the undersung yet overacted "My Man's Gone Now." If you don't want a Leontyne Price to sing Serena, then at least get a Nina Simone. *Porgy and Bess* is fundamentally a hybrid, an opera with Broadway numbers. I think it can work either way as long as Gershwin's great score remains its heart and soul. Tanglewood got it mostly right. The Cambridge production, for all its virtues, at least on opening night still seemed like a Broadway tryout.

A Damsel in Distress

November 15, 2011

A Damsel in Distress, which was released in 1937, four months after George Gershwin died of a brain tumor, was the third of only four films on which George and his brother Ira Gershwin collaborated. The star is Fred Astaire, but without Ginger Rogers. Their previous film together, *Shall We Dance?*, also with an unforgettable Gershwin score, hadn't lived up to studio expectations, and the now famous stars were taking a break from each other. This film has two substitutes for Rogers, one of the best and maybe the worst. Two songs from it became standards, and Astaire's longtime assistant, choreographer Hermes Pan, won an Oscar for dance direction for one of the most delightful production numbers in a Hollywood musical.

The story is based on a novel by P.G. Wodehouse, who also co-authored the screenplay. It's a mild satire of the snobbery of the British aristocracy. The heroine, the rebellious Lady Alyce Marshmorton, is played by eighteen-year-old Joan Fontaine (three years before she won an Oscar for *Suspicion*—the only actor ever to win an Oscar in an Alfred Hitchcock film). Her family thinks she has fallen in love with Astaire, who plays an American dancer visiting London with his publicist and his dizzy secretary, George Burns and Gracie Allen. It's directed by George Stevens, who's better known for such high dramas as *A Place in the Sun*, *Shane*, and *Giant*, but who had previously directed Astaire and Rogers in what many people consider their very best film, *Swingtime*.

One of the most famous songs from *A Damsel in Distress*—maybe the best song ever written about England—is "A Foggy Day." The British setting gives the Gershwins a chance to experiment. The score actually includes two madrigals. But the great number is the eight-minute sequence in a fun-house, in which Fred and George and Gracie slide down a chute and dance on a double turntable turning in opposite directions and in front of a series of fun-house mirrors that stretch them and shorten them and make them all legs with no bodies (a marvelously ironic image of Astaire). Burns and Allen are veteran vaudevillians, and their dancing is light as a feather, especially Gracie's hilarious non-stop trotting around that turntable, like some wonderful wind-up toy. The song that begins the number, deliciously introduced by Gracie, is called "Stiff Upper Lip."

The main problem with the film is that Fontaine was not a dancer. So the only romantic dance number in the film takes place in a woodland setting, and whenever possible, Fontaine is hidden by trees. It may be the only Astaire musical that doesn't end with a duet. The other great song in the film is "Nice Work If You Can Get It," with Astaire simultaneously dancing and playing drums with his feet.

Imagine a time in Hollywood when there were so many good movie songs that neither "A Foggy Day" nor "Nice Work If You Can Get It" was nominated for a best song Oscar. In fact, George Gershwin's only Oscar nomination was from the same year, another song introduced by Fred Astaire, "They Can't Take That Away from Me," from Shall We Dance? But it lost to a Hawaiian number called "Sweet Leilani" that Bing Crosby made popular. It would be my nomination for the worst decision ever made by the Motion Picture Academy.

Car 54

June 15, 2012

There's a holdup in the Bronx,
Brooklyn's broken out in fights,
There's a traffic jam in Harlem
That's backed up to Jackson Heights,
There's a scout troop short a child,
Khrushchev's due at Idlewild—
Car 54, where are you?

In case you're too young to remember, *Car 54, Where Are You?* was the TV comedy series about a mythical police station in the Bronx, created by Nat Hiken in 1961, his next brainchild after the Phil Silvers Show, *Sgt. Bilko*. It ran for only two seasons, but many people regard it as one of the funniest shows on television. I didn't watch it until I got hooked on it in syndication long after it was originally aired. So I was very happy to see the complete series of sixty episodes released on two DVD boxed sets. The episode in Season 2, "I Hate Capt. Block," about trying to teach a recalcitrant parrot to talk, and the way people are not much smarter than parrots, is one of the most hilarious things I've ever seen on television, maybe as inspired as Sid Caesar's foreign film parodies or Carol Burnett's version of *Gone with the Wind*.

I love the show for a couple of other reasons, too. For one thing, it was filmed on location in New York, where I grew up, but even more important, it was aware of what was going on in New York, starting with the line in Nat Hiken's memorable theme song about Khrushchev being due at Idlewild, which is what JFK Airport was called in 1960 when the Soviet premier had his legendary outburst at the UN. And how many other television comedies would refer to Leonard Bernstein conducting the New York Philharmonic?

One of my favorite episodes—the show's fifth—hits even closer to home. An elderly Jewish lady, played by Molly Picon, the enchanting musical star of the Yiddish theater, is being forced by the city to move from her apartment in the Bronx because her neighborhood is being torn down for an urban renewal project. That's exactly what happened to my family in Brooklyn. Picon's Mrs. Bronson became a prescient spokesperson for preserving real neighborhoods.

My other reason is Picon herself. My mother had a couple of old Molly Picon 78s, so I grew up listening to her bright singing voice and delicious comic timing. In the second season of *Car 54*, Mrs. Bronson is back. In order to get her to move out of her old building the city has given her a lease for an apartment in a new building. So she moves in, even though that building does not have walls yet. She of course charms all the officials trying to get her out, from the two police officers, Toody and Muldoon—Joe. E. Ross and Fred Gwynne—to the housing commissioner himself. She gives them homemade honey cake, and teaches them the touching turn-of-the-century Yiddish song "Oyfn Pripetshik." Songwriter M.M. Warshawsky's refrain can be loosely translated as:

In the fireplace
A little fire's burning
Warm the house must be
And the little rabbi
Helps the little children
Learn their ABC.

My grandmother used to sing me that song when I was a child. On the show, the words are never translated. However funny *Car 54* was, it was built on a bedrock of day-to-day reality that was one of the things that made it so deeply endearing.

My Parnassus

Artur Schnabel

May 13, 1987

I love Artur Schnabel—I wish I'd been around to hear him play the piano in person (one of the few reasons I'd want to be older). Of course, the reason I know him at all is that he recorded—he recorded a lot (in the '30s he became the first pianist to record all the Beethoven sonatas). And, fortunately, most of his recordings have been available at one time or another since his death in 1951. Now some of his greatest recordings have been issued by Arabesque on compact disc. These include most of his astonishing Schubert records (he was probably the most important re-discoverer of Schubert's piano music in this century) and his first complete set of the five Beethoven concertos (conducted by Sir Malcolm Sargent in the early '30s).

Schnabel is often classified among the "intellectual" musicians. But as is often the case, "intellectual" probably has more to do with intuitive emotional understanding than with any abstract theories. A Schnabel performance is characterized by the most poignant phrasing you've ever heard—with an uncanny lightness of touch and glistening tone that is never self-congratulatory but always at the service of some greater and deeper expression of the music. Take his timing in a remarkable transitional section from the slow movement of the Beethoven 4th Piano Concerto (I think you can often tell more about performers from the way they handle transitions than from the way they play either the big tunes or the ferocious virtuoso stuff—it's a sign of how deeply they understand an entire piece). At the beginning of the movement there's a sort of war going on between the orchestra and the soloist (Liszt compared this amazing passage to the story of Orpheus taming the wild beasts with his lyre). Gradually, with the quietest of voices, the piano begins to calm the rage of the orchestra—and finally succeeds. But for me, the greatest moment of all—and no one else I've ever heard plays this like Schnabel—comes in the sudden series of ominously rising trills and obsessive downward runs in the piano. This is the one sign that this effort, this attempt music makes to civilize our uncontrollable instincts, has its cost—if nothing else, a momentary but terrifying glimpse into the abyss. Then peace is movingly restored and both piano and orchestra can sail away into the practically undiluted joy of the last movement.

It's wonderful to have these Schnabel recordings conveniently available in the latest technology, though in the Beethoven concertos I actually prefer the scratchier but more spacious sound of the Arabesque LP versions (and, if truth be told, nothing comes near the warmth and clarity of the original 78s played on the best modern equipment). But, of course, the important thing is that they're available at all, and that someone in power feels that even after half a century it's still important to hear these performances which have never been equaled.

November 16, 1988

Artur Schnabel isn't as well-known for his Mozart or Bach as for his Beethoven and Schubert, but this has nothing to do with his artistry. He's the greatest Mozart pianist I've ever heard—his touch, his phrasing, his insights are as searching as they are in Beethoven and Schubert. But for as long as I can remember, his Mozart recordings have been harder to find. Much harder.

I remember a Schnabel record I found years ago. I was

spending a summer in Santa Fe trying to preserve a relationship that was going sour. I had lost my teaching job, and at summer's end I would have to return to Boston, probably alone and unemployed. One of the uncomplicated pleasures of Santa Fe was a small record shop run by a former classical music disc jockey from Chicago who was forced to retire because of his heart condition. He had wonderful out-of-print records—and great stories. I was broke. I barely had my fare home, which, in a way, made visiting a record store a very liberating experience. But a few days before I left, a record turned up that I'd been wanting for years: a long-out-of-print LP of Artur Schnabel playing two of Mozart's very greatest piano concertos—the powerful D-minor and the heartbreaking, heartbroken C-minor. They were Schnabel's last Mozart recordings and issued posthumously. I still remember the price: $12.50—a steal, really, but how could I afford it? The owner was willing to keep it for me, but I couldn't wait. I had to have it. And with practically my last cent, I bought it. I played it as soon as I got back to Boston—and it was everything I imagined.

These were among the most profound, moving performances of Mozart—of anything—I'd ever heard. They actually helped me see my life from a new and longer perspective. Later, my mother called to tell me that someone from a school I'd applied to in the spring had been trying urgently to track me down. A job had opened up, I wasn't going be destitute, and I had my Schnabel!

Now no one has to suffer to find Schnabel's marvelous Mozart records. They're all here. The sublime two-piano concerto that he plays with his son Karl-Ulrich. It's regarded as a lightweight piece, but as played by the Schnabels, it's not so much lightweight as weightless. There's the D-minor, with its dark rumblings of Don Giovanni, and the aching C-minor, with its notoriously modern cadenza composed by Schnabel himself. There's the tenderly playful No. 19 and the sensual No. 21. And No. 27, Mozart's last piano concerto, in which he discovered a radical and mysterious new simplicity.

Schnabel recorded only three Mozart sonatas: the last one, the tragic A-minor, and the ravishingly ambiguous F-major, now officially released in America for the first time. There's the great G-minor piano quartet, with members of the warmly remembered Pro Arte String Quartet. And finally, the A-minor Rondo, one of Mozart's most exquisite yet monumental miniatures—like Blake's world in a grain of sand. Music doesn't get much better than this.

Elliott Carter

May 20, 1987

I've been combing through the new releases of contemporary music and keep going back to a record that came out on Nonesuch a year ago that didn't get the attention it deserved. It contained the first recorded performances of two recent Elliott Carter pieces—the *Triple Duo* and *In Sleep, In Thunder*, his setting of six poems by Robert Lowell. It's a shocking comment on the state of contemporary music to realize that these works by our major living composer (might as well go out on that limb) took so long to be released (four years for the *Triple Duo*, five for the Lowell settings). They're marvelous and sometimes difficult works. Carter, now seventy-eight years old, has long since abandoned any conventional idea of melody and has become more interested in . . . well, character. Each instrument or group of instruments plays a part in the musical drama. They talk or they argue, sometimes all at the same time. They proceed at different speeds and in different rhythms. And there are often passages of the most aching lyricism (for me, the parts that keep Carter at the top of the "greatest living composer" charts).

The *Triple Duo* is Carter's Keystone comedy—a Rube Goldberg machine in which every turn of a cog triggers some unexpected but inevitable counter-reaction. As the title suggests, there are three pairings: a glittering toyshop of instruments you either stroke (violin and cello), strike (piano and percussion), or blow into (flute or piccolo and clarinet or bass clarinet). At one point, the pair might be as erotically harmonious as the piano and marimba you virtually can't tell apart; or as hilariously contradictory as the squeaky piccolo playing with the groaning bass clarinet; or as disorienting as the slow strings working against the fast winds. The opening gambit, a slapstick triple play, sets the whole piece in motion: piano to clarinet to flute to snare drum—bang! The banana-peel! The performers are the wonderful British ensemble, The Fires of London, to whom Carter dedicated the *Triple Duo*. It isn't ever likely to be livelier or more dazzlingly played.

I wish I could be as enthusiastic about the performance of *In Sleep, In Thunder*, which is a more difficult and demanding piece to begin with. The main problem is that it too is done by a British group—the London Sinfonietta with tenor Martyn Hill conducted by the British composer Oliver Knussen. It's almost grotesque to hear Hill, the proper Englishman, in the voice of Robert Lowell, singing stiffly about the modern Orpheus, with his murderous sons "dahncing with g-dateful gaiety rround the coook-out." These knotty, satirical, and moving poems need a singer who can capture Lowell's peculiarly American idiom. The players, however, get it right. In one delicious passage (please try to ignore the tenor), the solo trumpet, both bluesy and stentorian, mimics the failed Wagnerian soprano vocalizing across the yard from Lowell—Carter, in the process, giving us a portrait of Lowell himself: foolish, pathetic, heroic, and like nothing else you've ever heard.

December 14, 1988

On December 11, composer Elliott Carter celebrated his 80th birthday. Even a composer as valued as Carter still has a hard time getting his works recorded. The latest recording to include anything by Carter is an American song recital on the Nonesuch label by mezzo-soprano Jan de Gaetani and pianist Gilbert Kalish, two of Carter's most devoted advocates. It's a useful and revealing selection of songs from Stephen Foster to last year's Pulitzer Prize-winner, William Bolcom. The Carter songs are the most delightful pieces on the album—settings of two Robert Frost poems, "The Rose Family" and "Dust of Snow," composed in 1942.

It's been two years since the last important Carter release. New World Records issued brilliant performances by Michael Gielen and the Cincinnati Symphony of two of Carter's most ambitious orchestral works: the Variations for Orchestra, composed in 1955, and the Piano Concerto, from 1965, which pianist Ursula Oppens plays with phenomenal virtuosity and delicacy. But Carter did not stop composing in 1965 or 1975 or even 1985. His major new works—an oboe concerto commissioned by Heinz Holiger, an enigmatic chamber piece called *Penthode*, and his fourth string quartet, the deepest and most beautiful of his later masterpieces—have yet to be released.

One of the most interesting things about Carter is the continuity of his career. A first hearing of these recordings would barely suggest any connection between Carter's pretty and playful Frost miniatures and the two massive, intricate, and exhausting orchestral works. Yet the more you listen, the more they all seem the work of the same composer. Even as early as 1942—in fact, even earlier—Carter was already taking daring harmonic leaps and characteristically setting off one kind of rhythmic pulse against another—an impulse that led to his exciting explorations in what he called "metrical modulation." Since his later works seem to have abandoned anything we might ordinarily call melody, it's refreshing and reassuring to hear that he had a gift for irresistible tunes. Like discovering that an abstract expressionist painter could draw a convincing figure or beautiful landscape. Once you know that he actually wrote tunes, you begin to hear them everywhere, no matter how disguised or fractured they might be.

Let's close with Carter's "The Rose Family," his witty and affectionate setting of Frost's affectionate parody of Gertrude Stein's "A rose is a rose is a rose." I'll read the words first. Then imagine that Jan de Gaetani is singing them to Elliott Carter, on his 80th birthday: "The rose is a rose,/ And was always a rose./ But the theory now goes/ That the apple's a rose./ And the pear is, and so's/ The plum, I suppose./ The dear only knows/ What will next prove a rose./ You, of course, are a rose—/ But were always a rose."

January 18, 1989

Last month, on Elliott Carter's 80th birthday, I was lamenting that record companies have been ignoring his most recent work. Now the superb British ensemble the Arditti Quartet has recorded all of Carter's music for string quartet, from his early *Elegy* to his Fourth Quartet, composed in 1986—this is its very first recording. No matter how controversial Carter may be, his string quartets are almost universally admired. The Second and Third won him his two Pulitzer Prizes. All four probably make the greatest body of 20th-century chamber music since Bartok's six quartets, and this is the first time a single group has recorded more than two.

In 1951, Carter's First Quartet made him a world figure. It remains his longest and perhaps deepest work, large-scaled yet profoundly intimate and questioning. He's often repeated that it was written largely for his own satisfaction, and grew out of an effort to understand himself. When he composed it, he and his wife were living near Tucson, Arizona. It's desert music, full of open spaces, scurrying creatures, and the most aching isolation.

Carter said, "I regard my scores as scenarios—auditory

scenarios—for performers to act out with their instruments." His Second Quartet, from 1959, actually creates four distinct characters. Each one leads its own movement, while the others respond in various ways, including irritation and even deadpan silence. Movements are separated by flamboyantly individualized solo cadenzas. But chamber music to Carter also means teamwork. The Third Quartet, written in 1971, presents two teams—violin and cello vs. violin and viola—continuously pitted against each other.

The recent Fourth Quartet is more socially cohesive, more conversational. Sometimes one voice or another leaps from the chattery texture; or there's a moment of hesitation, when no one has anything to say. In the slow section, each player enters the intense discussion with a series of overlapping double-stopped chords (one critic called this passage Carter's "octet"). In the epilogue, the conversation turns into an argument—with the self. The rough beast within keeps interrupting the muted but persistent voice of sweetness and enlightenment. There's no solution, no exit. The stalemate finally ends in a little Charlie Chaplin shrug. We've done all we can, no?

The playing by the Arditti is secure, honest, and impassioned. I've heard riskier, more daring live performances of the Fourth Quartet by the Juilliard, who are about to record it, and the Composers Quartet, its dedicatees. Their classic recording on Nonesuch of the first two quartets has just come out on CD. But now with the Arditti, we can finally hear a unified conception of all four, which, like T.S. Eliot's *Four Quartets*, make a kind of inward epic, a long pilgrimage into some previously uncharted reaches of the lone spirit.

April 16, 1991

When Aaron Copland died last year, at the age of 90, he hadn't produced any new work for nearly twenty years. But at the age of 82, Elliott Carter is still going strong. In the past few years he has given us some of his most beautiful and vivid scores. Two years ago, there was a distinguished recording of Carter's four string quartets by the Arditti Quartet. Now there's an even better recording of the Fourth Quartet by the wonderful group it's dedicated to, the Composers String Quartet. Their recording of Carter's first two quartets was listed in *High Fidelity* magazine as one of the 50 great albums of the decade. The Fourth Quartet was written in 1986. It's in four continuous movements. The Arditti Quartet plays it in just over 20 minutes. The Composers Quartet takes nearly 4 minutes longer. But the Composers Quartet isn't so much slower as more spacious—the music has more time to expand, to breathe. Let me play you the extraordinary epilogue. Exuberant outbursts, sudden stops, and muted, inward-searching passages—we've heard them all earlier in the Quartet. Suddenly they begin alternating in rapid succession, like a series of double takes. Who's speaking? Who's interrupting?

Carter is the most democratic of modern American composers. For Carter, a community is made up of individual voices. He encourages each member of an ensemble to play with his or her own voice, at his or her own pace and rhythm. The Fourth Quartet may be Carter's most social and communal, and inter-communicative, piece. The group tries to solve the problems of the world, maybe the problem of existence itself. But there's no answer, or no one answer. I find that baffled little shrug at the end as touching, and as humble, as Keaton or Chaplin.

We can hear this democracy of voices in the four recent Carter pieces on an album that features the Swiss cellist Thomas Demenga. There are the almost weightless *Enchanted Preludes* for flute and cello and the pungent contrasts of *Esprit rude, esprit doux*, which was Carter's witty and touching 60th birthday tribute to Pierre Boulez. There's an 80th birthday *Riconoscenza*, or *Remembrance*, for the Italian composer Goffredo Petrassi, which incorporates many personality contrasts within the one solo violin. And there's Carter's most delicious later work, the hilarious and moving *Triple Duo* for three pairs of instruments, in which the opening gambit triggers a whole Rube Goldberg machine.

This Thomas Demenga album begins with his rich performance of Bach's C-major Suite for Solo Cello. In the liner notes, Heinz Holliger—the conductor, composer, and much admired oboist for whom Carter composed his recent Oboe Concerto—comments on this juxtaposition of old and new. He reminds us that Bach and Carter can be described with the same language. Great music creates a continuum. Holliger urges us to relax, lie back, remember the future, and try to foresee the past.

October 5, 1994

Ever since I first heard Elliott Carter's Cello Sonata and First String Quartet, I've been a devotee. His music is notoriously difficult. Yet I've found more and deeper pleasure listening to Carter than to just about any other contemporary composer. I don't actually try any more to figure out his multi-level cross-rhythms and intricate harmonic patterns. I just listen. But what I hear is insinuating, dramatic, and profoundly moving. The instruments themselves are living characters, making love, arguing, sometimes both at once. In one of Carter's knottiest masterpieces, *Duo*, from 1974, the violin keeps darting all over the place while the piano remains virtually stationary. Carter himself compared this music to a man trying to climb a glacier.

The violinist on this slippery ride is the remarkable Rolf Schulte; Martin Goldray is the icy, implacable pianist. Carter dedicated *Duo* to his wife Helen.

I'm glad the *Duo* and the seminal Cello Sonata are both included on this album. This lets us hear for ourselves how the new pieces, which are unusually small-scale for Carter, are founded on some of the same radical techniques. They're all short works for small chamber ensembles or solo instruments, and they're so fresh and youthful, they sound almost as if the violin, or guitar, or clarinet, or flute were improvising the music on the spot.

Flutist Harvey Sollberger plays the dream-like *Scrivo in Vento (I Write on Wind)*. Some of these new compositions are dedicated to celebrated figures Carter admired: the Italian composer Goffredo Petrassi, the writer Italo Calvino. Last year he wrote an exuberant clarinet solo called *Gra*, which is Polish for "play," for the Polish composer Witold Lutoslawski who died early this year. Running through all these pieces is a complex interweaving of playfulness with elegy that reminds me of what Yeats, in his 70s, called "tragic joy." Is Carter, in his 80s, now feeling that all art is "written on wind"? Is that transience a kind of liberation? In his poem "Lapis Lazuli," Yeats describes a Chinese carving of three old men on a mountain staring down "On all the tragic scene." "Their eyes mid many wrinkles," Yeats writes, "their ancient, glittering eyes, are gay."

August 13, 1998

I went up to Elliott Carter after a wonderful performance at Tanglewood of his recent Clarinet Concerto. I'd been particularly moved by the slow sections, and I told Carter that I thought he wrote the best slow movements since Schubert.

"But what about the fast movements?" Carter asked. "Those are good too. They're a lot more work because there are so many more notes to write down." For me, Carter's exhilarating extremes of tempo represent two different kinds of soul-searching—one scurrying, frantic, or comic, like a Keystone Kops chase; the other calm, eerie, more inward, even ecstatic. Each needs the other. The amazing transition from the Presto of the Clarinet Concerto Carter wants the woodwinds to play "as fast as possible." Then suddenly we're in a slow movement for clarinet and strings, where time seems to stop.

I just heard Carter's Clarinet Concerto at Tanglewood—the East Coast premiere—played by the Boston Symphony Orchestra's brilliant clarinetist Thomas Martin and a group of impressive young Tanglewood fellows under the direction of Stefan Asbury—maybe the perfect group to bring out Carter's own astonishingly youthful energy.

Carter's 90th year has been a good one. He's in fine health, and has been working hard. He just completed his very first opera, called *What Next?*, which was inspired by the Jacques Tati comedy *Traffic*. And his music is even being performed in his own country! I can remember back in the early-70s, waiting in the crowd trying to get into Harvard's Sanders Theater to hear the Juilliard Quartet play the first Boston performance of Carter's Third String Quartet. The cultural climate is different now. Audiences have been seduced by the simplicities of minimalism. Schools rarely teach music anymore. Where's an educated young audience for serious music going to come from?

They love Carter in Europe, though. *What Next?* will have its world premiere next year in Berlin. At least landmark birthdays are useful, as Tanglewood's Contemporary Music Festival proved. And despite Carter's reputation for difficulty, his new pieces are not hard to follow. Both the Clarinet Concerto and the Fifth String Quartet have similar structures: he's exchanged his earlier outpouring of melody for "character" movements (Joking or Tranquil or Agitated) that alternate with more chaotic "intervals," sometimes very brief, that recall—or anticipate—fragments from earlier or later sections. It's one way music, Carter says, expresses how the mind works. He compares the witty/edgy opening of the Fifth String Quartet to something you might overhear at a rehearsal, each player warming up or tuning up independently of the others.

It's the ultimate democracy. Carter dedicated it to the Arditti Quartet, who played it magnificently at Tanglewood.

I wish I could play excerpts from all the recent Carter recordings, especially Charles Rosen playing Carter's complete solo piano music, on Bridge Records, and on CPO the dazzling Ensemble Contrasts from Germany, playing Carter's delicious and profound chamber music for winds. Carter has been lucky with finding great performers who've loved his music, and the level of expertise keeps going up. What was challenging twenty years ago now seems almost effortless. The musicians are hearing not only the notes but the music. So we can hear it too.

March 16, 2000

People who love Elliott Carter's music had probably given up hope that he would ever write an opera. But now they finally have their wish. The aptly named *What Next?* is a delight, an inventive, semi-absurdist one-act comedy that you'd never guess was composed by someone about to turn 90. Carter says he waited so long because he just couldn't find a situation that convinced him it should be sung. British novelist and *New York Times* music critic Paul Griffiths has given him a libretto that couldn't be anything else BUT sung—a kind of "Six Characters in Search of an Opera." *What Next?* literally begins with a bang, a brilliantly orchestrated crash, with trash cans and brake drums joining the almost comically extensive battery of percussion instruments.

There's been an accident. Six characters are starting to come to, trying to figure out who they are and where they were going. They never entirely succeed, though 45 minutes later they're a little wiser, more self-aware than when they began.

The central character is a self-centered soprano, a diva named Rose. She almost never stops singing, mostly about how wonderfully she sings. Then there's an oddball named Harry or Larry. He and Rose may be on the way to their wedding. A woman named Mama might be Harry—or Larry's— mother. A burbling Hippie-ish philosopher, named Zen, might be Mama's ex-husband, and a learned astronomer, Stella, might be Zen's new girlfriend. In Griffiths' sometimes too schematic quasi-allegory, Zen and Stella represent polar opposites. Stella wants everything measured; Zen wants to live by chance, by "accident." They're like the history of 20th-century music. There's also a hungry little boy, called simply Kid, who wakes up dying for a Big Mac.

Carter's music is not what most people would call melodic (he gave up traditional "melody" years ago), but it ranges widely from the most jaggedly edgy and chattering to the long-breathed and lyrical. The singing starts with a hissing sound, as if air were leaking out of a tire, but this sibilance is actually the beginning of the word "star." The soundings-out of these delicate syllables are like ethereal vocal warm-ups.

In the middle of the opera, the characters leave the stage and the orchestra plays one of the most ravishing passages Elliott Carter ever wrote, a haunting nocturne with a wreathing solo for English horn.

Carter has often said that everything he's written has been a kind of character piece, with each instrument or section of the orchestra expressing a different point of view. Some of his favorite musical reference points are the complex banquet scene from *Don Giovanni*, in which three separate orchestras play on stage, or the famous sextet from *Lucia di Lammermoor*. *What Next?* is really another sextet, in which the six characters simultaneously express their diverse and conflicting—not to say conflicted—feelings. It's one of the things music can do best. And one of the things Elliott Carter can do better than almost anyone else.

December 22, 2008

In the upstairs bar at Boston's Symphony Hall, there's a photo exhibit honoring Elliott Carter. In one picture taken in 1939, he's a grinning-30-year-old, but he looks 18. If I were making a movie called *The Elliott Carter Story*, I'd cast Matt Damon. Now at 100, Carter still looks younger than his years, and he's composing some of his most vital and youthful work. This Carter landmark has been a source of world-wide celebrations—the most extensive of which was at Tanglewood last summer, where the annual Festival of Contemporary Music was devoted entirely to him. And there he was, obviously enjoying the nearly fifty performances of his music, including two world premieres.

Carter celebrated his actual birthday at Carnegie Hall, where James Levine led pianist Daniel Barenboim and the Boston Symphony Orchestra in his dazzling, ambitious, and emotionally complex new piece, *Interventions*. He had already attended the world premiere in Boston the week before. And all year long, exciting new Carter recordings have been appearing. Pianist Ursula Oppens, Carter's longtime champion and friend, has a new CD called *Elliott Carter at 100: The Complete Piano Mu-*

sic—a title which will probably soon become obsolete.

On it is the very first recording of the 2-minute gem that Carter wrote for the 92nd birthday of maestro Levine's mother. It's called *Matribute*—Carter was an English major at Harvard and loves to play with words. The right and left hand are like two characters having a conversation. It's a typical Carter stratagem, which is nothing less than a view of the world, where musical lines, like individual lives, intersect at changing speeds in endlessly changing contexts, and sometimes, maybe only for a moment, come together. His pieces usually end not with a grand heroic climax but a whisper, or a shrug. In *Matribute* it's a single note—a quiet little C.

Benita Valente

June 3, 1987

For twenty-five years, American soprano Benita Valente has been a connoisseur's delight, a musician's musician—in opera and recitals, in Europe and with practically every important orchestra or opera company in this country (including the Met). Yet she's never acquired the celebrity status of some of her equals—or inferiors. Partly, I suspect, it's a matter of temperament. She projects humility and reticence rather than the aggressive glamour of the typical prima donna. She seems to care more about her music than her image. Which, of course, is part of her charm. It's what makes her self-sacrificing Gilda in *Rigoletto*, for example, so convincingly youthful. And it's what must be at least partly behind the touching sweetness and transparency of her Mozart and Handel. With that tear dissolving in her voice, or the sunburst of joy, she's the ideal musical heroine.

But probably the main reason for her relative obscurity outside the musical world is that she hasn't recorded much. Some twenty years ago, she made a famous record of Schubert's "The Shepherd on the Rock," with Rudolf Serkin and Boston Symphony clarinetist Harold Wright—it's still a collector's item. Her few other recordings, on small labels, have virtually disappeared.

But this situation is being remedied. Lately she's been recording again, and the Pantheon label has been releasing a series of four solo records and CDs: there are Wolf and Strauss songs, Mozart and Handel arias, some vocal chamber music (mostly French and Spanish), and a wonderful album of Haydn, Mozart, and Schubert songs that includes a new version of "The Shepherd on the Rock" with pianist Cynthia Raim and once again clarinetist Harold Wright (better than ever). In the last few minutes of this ambitious work, possibly Schubert's last song, Valente and Wright capture the repressed pain and uncertainty behind the lonely shepherd's springtime optimism.

Valente is one of a sadly dwindling number of singers who specializes in the art of the art song. Among her teachers were Lotte Lehmann, one of the greatest lieder singers of this century. Valente's many virtues—and a few limitations—are present on this disc: every so often, a vocal turn emerges a little less delicately than it might have ten years ago, but her tone is still rich and exquisitely limpid. Her German, Italian, and even English diction is impeccable, immaculate, comprehensible without being pretentious. And that comes in handy, in case no texts or translations are included with your CD (there weren't any with my copy). On the other hand, her French strikes me as a little un-aromatic. Still, you can't help feeling over and over again what a superb and moving artist she is, how little she needs to sacrifice either dramatic urgency or beauty of tone because her understanding of both the music and the words seems to spring from the same expressive impulse.

September 22, 2010

Soprano Benita Valente has retired from singing, though at 75, she's still remarkably active behind the scenes as an educator, organizer, and fund-raiser. She may not be the world's most famous singer, but a selection of her recordings lead off a new series on Bridge Records called *Great Singers of the 20th Century*. It's hard not to love Valente. She had one of the most exquisite soprano voices in opera, and at 75, maybe still has. But a lot of opera singers have pretty voices without being nearly as admirable. What makes Benita Valente so special? We could start with almost any track on her latest CD—a compilation of recordings, some of them live performances, from between the late '60s to the late '80s. Let's take Mozart—maybe the hardest composer to get right because mere vocal pyrotechnics aren't a sufficient substitute for the complete honesty of musicianship and feeling his music requires. This sublime aria from the last act of *The Marriage of Figaro*, for instance, is part of a complicated plot to expose the lechery of the Count Almaviva. His wife's servant Susanna is in the garden, serving as a decoy, pretending to have an assignation with the Count. She seems to be singing him a love song: "Deh, vieni, non tardar"—"Oh, please don't be late." She knows that her fiancée, the Count's barber and factotum Figaro, will also be spying on her. Susanna wants to test him too. But we know that she loves Figaro and her love song is really directed at him. In the midst of the farce, this aria is one of the purest expressions of true feeling in all of opera. Valente effortlessly captures this depth of feeling, and still manages to retain Susanna's little sparkle of mischief.

One way to judge an artist is through his or her associates. Valente's collaborators here include conductor Alexander Schneider, who is probably best known as the second violinist of the legendary Budapest String Quartet. Her piano accompanists are Richard Goode, Lydia Artimiw, and David Effron, who also conducted the Mozart we just heard. The most famous of Valente's recordings on this CD is Schubert's ambitious "The Shepherd on the Rocks," with pianist Rudolph Serkin and clarinetist Harold Wright, recorded at the Marlboro Music Festival in 1969. That performance made her a star. She sings Italian arias, and songs in German, French, and Spanish. Valente's gift for languages is impeccable, which is a sign that she cares about what words mean in every language. Another of my favorite tracks, "Auch kleine Dinge," is a song from Hugo Wolf's *Italian Songbook* "In Praise of Small Things"—a short song, of course. The last lines of the song are: "Think of the rose—how small it is, and yet how lovely it smells—as you know." It could be Valente's anthem. She didn't have a huge voice and was never a diva who exulted in her own grandeur. And yet what a precious artist she is, and how precious she made everything she touched.

Pierre Boulez

June 10, 1987

As conductor, composer, and writer, Pierre Boulez has developed a forbidding reputation for technical precision, intellectual incisiveness, and emotional detachment. He appeared once on the *Tonight* show and demonstrated his perfect pitch by correctly identifying any note played at random. A cool character! How could any other kind be interested in the cold abstractions of 20th-century music?

I think people who believe this have never heard—or at least never *listened* to—a Boulez performance. Of course, the textures are always prismatically, "scientifically" clear: on a Boulez recording you can hear *everything*. (And if you've ever heard him conduct in person, you know it's not just the recording engineers who are doing the clarifying.) What *isn't* there are the excesses, the exhibitionism, the melodramatic revving-up you hear from so many conductors who think you have to be heavy to be deep. Boulez doesn't need to inflate, because he's right there with the composer, carefully observing, following, and empathizing with every nuance of a score. Technically, this comes out in the process of balancing—the kind of analytic approach that makes sure no instrument is drowning out or blending too much with another. And in the process of phrasing, which is a more subtle matter of rhythmic continuity. In a Boulez performance you don't just hear notes but urgent, unstoppable waves of music.

Naturally, this approach is especially useful for new music, or music we don't get to hear very often. But a Boulez performance of a work like the Beethoven Fifth Symphony will also sound like something you're hearing for the first time. From large-scale Mahler and Wagner to delicate Mozart serenades and early Schubert symphonies (which he's never recorded), his versions are among the most moving, affectionate, and unpretentious I've ever heard.

I'd also like to call your attention to two new CBS Masterworks compact discs that include several of his greatest recordings from the '70s: One has his exuberantly colorful and touching performance of Stravinsky's *Petrushka* with the New York Philharmonic, when it was still a great ensemble (the late Paul Jacobs is at the piano),—and an overwhelming *Rite of Spring* with the Cleveland Orchestra (which still is a great ensemble); the other has Bartók's *Concerto for Orchestra*, also with the Philharmonic, and his *Music for Strings, Percussion and Celesta* with the BBC Symphony. The Stravinskys are the most vivid recordings of these masterpieces after Stravinsky's own, and technically even more authoritative. The Bartóks are on a completely different level from any other performances I've heard—sweeping yet delicate, and totally mesmerizing.

In the "Interrupted Intermezzo" from Bartók's *Concerto for Orchestra*, the "Interruption" is a jaunty little clarinet theme from *The Merry Widow*. Shostakovich quoted it in his *Leningrad Symphony*, which Bartók heard on the radio, couldn't stand, and immediately had to use.

The CDs are in splendid sound and of course provide the advantage of not having to interrupt the music by changing sides. With both Bartóks on discs, they're also phenomenal bargains.

March 24, 2000

Pierre Boulez is not only a conductor, a composer, and a theorist, but a cultural icon, perhaps the greatest living spokesperson for Modernism in music. He's been a hero for more than thirty years. When I was a graduate student, my music-loving classmates were particularly excited about a handful of contemporary musicians: Pierre Boulez, Maria Callas, and the Beatles. We would gather at someone's dorm room to listen to and argue about their latest recordings.

Boulez was the most outspoken, iconoclastic champion of the music of our own time, the musical equivalent of Rimbaud's dictum: "One must be absolutely modern." At one point he even considered Stravinsky out of date! Over the years, he recorded not only the 20th-century masters but also the earlier composers (Berlioz, Wagner, Mahler) who influenced them. These recordings were profound considerations of a crucial historical continuity. They were also the most extraordinary performances. Yet, Boulez was not embraced by the American press. He was regarded as a cold fish, analytic, mathematical, precise. But these adjectives didn't seem to fit the tenderness and passion of his performances. Now, in his 70s, Boulez has become a star. He's been making wonderful new recordings. He even wins Grammies. So when I was invited to a publicity lunch for Boulez in New York, preceding a remarkable weekend of concerts he was giving at Carnegie Hall with the London Symphony Orchestra, how could I not go? I even got to sit next to him at lunch. He was surprisingly relaxed, unintimidating, and charming. After a Q&A, when dessert was announced, the maestro quipped: "I thought I was the dessert." More seriously, he talked about the horrible bind that Austrian artists are now finding themselves in. The West wants to boycott the very figures the new right-wing would love to keep quiet. Wouldn't such silencing be giving the neo-Nazis exactly what they want?

This series of concerts was part of an international tour (including Vienna) organized to celebrate Boulez's 75th birthday, March 26. Carnegie Hall, one of the tour's sponsors, was the only American venue, and some members of the orchestra told me they were especially excited to be playing there. Each of the four different programs juxtaposed an early 20th-century masterwork with an American premiere. The most beautiful new piece was *Palimpsest*, by George Benjamin, the forty-year-old British composer who'll be directing the contemporary music concerts at Tanglewood this summer. The superstar soloists included pianists Maurizio Pollini, who played a brand new piece by the Italian composer Salvatore Sciarrino, and Daniel Barenboim, who gave an absolutely riveting account of the Schoenberg Piano Concerto. The young German violin virtuoso Christian Tetzlaff played the mercurial and mysterious Ligeti *Violin Concerto* (with its haunting ensemble of ocarinas!). On the last program, Boulez led one of his own pieces. The performances were mind-boggling. Even the most familiar works sounded like you were hearing them for the first time. How could anyone who heard Schoenberg's erotic, almost lurid early tone poem *Pelleas* and *Melisande* think Boulez was chilly? In Stravinsky's *Petrushka*, he was like a great director filming a kaleidoscopic montage of a Russian Mardi-gras fair, with a puppet (or is he the artist?) as the tragi-comic hero. Was music ever more exhilarating, or enchanting, or poignant? I've thought for years that Boulez was our greatest living Mahler conductor. And now I was finally getting to hear him do a Mahler symphony—the tragic *Sixth*—live. Every note seemed completely felt, as intense as any music I've ever heard. I don't cry easily, but suddenly tears were streaming down my face.

The evening after the luncheon, I ran into a friend from the *New York Times*, who had just come from a rehearsal. "They let you into a rehearsal?" I asked. It hadn't occurred to me. The next afternoon, I started going to rehearsals. And they were fascinating. After performances in London, Vienna, and Paris, the orchestra was in terrific shape. Boulez has one of the great "ears" in music, so he was asking the musicians—in the most straightforward way—for only the subtlest readjustments. He was also quite playful. "Do you know what we're playing?" he asked Barenboim at the beginning of the Schoenberg rehearsal. Barenboim responded by playing the opening bars of Beethoven's Fourth Piano Concerto. "What IS that?" Boulez asked. Later on, Boulez missed a beat and stopped: "My mistake," he apologized. "Thank God!" Barenboim exclaimed. "I've been waiting all my life to hear you make a mistake." During the ovation at the end of the last performance, the concertmaster suddenly raised his bow and the orchestra burst into "Happy Birthday!" Isaac Stern—"Mr. Carnegie Hall"—emerged from the wings with a huge bouquet. The audience went wild. It was such a rare opportunity for everyone who loves Boulez to convey not only their admiration but their affection, and maybe an even rarer occasion for him to accept it.

March 21, 2001

I was invited to a rehearsal for a concert by the Ensemble Sospeso of music by Pierre Boulez. I asked one of the brilliant musicians what it was like rehearsing with Boulez. "Everything he said makes sense," the young musician told me. "It's extremely obvious he knew exactly what he was doing and hears exactly what he writes. He could be God—or the Devil."

This rehearsal was in conjunction with the weekend of concerts Boulez was conducting at Carnegie Hall with the Vienna Philharmonic Orchestra. Boulez is surely the most important living musician with a hyphenated career: conductor-composer. Or is it composer-conductor? Which comes first? That's the question Boulez has been asking himself. Beginning in September, the septuagenarian conductor is taking a year off to compose. His work is difficult, but elegant. One piece called *Sur incises* (French for "cuts"—as in film or sound editing), which Boulez worked on from 1996 to 1998, just won what is probably the most prestigious award in music, the $200,000 Gravemeyer Prize.

The music started as a four-minute piano solo. Boulez expanded this germ into a hypnotic 45-minute fantasy for glittering sprays of glissandos and arpeggios on three pianos, three harps, and three sets of percussion instruments that can sound like bells (marimba, vibraphones, steel drum, glockenspiel). These real instruments seem to imitate the textures of electronic music, only here they sound more colorful, jazzier, moodier, and more erotic. As I've gotten to know Boulez's music better, I've discovered that—like his conducting—it has a deeply human side. On a marvelous new recording, Boulez leads nine players from the Ensemble InterContemporain.

Boulez the conductor also just happens to be at the very top of his form. He's been making astonishing new recordings with some of the world's greatest symphony orchestras: Cleveland, Chicago, the Berlin and Vienna Philharmonic. Last year, he played an extraordinary series of concerts at Carnegie Hall with the London Symphony, in which he programmed brand new pieces, including one of his own, along with masterpieces of late Romanticism and early Modernism—works that interest him as the seeds of contrasting aspects of contemporary music. This year, with the astounding (and anachronistically still virtually all-male) Vienna Philharmonic, the most recent work was Stravinsky's explosive post-World War II Symphony in Three Movements, which Boulez followed up with something I've never heard him do—an encore(!): Stravinsky's *Circus Polka*, commissioned by George Balanchine for his dancing-baby-elephant ballet at Ringling Brothers/Barnum & Bailey. Boulez has a sly sense of humor—it was delicious to hear him in a mood of unbuttoned, practically inebriated hilarity.

The biggest works were by Bruckner and Mahler—the Vienna Philharmonic's chicken soup. I was allowed to attend rehearsals, and it was fascinating to witness Boulez go over and over again a tiny phrase, to get from these spectacular players the precise rhythmic articulation he was looking for. In Mahler's Third Symphony, he got the American Boychoir to sound less like boy sopranos than like real boys imitating bells. On the podium, Boulez has an uncanny instinct for exactly what it takes for each note, each phrase, to sink in. The Mahler seemed to come not so much from the orchestra as from some place inside my own body. I was so choked up by it I could hardly speak; so transported to another world, I took a subway going in the wrong direction. Do I want to hear more new pieces by composer Pierre Boulez? Of course. Do I want him to give up conducting on this level, even for a year? What do you think?

Otto Klemperer

July 29, 1987

I'd like to call your attention to a record company: Music and Arts Programs of America, Inc., the latest incarnation of what used to be officially known as—and is still sometimes called—The Bruno Walter Society, or Discocorp. It's an organization I'm devoted to because they perform an invaluable service to music lovers and record collectors. Along with some excellent new recordings, they release—in the best available sound—historic recordings, most of them from actual live performances. They have superb taste in the musicians they concentrate on, including some of this century's greatest conductors: Arturo Toscanini, Wilhelm Furtwängler, Otto Klemperer, and, naturally, Bruno Walter. As Music and Arts, they're now producing only CDs, although some of their earlier LPs are still available.

Of course, even at its best, the sound of a live recording dating back thirty or forty years doesn't have the glamorous sheen of today's digital engineering, and some of the performances lack the technical finish that can only be created in a recording studio. But it's the rarity and vitality of the performances themselves that make these discs so precious. For example, there's their new issue of the Bruckner 6th Symphony that Otto Klemperer performed with the Concertgebouw Orchestra of Amsterdam in 1961. Klemperer shows us just how Bruckner, in this marvelous but relatively ignored work, takes his two idols, Beethoven and Wagner, and makes them sing with his own eccentric but heroic combination of solemnity and naiveté.

Three and a half years later, Klemperer made a studio recording of this with the New Philharmonia, and it's one of his most beautiful Bruckner performances. (Angel Records has just re-issued it on cassette.) With all its precision and beauty, and the authority of a conductor admired for his deep penetration of this music, you wouldn't imagine much was missing—until you hear the more personal inflections of the live performance, the more exciting sweep from phrase to phrase and movement to movement. In spite of some raggedness in ensemble and the feeling of listening to an old radio broadcast, no other performance can take its place. This CD also includes a fascinating live performance of the Brahms Variations on a Theme by Haydn.

The Music and Arts catalogue currently lists such choice items as Toscanini's live Verdi *Requiem*, his Beethoven *Missa Solemnis*, and even a two-disc set of rehearsals for his famous recording of Verdi's *Falstaff*. There's the Furtwängler *Don Giovanni*, a Klemperer Beethoven *Ninth*, a Mahler *Kindertotenlieder* sung by Marion Anderson and conducted by Jascha Horenstein, and many more. Even aside from the historical and musical value of these recordings, it's important to be reminded that making music is primarily a living experience, not only an electronic one.

March 7 and 14, 1990

In 1907, when Otto Klemperer was not quite twenty-two, he played for Gustav Mahler a piano arrangement he'd made of the Scherzo of Mahler's gigantic 2nd Symphony, and he played it from memory. Mahler was so impressed he wrote the young conductor a recommendation that helped launch his career—a career that took him to Berlin, Budapest, Los Angeles, and finally London. In 1951, the powerful British record producer

Walter Legge, who was head of EMI, the parent company of Angel records, hired Klemperer to conduct the Philharmonia Orchestra, which Legge himself had founded. After years of illness, neglect, and bad luck, Klemperer became the idol of London. At the age of sixty-seven, he began his magnificent series of recordings with the Philharmonia, and later the New Philharmonia. It was a relationship that lasted nearly twenty years. Klemperer is still associated with the music of Mahler and two of his greatest Mahler recordings—the 2nd and 9th Symphonies—have recently been re-released on compact discs. Here's Klemperer conducting, with delicate wit, the very music he played for Mahler over half a century earlier.

Mahler and Klemperer had a number of things in common. Both were Jewish, both became Roman Catholics. Klemperer's monumental scale and crystalline textures owe a lot to Mahler. The cliché, about Klemperer is that his tempos are very slow and heavy. Though he conducts some passages faster than anyone else, his most characteristic tempos certainly are slow. But they're so rhythmically alive, there's nothing heavy about them. Their spaciousness actually allows you to hear every note. His Brahms Third Symphony has surely never had a graver beauty. In Klemperer's slow motion, even the little transitional phrases have unforgettably melodic lines of their own.

Klemperer underwent more than his share of mental and physical suffering. He was chronically manic-depressive. During a rehearsal in 1933, the podium rail gave way. He fell backwards and hit his skull. Later, a brain tumor left him partially paralyzed. A broken leg put him out of commission for over a year. At 81, he broke his hip. Once he fell asleep smoking and ignited his bed. What he used to extinguish the fire turned out to be liquid camphor. It was amazing he survived. Klemperer was a large man, six feet-four, and his endurance must have been phenomenal. Perhaps all this suffering gave him a special insight into works like Mahler's crushing yet sublime 9th Symphony. Almost everything he played glowed with a spiritual flame. But Klemperer was also famous for his caustic wit, a quality perhaps inherited by his son, the character-actor Werner Klemperer (who played Col. Klink on *Hogan's Heroes*). At the recording session of Beethoven's *Pastorale* Symphony, Walter Legge questioned Klemperer's radically slow tempo for the peasant merrymaking. Klemperer told him he'd get used to it. A few minutes later Klemperer phoned Legge in the control booth and asked: "Walter, are you used to it yet?"

* * *

Last week, I played selections from three of the composers most closely associated with Otto Klemperer: Mahler, Beethoven, and Brahms. Klemperer hewed to the German tradition in music. Except for Stravinsky and Berlioz, whom he performed with great beauty and clarity, the few non-German composers Klemperer played, like Franck, Dvorak, and Tchaikovsky, were heavily under the German influence. Trendy early-instrument performances have made the earliest composers Klemperer recorded, Bach and Handel, seem old-fashioned in their rich textures, though they remain soul-stirring. Less well known are Klemperer's recordings of the high-classical repertoire. His Haydn and Mozart symphonies are among the most beautiful ever made. I've never heard a G-minor Symphony more moving than Klemperer's 1957 performance, though some people find his tempos almost perversely slow. He recorded the symphony more than once—I'm glad it's this version Angel chose for its new three-disc Mozart set. One of Klemperer's greatest Mozart performances is not a symphony but the extraordinarily ambitious Serenade for 13 Winds. Here Mozart transcends the simple music-for-entertainment origin of the serenade. Klemperer's recording with the London Wind Quintet and Ensemble presents a profound insight into the way Mozart can be simultaneously ravishing and heartbreaking.

Klemperer's earlier Mozart symphonies—like the "Little" G-minor Symphony, No. 25 and the "Paris," No. 31—have the transparency and shapeliness of chamber music. One of the ways Klemperer makes the architecture of a work so vivid is through orchestral balances. When a theme or melody arrives that has important structural significance, Klemperer highlights the instruments that play it. His broad tempos allow him to keep his textures unhomogenized; even in the thickest ensembles, each musical line seems outlined in air. Klemperer's best known Mozart album is probably *The Magic Flute*. He plays down the comic elements and even the all-star cast, but the most serious music, growing out of Mozart's affiliation with the Masons, has seldom sounded more consequential.

One of Klemperer's earliest professional experiences was in opera. He actually conducted Caruso in *Carmen*. He didn't make many opera recordings. His three Mozart Italian operas—*Figaro*, *Don Giovanni*, and *Così fan tutte*—have been attacked for their lack of humor. These have not yet appeared on compact disc. One that has, Klemperer's version of Beethoven's *Fidelio*, is rightly considered one of the greatest opera recordings ever made, and his Flying Dutchman may be more controversial for the singing than for his exhilarating conception of Wagner's score.

Not every Klemperer performance works, but everyone is heroic in dimension and noble in impulse. How much smaller most of today's music-making seems in comparison.

Arturo Toscanini

August 5, 1987

It's one of the great ironies that the most popular conductor ever recorded should have been recorded so poorly. The thin, dry, tinny sound of Arturo Toscanini's records is notorious—and I'm talking about records made not in the early days of 78s but in the late '40s and early '50s when hi-fi was the new rule. Fortunately, digital and half-speed remastering and CDs have helped restore some sonic life to the old records—a new clarity and presence if not an actual change in the character of the sound itself.

Toscanini is somewhat under a cloud these days, partly, I suspect, as a reaction to his extreme popularity and partly, I think, because the conductors who most obviously imitate him don't have his musical genius. It seems that anyone who gets an orchestra to play fast and loud, with cold, hard-driven precision, is considered a disciple of Toscanini. But most of his recordings reveal that the crisp, precise attack he so ruthlessly demanded is there not only to create socko climaxes but actually to ensure a delicacy and variety of touch throughout, hairpin turns in dynamics and rhythm that help create a soaring, singing musical line. He was one of the first conductors dedicated to following the letter of a score but he was never just a human metronome.

Another common oversimplification about Toscanini has to do with his repertoire. Some people think he conducted only Beethoven, Italian operas, and short "Pops" favorites. But that ignores his lifelong devotion to Wagner, his sublime performances of Haydn and Mozart, his rhythmically exhilarating Schumann, Mendelssohn, and Brahms, his muscular, energized

Debussy. It's true he never liked or understood Mahler, but then no one complains about Wilhelm Furtwängler's lack of interest in Rossini or Verdi.

Or Berlioz, who's another composer we don't usually associate with Toscanini either. Take the kaleidoscopic third-movement Serenade from Berlioz's *Harold in Italy*, recorded at a live broadcast from Carnegie Hall in 1953, and just reissued on a new RCA CD. The eloquent soloist is Carlton Cooley, principal violist of the NBC Symphony. Toscanini gave the first American performance of *Harold in Italy* with the New York Philharmonic in 1929. He recorded his first Berlioz in 1920—the *Rakóczy* March from *The Damnation of Faust*—with the La Scala Orchestra. His breathtaking 1945 version is included on this new CD, along with the Roman Carnival Overture, and the dazzling, dazzlingly executed *Queen Mab* Scherzo. These lean and brilliant performances emphasize the sinuous, insinuating curve of Berlioz's melodies and the uncanny alternation of tension and release that is impossible to convey only in an excerpt. Six months after this youthfully exuberant recording of *Harold in Italy,* Toscanini, at the age of 87, would lead his own great orchestra for the last time and retire.

March 2, 1988

One of the most extraordinary recent opera recordings is a rehearsal for a radio broadcast of the second and third acts of Verdi's *La Traviata* with Arturo Toscanini and the NBC Symphony. It was taped, without Toscanini's knowledge, of course, in December 1946. Toscanini rehearsals are the stuff of legend. There are dozens of stories about his violent temper—breaking batons, even smashing his watch. "Put something—put your blood!" he cried at one rehearsal of a minor Italian overture.

No music was too trivial for Toscanini to demand everything from an orchestra. In the *Traviata* rehearsal, Toscanini suddenly blows up at the basses and mimics their sloppy playing. These are short notes, and sweet; they must be played that way. A moment later he's all sweetness, indicating how lightly (tutti leggieri) the next passage must sound, and then he loses patience again. Lighter! Softer! Sweeter! "Don't run away, it's fast enough!" "Sing!" he tells the orchestra over and over, sometimes paternalistically, sometimes almost childlike. And he always gets results.

At one point, he tells them a story about when he played cello under Verdi himself. One passage in *Otello* was marked pianissimo, 4p. Verdi stopped the rehearsal and asked, "Who is the second cello?" "I was so confused," Toscanini admits to his musicians. "I stood up. `I, maestro.'" Then Verdi tells him: "Play a little louder." The moral is that cellos in Verdi have to play out, whatever the score says. Toscanini is a practical musician. Throughout the rehearsal, he keeps modifying the instrumentation. Later in the rehearsal, the street chorus outside Violetta's house sounds too loud, too near. He tells them to try putting their hands over their mouths. ("Try, try, try. Don't be afraid. Put, put, put.") Finally, the solution is to mute the trombones.

But what comes through clearest in the rehearsal is Toscanini's desire for a singing line. Even on the final recording of the *Traviata* broadcast, you can hear Toscanini's hoarse voice grunting in the background. In this rehearsal for the orchestra, the only singer is the 79-year-old maestro. One of the most poignant things I've ever heard is Toscanini on this disc trying to croak out the dying Violetta's tragic last-act aria, "Addio, del passato": "Every hope is dead. Farewell, sweet laughing dreams of the past. The roses of my cheeks are already growing pale." I think the deepest source of Toscanini's greatness is that he himself wanted to sing but couldn't. That's why you can hear him on his recordings. That may be why he chose the cello. That's why he worked harder than almost any other conductor to get the whole orchestra to sing.

July 26, 1989

Arturo Toscanini's most widespread popularity came not so much from his concerts as from his radio broadcasts and his records. And he helped the recording industry at least as much as it helped him. But he hated making records. Imagine someone with his concern for continuity having to stop every four minutes for the end of each side of a 78 rpm disc. In the 1940s and '50s, his radio broadcasts with the NBC Symphony were recorded in front of live audiences, so that many of his most famous recordings were the equivalent of live performances. But he was already in his 80s by then, and radio itself seemed to make him nervous. Toscanini's official broadcasts were often more rigid and driven than his rehearsals (many of which were secretly recorded by his own musicians). Not many examples of Toscanini's pre-World-War-II live performances have survived, and few of them are commercially available. EMI-Angel's latest batch of Great Recordings of the Century, includes two CD's that contain live performances of Toscanini in London conducting the BBC Orchestra in 1935!

La Mer was one of Toscanini's favorite pieces. His 1950 Victor recording is one of his most brilliant—it's a scintillating corrective to the cliché that all of Debussy's music is shapeless and dreamy. But this 1935 live performance is even more astonishing, richer and more subtle. Each note is like an inflection in a longer phrase; each phrase is a new turn in a fascinating story. Some of Toscanini's later recordings steamrollered you into submission. But here he spins an intricate web of sound that holds you spellbound.

The other selection on this Toscanini disc is Elgar's *Enigma Variations*—a tone poem made up of a series of musical portraits of Elgar's wife, himself, and a dozen friends. Though it's not a piece you associate with Toscanini, it's a piece he loved. His later commercial recording is wonderful but this live performance with the BBC Symphony is even warmer, funnier, more loving, more moving. And Elgar is in *this* orchestra's blood.

A separate disc includes two live Toscanini Brahms performances—his famous version of the *Tragic Overture* and a Fourth Symphony that has never been issued before. Toscanini's Brahms was always fat-free and sinewy. His 1935 Brahms Fourth has a grave, flowing beauty, only slightly scarred by the noisy surfaces of the old acetates. The last movement achieves the tragic intensity and grandeur of Toscanini's greatest work. How lucky we are to have it restored and rescued from oblivion.

Leon Goossens

August 19, 1987

The greatest oboe player of this century—no one else comes even close—is Leon Goossens. He's probably best known as the first oboist in the pre-War London Philharmonic Orchestra. With its conductor, Sir Thomas Beecham, hand-picking the players, it was perhaps the most perfect orchestra ever assembled. And it was by the Goossens oboe that you could immediately identify the old London Phil. Goossens is the Olivier of musicians. His oboe doesn't just play the notes, it sings them and talks them and recites them. The way Goossens turns a phrase gets etched in your memory—you know no one will ever play a passage like that again, that no one else's version will have the color, the drama, the intimacy, the long-breathed rhythmic daring. The first time I ever thought that *Swan Lake*, for example, might actually be great music was after I heard the uncanny phrasing by Leon Goossens of the mysterious Swan theme.

Not many London Philharmonic records are available in this country anymore and little of Goossens's solo work remains in the catalogue. But recently, a friend of mine discovered a remarkable recording on the British Chandos label. It's called *Elgar Miniatures*. It's a charming selection of Elgar's early works, or later works based on early sketches. They're all sweetly melancholy and pastoral in tone, nothing over five minutes long, and all lovingly performed by Norman del Mar and the Bournemouth Sinfonietta. But the great thing on the disc is a 3-minute-and-50-second piece, with Leon Goossens as guest soloist, called *Soliloquy for Oboe*, recorded a little over a decade ago when Goossens was 79.

In 1933, the year before Elgar died, he conducted one of his early overtures with the London Philharmonic. Later, when he heard the recording, he was overwhelmed with Goossens's playing of the oboe passages. Half a century earlier, Elgar had written oboe solos for his gifted younger brother (whom he outlived). Now Elgar was inspired to compose a Suite for Oboe and Orchestra for Goossens. He didn't live to finish it, but one movement existed in short score with full indications for what he wanted the orchestra to do. Goossens asked Gordon Jacob to flesh out the orchestration. It's probably Elgar's last work, certainly one of his most poignantly beautiful and yearning. This is its first recording; there won't be a better one.

Mieczyslaw Horszowski

September 2, 1987

Mieczyslaw Horszowski's name has been one I've valued for years, but only in conjunction with other names I value. In other words, I think of him primarily as a chamber music specialist, a partner to some of the greatest musicians of this century: Pablo Casals, violinist Joseph Szigeti, clarinetist Reginald Kell, the Budapest Quartet. He also made several marvelous chamber-music recordings as a member of the short-lived New York Quartet. In fact, because I never heard him play a recital, I never really thought of Horszowski as a soloist, even though he recorded the Chopin First Piano Concerto (over thirty years ago) and has performed complete cycles of Beethoven and Mozart sonatas in concert.

Nonesuch records, however, has remedied this misconception with its recent release of a Horzsowski solo album, recorded last year when he was 94 years old. This is no mere souvenir of a once-distinguished artist or a feat of inventive engineering. These are very much performances that show the wisdom and rediscovered innocence of old age. Even the Debussy *Children's Corner Suite* has an air of profound retrospection, the great-grandfather watching the young ones with nostalgia and infinite sympathy. (Though Horszowski has no direct descendants of his own. The liner notes tell us he married for the first time in 1981, when he was 89.) His touch is tenderly secure and eloquent; his tempos are on the slow side but rhythmically alive—the pace never flags. What we get isn't so much a performance as a vision.

The most extraordinary selection on the record is Mozart's achingly beautiful Fantasia in D minor—one of those archetypal Mozart works that gets deeper and sadder the more beautiful it gets—a piece that in its very brevity seems both to question and accept the mystery of time itself and the pain of its inevitable passing.

Horzsowski is a direct musical descendant of Beethoven and Chopin. His great teacher, Theodor Leschetitzky, was a student of Beethoven's pupil Czerny; Horszowski's mother studied with a student of Chopin's. This new record includes two Chopin Nocturnes and Beethoven's Second Sonata. It's a generous selection and demonstrates the generosity of its performer. This entire record makes me think of what Yeats toward the end of his life called "tragic joy," and especially these lines from his extraordinary poem "The Apparitions," which he wrote when he was a mere 73:

> When a man grows old, his joy
> Grows more deep day after day,
> His empty heart is full at length,
> But he has need of all that strength
> Because of the increasing Night
> That opens her mystery and fright.

Maria Callas

September 23, 1987

Much has been written about Maria Callas since her death in 1977, most of it sad and some of it true. There's no doubt she was a volatile personality—her life makes a good story. But her greatest importance still lies in her recordings. No opera singer in history brought such an extraordinary dramatic range to records. Of course, everyone talks about what a great actress she was, but she always acted through the music. The drama was in her voice—in the different color that she gave each character, each mood, each phrase, each word. She could make even passages without words, like the runs and trills in the "Mad Scene" from *Lucia*, seem the expression of deep and complex psychological states. She not only understood the text but the sub-text (how many opera singers literally don't know what they're singing about?). Her daring sense of rhythm gave unique conviction and urgency to her phrasing. With Callas, the words themselves became music.

There's an extraordinary passage from a recital album that she recorded in 1955 and has just been reissued on a new CD called simply *Operatic Arias*. Though Callas is most famous as a tragedienne, this is one of her rare comic numbers: Rosina's "Una voce poco fa" from *The Barber of Seville*. In it she sings of how obedient she can be—unless she's crossed. Then she'll turn into a viper and play a hundred tricks. In a diabolically teasing way Callas builds up her tongue-in-cheek declaration of docility until she punctures it with the tiny word "Ma!"—"But!" Of course no single aria can show us how she brought an entire role to life or the uncanny way she illuminated recitative. Fortunately, Angel Records has remained committed to Callas, and lots of complete Callas operas are now available on CD, including *The Barber of Seville* and her other great comic part, the resourceful heroine of Rossini's *The Turk in Italy*. But no other recording of hers surpasses this early recital in conveying her phenomenal technical and dramatic range. The CD, with its expanded dynamics, reveals a vocal freshness you couldn't always hear on LP. It includes the best recording ever made of Catalani's "Ebben? ne andro lontana" (the aria from the movie *Diva*), a bone-chilling performance of Margherita's prison aria from Boito's *Mefistofele*, and even an aria one hardly associates with Callas, the "Bell Song" from *Lakme*, in which the brilliant singing is for once not merely a display of vocal fireworks but part of a touching characterization. Everything on this CD, including four additional selections from a later record, is conducted—with delicacy and fire—by Callas's great mentor, Tullio Serafin.

January 4, 1996

Soprano Maria Callas is in the news again. Last month, *The New Yorker* published a long profile on her by critic Will Crutchfield. A new play about her by Terrence McNally, *Master Class*, has just opened on Broadway. And in conjunction with that play, EMI has just reissued its 3-CD set called *Maria Callas at Juilliard—The Masterclasses*.

Callas stopped appearing in complete operas before I ever got to see her perform. My very first glimpse of her was at Carnegie Hall. But she was just a member of the audience. She was sitting in the equivalent of the royal box. I don't remember too much about the performance but I sure as hell remember Callas. So when in the fall of 1971 it was announced that she'd be teaching a series of Master Classes at the Juilliard School and that the public was welcome (for $5!), I knew I'd have to go down to New York. I got to two classes. I still have the notes I took, though they're sadly skimpier than I remembered. A few years ago, EMI released a set of excerpts from these classes, which also includes Callas's own recordings of some of the arias she was working on with these students—only a few of whom went on to have substantial careers.

The procedure was simple: a student came onstage and sang an aria, accompanied by pianist Eugene Kohn, while Callas listened from a stool next to a card table with her scores. Then she'd ask the student to begin again, only this time she felt free to interrupt. She commented on the subtlest issues of style and meaning. She talked about rhythm, dynamics, ornamentation, pronunciation, where to breathe—always insisting on absolute fidelity to the score. She compared singing Italian with singing French. She even offered advice about what to wear to auditions.

The most riveting session I heard—and it's included on these discs—was Callas working with a young baritone on Rigoletto's aria "Cortigiani, vil razza dannata" ("Courtiers, you cowardly and damned race"). Rigoletto, the Duke of Mantua's court jester, sings it when he discovers that his daughter has been abducted by the very noblemen he's been ridiculing mercilessly. He can barely contain his anger even as he abjectly begs them to take pity on him. Callas tells the student to sing the notes, but to forget about his voice. Rigoletto, she says, "should be a real animal that's trying to dominate himself." He hates being obliged to beg them. And since it's his own daughter, he's fiercely savage. And she demonstrates this.

Callas, of course, never sang Rigoletto, or any baritone part. But these few moments are electrifying. "Who'd have thought the world's greatest Rigoletto would be a woman?" someone remarked after the class. Callas was too serious an artist ever to do anything as bizarre as record an album of baritone arias, but I bet everyone present at Juilliard that day wished she would. Why shouldn't she "be" Rigoletto as easily as she became Carmen or Violetta? She could obviously identify with the way the hunchbacked jester had to overcome impediments of appearance and temperament.

Years before, she lost over sixty pounds to transform herself from an overstuffed young prima donna into a convincing and mercurial actress. She lightened the natural weightiness of her voice to create an instrument of phenomenal technical—and dramatic—flexibility. She even turned her increasing vocal problems into a means of even more nuanced expression. All this while she was playing to an audience who was often more interested in the melodrama of her life than in her real artistic achievements.

But these classes never turn into a showcase for herself. She never forgets she's there to teach. She interrupts her own singing mid-phrase to make a point. And despite her obvious frustration when some of these students seem dense or unprepared ("Are you after expression," she says to one of them, "or are you after fireworks?"), she's remarkably patient. She makes them do what she tells them over and over until they get it right. She seems resigned that they'll probably never comprehend the deepest message or mystery of her art. Yet who could blame them when it's probably something she herself never completely understood?

February 1, 2005

Have you ever seen a performance of *Romeo and Juliet* in which Juliet delivers her most famous line as: "O Romeo, Romeo, wherefore ART thou Romeo?" Juliet, of course, hasn't known

Romeo long enough yet to be concerned with his whereabouts. "Wherefore" doesn't mean "where" at all, but "why." She's asking WHY he's Romeo. Why did she have to fall in love with a Montague, her family's arch-enemy. The line should read: "O Romeo, Romeo, wherefore art thou ROMEO?" I hear a similar misunderstanding in most performances of a famous soprano aria—Puccini's "O mio babbino caro," from his short opera *Gianni Schicchi*. In the aria, the heroine, Loretta, is threatening to throw herself off the Ponte Vecchio, the famous bridge in Florence, and most sopranos emphasize this potential tragedy. But the opera it's from is actually a comedy. Loretta isn't really going to attempt suicide. She's begging her "babbino caro"— "her dear daddy"—for permission to buy a wedding ring so she can marry the young man she loves. "If you don't let me buy it," she wheedles, "I'll throw myself into the Arno. So come on, have pity, have a heart."

Sopranos love this aria—it's pretty, it's short, and it's not very high. But one of the very few who really understood Puccini's tone was Maria Callas. On her famous early album of Puccini arias, she captures the aria's playfulness. But in a 1965 concert on French television, Callas, in terrific voice, suggests even further how Loretta's mercurial emotions flicker from romantic love to tender affection for her father to that comic wheedling threat. Callas offers a kind of roadmap of the aria, showing all the different directions the emotions take. It's thrilling to hear it done right, and it makes almost every other performance—no matter how beautifully sung—seem misguided.

It's even better when you see it. EMI has issued this performance on DVD, along with two other arias Callas did on that French TV show. They are so important, EMI released them in two different formats. On one DVD, the three arias are coupled with Callas's fascinating television interviews about her career, her range of roles. She talks about how singing is really about life. The other version is a mixed CD and DVD, with seven of Callas's greatest Verdi recordings. Films of Callas performances are extremely rare, and they're all amazing. But this one stands out even in that rarefied context.

Glenn Gould

October 28. 1987

In 1955, Glenn Gould made his American debut and his first major recording for Columbia, Bach's *Goldberg Variations*. Soon he was an international star. Nine years later, he stopped giving public performances and devoted himself exclusively to the recording studio. In 1982 he died of a stroke at the age of 50. Nothing about his life or career was commonplace or predictable. As a pianist he could be maddeningly perverse. He did a series of Mozart sonatas, for instance, that had the mechanical rinky-tink hysteria of a silent movie soundtrack (I actually like them for that reason). Some of his later Bach recordings strike me as detached to the point of desiccation, brittle and flavorless. But his greatest recordings, which include Mozart and Haydn, the Five B's (Bach, Beethoven, Brahms, Byrd, and Berg), and even Wagner (Gould's own transcription of the *Siegfried Idyll*), are intensely clear illuminations of some of the greatest music ever written.

Gould had all his power early on. He was only 22 when he recorded the *Goldberg Variations*. His Haydn E-flat Sonata, three years later, is probably the greatest solo Haydn recording ever made, and his exquisite and searching versions of Mozart's C-major Fantasy and Fugue and 10th Sonata came long before the ruthlessly anti-lyrical manner of those later Mozart efforts. After a long disappearance these are now available again in a wonderful Haydn/Mozart/Beethoven box from CBS. The *Goldberg Variations*, never out of the catalogue, has just been issued, also by CBS, on a budget-priced CD.

Glenn Gould's first recorded performance of Bach's *Goldberg Variations* seems as fresh and crisply modern now as it did thirty years ago. What keeps it ticking, even beyond the delicate electricity of his touch, is his structural balancing act—the tactful, intuitive contrasts between brilliantly-faceted fast variations and breath-holding slow sections. Gould's uncanny timing takes on an architectural grandeur that can afford to embrace both his headlong, youthful energy, and his joy in exploration. This performance never allows itself to become merely a marathon of little numbers (and on CD it can build without your having to stop and turn over the record—though Gould's notorious humming and muttering are also clearer than ever). Later on, you couldn't rely on Gould's tact, or his joy either—though even without them, as in his later recording of the *Goldbergs*, he was still one of the most fascinating musicians around. But at his paradoxical best, his combination of "depth, delicacy, and display," the very qualities he said he admired in the *Goldberg Variations*, transcend the quirks of self-expression, and his unique style, at once Romantic and Modernist, leads you into the heart of the music through a door nobody had ever opened before.

Mravinsky Tchaikovsky

November 11, 1987

The first classical music I ever loved was Tchaikovsky. The unforgettable tunes, the grand sweep, and probably even the romantic melancholy were just what I thought music should be. Then I learned better: Tchaikovsky was sentimental, melodramatic, definitely not sophisticated or for sophisticated tastes. Mozart was the greatest genius, Bach the most magnificent and spiritual, Beethoven—especially the late string quartets—music at its most exalted and profound. Some moderns were also OK—Stravinsky and the Viennese school—even Mahler and Debussy, as long as you liked them for the right reasons. That was the beginning of my musical education.

But after years of being embarrassed by my earlier tastes, I started listening to Tchaikovsky again. After all, even Stravinsky loved Tchaikovsky and actually wrote a ballet, *The Fairy's Kiss,* using Tchaikovsky themes. I was also learning to distinguish good performances from bad. A friend played me Toscanini's recording of the *Romeo and Juliet* Overture, which I was ashamed to admit had once been my favorite piece of music. But suddenly it wasn't just the saccharine theme song for a hundred soupy movies but a dazzling, elegantly fleet, and extraordinarily moving new score—a revelation.

The same thing happened again with Tchaikovsky's last three symphonies when I heard about—and then heard—the famous 1960 Yevgeny Mravinsky recordings with the Leningrad Philharmonic. I could hear in the music not Tchaikovsky's heart's blood dripping down his sleeve but the dark courage and toughness of the Russian character. No wallowing in self-pity, but backbone, a tensile mixture of power and suppleness.

Deutsche Gramophon has just issued them on CDs, and they hold up brilliantly.

Mravinsky gets some eloquent playing out of the Leningrad Philharmonic in these Tchaikovsky symphonies—actually a lot closer to Toscanini's nobility and refinement than to the usual pseudo-Slavic excesses and distortions. The cantabile or canzone movements really sing, passionately yet with a rare tenderness; even the grand climaxes have an elasticity of inflection that sounds more like someone speaking than someone making a speech. Like Toscanini in his recording of the Pathétique, Mravinsky gives the march a ferocious yet lilting concision, and the slow finale, marked Adagio lamentoso, a philosophical weight. Mravinsky injects all the loneliness and melancholy with a certain stoic reticence—almost like Sibelius, but warmer, more open-hearted. The music may be autobiographical, but it's not merely autobiography. Tchaikovsky's lament is for all of us. In his commitment to conducting the scores as written, Mravinsky—like Toscanini—restores to Tchaikovsky his dignity as a composer.

Jussi Björling

December 2, 1987

If I had only one vote to cast for the greatest operatic tenor of this century, I'd cast it for Jussi Björling, the singer who was born in Sweden in 1911 and died before he was fifty in 1960. Part of my reason would be sentimental. Björling was the tenor on one of the first complete operas I ever owned, the great Victor recording of Verdi's *Il Trovatore* with Zinka Milanov as Leonora. His "Di quella pira" still rings in my memory as the most impassioned and elegant I've ever heard. He's also on the wonderful Victor *Turandot*, with Birgit Nilsson and Renata Tebaldi. "Nessun dorma" is currently Luciano Pavarotti's theme song, and Pavarotti is no slouch; but Björling's version remains definitive because its clarity and heroism pour forth so effortlessly. Pavarotti sounds like a soldier, a warrier; Björling is the prince Puccini wrote the aria for. That unmistakable sunlight-shot-through-with-moonlight voice is the ideal instrument for both lyricism and power. Björling's phrasing is both sensitive and unmannered, natural without any compromise in volume, diction, or intonation. Perhaps being Swedish allowed him to combine Italian passion and French suavity.

There's a new CD on Legato Classics that would make a wonderful introduction to this glorious artist and might also be a find for Björling enthusiasts. It's a collection of live Björling performances, recorded between 1929 and 1960. There are songs and arias in Italian, Latin (the magnificent Ingemisco from the famous Toscanini performance of the Verdi *Requiem*), French, Swedish, and English (American singers could learn from his English diction). There's a stirring passage from a 1960 *Trovatore* that may have been his last performance.

It's amazing to discover that the quality of Björling's voice had only slightly coarsened between the earliest and the latest selections on this disc, a period of over thirty years. "Sorrento," recorded in Swedish in 1929, isn't your typical Italian performance with sobs and emotional outbursts. But it's typical of Björling's inwardness, the conviction of his understatement that could only spring from a secure emotive and artistic center.

The sound quality of the transfers is spectacular, except for the wavering pitch on "Nessun dorma." Some of the older acetates are scratchy, but to my ears not annoying. Legato Classics offers no information about the sources of these recordings, and at least my copy of the disc does some peculiar things (like skipping back to a previous band instead of moving forward). But the opportunity to hear Björling unfiltered by the recording studio makes almost any inconvenience minor.

Pablo Casals

December 30, 1987

Pablo Casals was not only one of the most profound musicians of our century, he was also a moral force, even in non-musical matters. He left Spain at the end of the Civil War in protest against the fascists and took a vow of musical silence. He made no public appearances after that until 1950. He was a great teacher. He taught that a musician must serve the music—that playing music was a selfless, spiritual quest to discover what lies within it. You can hear his integrity, his passionate honesty in every note. There's no self-indulgence. Even his most passionate outbursts have a kind of austerity. His cello doesn't always make the prettiest sound. It has a dark edge—it growls, it bites even as it caresses. But Casals's astonishing rhythmic vitality transcends the glamour of mere tone. His emotional directness allows you to follow a work's essential structure—every phrase sings with meaning.

The first CD versions of Casals playing the cello have finally been released, and they immediately become the most important cello recordings to appear on CD. One of these releases is no surprise: the complete set of Bach's six Suites for Unaccompanied Cello, issued on two separate CDs on Angel's wonderful new batch of budget-priced Great Recordings of the Century. They are probably Casals's most famous recordings. He was practically the first musician since the time of Bach to take these works seriously. Casals studied them for twelve years before he played them in public. Till his dying day at nearly 97, he would practice a Bach Suite first thing every morning. And he was the first cellist to record them all. These performances, recorded in the late '30s, remain a kind of spiritual testament, besides being the most exploratory, the most moving, and also the most playful versions ever made.

The other Casals issue is more surprising. Philips records, in its excellent Legendary Classics series, has reissued a pair of rare live performances of Beethoven trios—the *Archduke* and the *Ghost*—from later in Casals's public career. Perhaps the greatest Archduke on record is the one Casals recorded thirty years earlier with his famous collaborators—pianist Alfred Cortot and violinist Jacques Thibaud. This one from 1958 with Mieczyslaw Horszowski and violinist Sandor Vegh is far from its most refined performance. Yet it's still remarkable—witty, buoyant, clear and compelling in conception. The *Ghost*, recorded in 1961, with Vegh and Karl Engel, is even more astonishing, especially the literally haunting slow movement which gives the work its nickname.

September 12, 1990

Schubert's String Quintet in C is his last masterpiece, his greatest work of chamber music. It was written barely two months before he died at the age of 31. Its sumptuous melodies and passionate intensity make it one of the most gratifying pieces of music to play. Schubert himself probably never heard it performed, and now it's as if musicians are playing it for him. The greatest performance I know of the String Quintet was recorded at the Prades Festival in 1952. Prades is a little French village near the Spanish border where, after the Spanish Civil War, the great cellist Pablo Casals vowed to remain in self-imposed exile and musical silence until Franco was defeated. Violinist Alexander Schneider suggested that if Casals wouldn't leave Prades, the music world should come to him. Schneider gathered some pretty great musicians, and Casals agreed to participate in a festival.

Casals is clearly the spiritual center of this performance. Listen to the calm and delicacy of the heartbreakingly beautiful melody introduced by the two cellos in the first movement. It's actually played a little faster and lighter than you'd expect, less intense but much more spontaneous. It's Schubert singing quietly to us from beyond the grave, as if he was sure that's what his music would eventually do.

The two violinists on this recording are Schneider and Isaac Stern. Milton Katims is the violist, and the two cellists are Casals and Paul Tortelier. Schubert scored the Quintet for one viola and two cellos instead of the more usual other way around. The calm Adagio is one of Schubert's most uncanny inspirations. The pizzicato cello, as in a serenade, makes the elegy also a kind of love song.

One of the things I love most about this performance is what makes it less than fashionable. This is not a smooth, impeccable blend manufactured in the control booth. It's got the uninhibited rough edges of a group of friends getting together to play music they love in a room, a chamber of one of their own homes.

The sound quality is that of good but not great 1950s monaural LPs. The digital remastering for the new compact disc doesn't change that quality. The great thing is that it's available again after decades of absence. The Masterworks Portrait series also includes Casals in the Brahms Sextet, the wonderful Schumann First Trio, with Alexander Schneider and Mieczyslaw Horszowki, and in three tremendous Beethoven sonatas with Rudolf Serkin. Casals also played in Schubert's two magnificent Trios, and these desperately need to be reissued. Unfortunately, these Masterworks Portraits are a limited imported edition. But if they spark enough interest, maybe Sony will return to the CBS vaults and begin to dispense more of these lost treasures.

Cortot, Thibaud, Casals

June 23, 1993

Musicians at the beginning of this century seem to have been more interested in music than in merely furthering their solo careers. One reason I have for saying this is that so many of the greatest musicians of that time made such an extensive commitment to chamber music. (Maybe they were so great because they were devoted to chamber music.) Between 1926 and 1929, some of the central masterpieces in the chamber repertoire were recorded by three musical giants, two Frenchmen, the dazzling pianist Alfred Cortot and the elegant violinist Jacques Thibaud, who was killed in a plane crash in 1953, and a Catalonian Spaniard who was one of the world's greatest musicians on any instrument, cellist Pablo Casals. They were a perfect combination because they balanced refinement and energy, witty almost-conversational repartee and lilting, soaring melody. Listen to the lullaby that opens the slow movement of Schubert's B-flat Trio.

Cortot, Thibaud, and Casals played not only with profound respect for the music but also with a deep spirit of courtesy, of cooperation, of respect for one another. You can hear this in every phrase. Yet the wonder of chamber music is that the individual participants never have to give up their individuality. Each player has a turn to shine. Each player lets the others shine, as in the opening of the Mendelssohn Trio in D-minor, with its tender song for solo cello.

This 3-CD set contains the complete recorded collaboration of Cortot, Thibaud, and Casals. Besides the Schubert and Mendelssohn we've heard, there are trios by Haydn, Beethoven, and Schumann. Cortot was a distinguished conductor as well as a pianist, and he leads an extraordinary recording of the Brahms Double Concerto with Thibaud and Casals as the two soloists. There are two duets: Cortot and Thibaud in their famous rendition of Beethoven's Kreutzer Sonata and Cortot and Casals doing Beethoven's Magic Flute Variations. But the heart of this set are the trios.

In a way there isn't even much to be said about these supreme performances. They're indispensable models of natural, unmannered, alert, and flawlessly beautiful playing. Nothing is taken for granted—each note seems to be a discovery. Each phrase is moving toward some greater harmony. These recordings are the absolute standard by which all later performances must be measured.

Casals Festival at Prades

October 10, 2005

When I first started collecting classical records an especially admired series was already long out of print. They were the recordings made in the early 1950s at annual music festivals in the small Catalan towns of Prades and Perpignon, in France right near the Spanish border. That's where the great Spanish cellist Pablo Casals was living to avoid a death sentence imposed by Franco's fascist government. I remember going into the Grammophone Shop on Manhattan's 8th Street and seeing a used copy of one of these boxed-sets of LPs for $300—way beyond anything I could afford. Years later, some of these recordings began to appear on CD, but many of them have remained unavailable in any form. So I'm especially glad to see three new double-CD albums on the British label Pearl—all devoted to the music of Bach played at the very first Festival at Prades in 1950.

Styles in music change almost as often as styles in clothing. These days, there seems to be only one respectable way to play Bach—in so called "historically-informed" performances, on instruments that were either made in the 18th-century or are reproductions of those instruments. Of course, there are many excellent performances under these conditions, but Bach was a composer for whom the particular instruments didn't necessarily matter. He took pieces he (or other composers) wrote for one instrument and arranged them for other instruments. In one case, The *Art of the Fugue*, we aren't sure he had any particular instrument in mind. But however out-of-date a style of playing might be, it seems to me we should never overlook a great performance. The warm expressiveness, the drama, and the sublime beauty of these Prades recordings, played and conducted by Casals with some of the most searching musicians of the time (including Joseph Szigeti and Isaac Stern), should be a reminder that we mustn't allow any one style to dictate how music ought to be played.

There's also a spectacular 13-disc, less-than-half-price set on the Music & Arts label of actual live chamber music performances from Prades—more Bach, but also Mozart, Beethoven, Brahms, Schubert, Schumann, and Mendelssohn—some even more ravishing than any of the commercial versions, some of unusual pieces these artists never recorded in a studio. And what a few of them lack in perfection they make up in urgency and spontaneity.

Kolisch Quartet

February 3, 1988

The name Rudolph Kolisch is probably unfamiliar to the general public, but among musicians it still inspires admiration and awe. Scholar, philosopher, and left-handed violinist, he was a member of Arnold Schoenberg's inner circle in Vienna, along with Anton Webern, Alban Berg, and the pianist Eduard Steuermann. In 1922 he founded a string quartet which five years later became known as The Kolisch Quartet. This group also included violinist Felix Khuner, violist Eugene Lehner, and cellist Benar Heifetz (no relation to Jascha). Schoenberg's third and fourth quartets were written for them, Berg's Lyric Suite, Webern's Trio and Quartet, and Bartok's last two quartets. Their recordings of the four Schoenberg Quartets are the most moving I've ever heard. The other recordings of theirs I know of are standard repertoire pieces—Mozart, Schubert, and Schumann. In fact, they made very few recordings, and most of them have probably been out of print for close to forty years. Recently, the German label Schwann has issued LP and CD versions of two Kolisch Mozart Quartet performances, and they are so effortlessly and heartbreakingly eloquent, so artfully structured yet so spontaneous, they make me wish even harder for the rest.

The Kolisch Quartet worked in some remarkable ways. For one thing they didn't rehearse from parts. Each player worked from a complete score. So each player could see what the other players were up to at every moment. Too often with string quartets you get the feeling that each player thinks he or she is playing a concerto—showing off his own part with little regard to how it fits into the large scheme of things. The greatest chamber players know when to hold back, when to allow their partners the spotlight. This is called courtesy. It's also called musicianship. The Kolisch Quartet seems to weave its way through the mysterious introduction to Mozart's so-called "*Dissonant*" Quartet in C major (not the key you'd expect it to be in). This recording dates from 1941, the Kolisch's last year. Jascha Veissi plays viola, Stefan Auber cello. Kolisch and the Quartet did something even more amazing. They performed from memory—which in chamber music means learning not only your own part by heart but everyone else's too. Their eye contact during a performance must have given them an astonishing flexibility. There's a freedom, a dramatic—but not melodramatic—sense of pace and continuity in the Trio of the third movement of the "*Dissonant*."

Ironically, Kolisch himself was allegedly unhappy with these recordings because the short time span of the old 78s kept them from taking all the repeats that Mozart asked for, structural elements Kolisch considered crucial to the way Mozart built an entire work. Of course Kolisch would be harder than anyone else on his own performances. We can forgive such lapses because he's given us so much else to think about and be grateful for.

Lorraine Hunt Lieberson

February 10, 1988

Seiji Ozawa has a reputation as a technician, as a conductor who can keep the orchestra from falling apart even in the most difficult pieces. Audiences are impressed by the way he conducts every score from memory. In Preston Sturges's movie *Unfaithfully Yours*, a reporter wants to know why conductor Rex Harrison uses a score. "Because I can actually read music," he replies. Of course, Ozawa can read music, but his memorized performances tend to gloss over details. He favors a coarse blending of sound instead of encouraging individual voices and colors. The orchestra plays soft and loud—especially loud—but with very little dynamic variety in between. For such an athlete, practically a ballet dancer on the podium, Ozawa has surprisingly little rhythmic flair. His phrasing is square, unimaginative—even plodding—without style or the conviction that music means anything. Every composer comes out sounding the same.

Lately, though, there seems to be cause for mild optimism. People are talking about the "new Seiji." He's not so cute anymore. He's given up wearing beads. He's getting older, and he seems more serious and thoughtful. He's still better at big climaxes rather than at what leads up to them. But in music that relies more on tunes than on architecture—Ravel rather than Beethoven—he can make a passable if not memorable impression. As on his latest CD, an album of some very pretty music composed by Gabriel Fauré, though for the most part orchestrated by others.

In 1898, Fauré wrote some incidental music for an English production of Maetterlink's play *Pelléas and Mélisande*. Later, he turned some of this music into an orchestral suite. This new CD also includes a song that Fauré didn't use in his suite, a haunting ballad— in English—that Mélisande sings at the window as she's combing her hair. It's about three blind sisters waiting to be rescued from their prison tower. I first heard this song at a BSO concert, a little over a year ago. It was sung, at short notice, by a remarkable young soprano with a sumptuous voice—Lorraine Hunt, who has done impressive work in a couple of Peter Sellars opera productions, and in the world premiere of John Harbison's *The Flight into Egypt*, last year's Pulitzer Prize winner. Ozawa's smartest musical decision was keeping her for the recording.

The CD also includes a well-played but droopy, unatmospheric performance of the famous *Pavane* in Fauré's choral version, with pastoral verses written by the Comte Robert de Montesquiou—Proust's Baron de Charlus. There's also the *Elégie*, with BSO cellist Jules Eskin, and the syrupy *Dolly Suite* (which is much livelier in Fauré's own original piano four-hand version); here it's French perfume with no smell. But if this album is remembered for anything it will be as the recording debut of Lorraine Hunt.

April 8, 1996

Since her first appearances in productions of Handel and Mozart directed by Peter Sellars, mezzo-soprano Lorraine Hunt has become a star of the early-music circuit. A few weeks ago, she was profiled in the Sunday *New York Times*. She actually started out as a viola player. Lately, critics have been comparing the dark, rich timbre of her amazing voice to the tone of a viola. But unlike many singers who specialize in Baroque and Renaissance music, there's nothing merely instrumental about

Hunt's singing. In the Peter Sellars production of Handel's *Julius Caesar,* which you can see on videotape, she played Sesto, the Hamlet-like son of the murdered Pompey who is burning to avenge his father's death. Her searing ferocity was one of the many unforgettable events of that magnificent performance. Since then, she's made a number of Handel recordings, including some complete operas, under the direction of Nicholas McGegan, a British conductor who has become an early-music institution in San Francisco. McGegan is the kind of conductor who seems more concerned with historical authenticity—the early-music version of political correctness—than with creating intense dramatic experiences. Hunt has sounded pretty tame under McGegan's direction. Last year, in the title role in Charpentier's *Medea,* conducted by William Christie, her straitjacket was off and she was hair-raising. She's back with McGegan in the title role of another wonderful Handel opera, *Ariodante.* McGegan remains a pedestrian conductor, but at least he's learned to give Hunt more latitude. Or she's simply taking it. This is one of her very best recorded performances, and she sings some of the greatest music Handel ever composed.

One aria is worth the price of the whole 3-CD set. In a plot from Ariosto's *Orlando Furioso*—a plot that Shakespeare also borrowed— the hero thinks he sees his girlfriend spending the night with the villain. It's actually the villain's girlfriend dressed in the heroine's clothes. "Scherza infida"—Ariodante sings—"That faithless woman enjoys herself in the embrace of her lover, while because of her, betrayed, I now go to embrace death."

Hunt's fellow singers range from more than competent to—let's just say—less so. The Freiburger Barockorchester sounds OK. But under McGegan they just keep chugging away. *Ariodante* was a big hit for Handel. This complete recording also includes some very attractive music that he replaced in later performances. But besides the music itself, the only real interest in this recording is Lorraine Hunt. And that's a lot more than most opera recordings have going for them these days.

July 7, 2006

Lorraine Hunt Lieberson had everything. Her sumptuous voice could turn from blue velvet to molten gold. Her uncanny ability to enter the spirit of whatever music she sang also allowed her to identify completely with every character she played. She went from triumph to triumph yet never became a diva, never lost her sense of humor about herself. I was lucky to hear her from the beginning of her vocal career, especially in a couple of the famous Mozart and Handel productions staged by Peter Sellars, as well as with the Boston Symphony Orchestra, and in leading roles at the Metropolitan Opera. As Dido, Queen of Carthage, in Berlioz's epic opera *The Trojans*, she achieved a truly tragic stature. She was such a regal presence that her suicide when Aeneas deserts her was all the more heartbreaking. As Carmen, a role she sang only once, she was a scintillating, charismatic, complicated heroine, not a hip-swinging cliché.

Beautiful and sexy, she also excelled in so-called "trouser" roles. In Handel's *Julius Caesar* she played the vengeful son of the assassinated Roman leader Pompey. Her ferocity was terrifying. She never held back. Yet her singing was always magnificent—with pitch-perfect accuracy even in the most astounding coloratura, and that remarkable tonal beauty. She was originally a viola player, then started singing as a soprano, but her voice settled more comfortably into the mezzo-soprano range—her dark, rich timbre and seamless phrasing even sounded like a viola. An aria from a Bach cantata ("Schlummert ein"), conducted by her friend Craig Smith, is a lullaby sung by the soul to eyes that have grown weary of the world.

One of her most recent appearances was with the Boston Symphony Orchestra in the gorgeous *Neruda Songs*, a series of love poems composed for her by her husband, Peter Lieberson, a work that was a finalist for last year's Pulitzer Prize. Hearing her sing these songs with such passionate intensity, you couldn't imagine how seriously ill she must have been. Lately, her cancellations made almost as much news as her performances. It's understandable. What could be more disappointing than missing someone you wanted to hear so badly? Like the beloved British contralto Kathleen Ferrier, who died too young half a century ago, Lorraine Hunt Lieberson's star was still rising. She died of cancer last Saturday, at the age of 52. We wanted her to go on forever.

January 3, 2007

At a memorial tribute to Lorraine Hunt Lieberson at Boston's Emmanuel Church, where the late singer started out as a violist in the church orchestra before she really launched her professional singing career, her friend and colleague soprano Susan Larson talked about Hunt Lieberson's live—almost unbearably live—performances: "So chock-full of ideas and heat and intimacy and surprise . . . She colored words like a jazz singer . . . she could start a tone from nowhere—or from inside her mind, or from another planet . . . When I heard her sing in person, I never wanted it to end."

Three CDs have just been released of live recordings of Hunt Lieberson singing song cycles by two of the composers she was closest to: her husband, Peter Lieberson, and John

Harbison, in whose opera *The Great Gatsby* she made her stunning Metropolitan Opera debut. The Harbison cycle is called *North and South*, a setting of six poems by my favorite 20th-century American poet, Elizabeth Bishop. I heard this performance in Chicago, in 2001, with the superb Chicago Chamber Musicians, so for me this new release is also a precious souvenir of a memorable event. Each of the cycle's two parts begins with one of Bishop's "Songs for a Colored Singer"—Harbison calls them "Ballads for Billie." Bishop first published these poems in 1944 and secretly hoped Billie Holiday, whom she knew, might someday sing them. Hunt Lieberson is completely at home in their bluesy element.

All six poems in *North and South* have something to do with either love or music, or both. Each part ends with a love poem Bishop never published in her lifetime, and I have a special fondness for these poems because, as the liner note explains, I had a hand in locating and preserving them. In "Breakfast Song," a waltz, Bishop is at her most autumnal, like Shakespeare, facing the inevitability that she will die before her lover. It's a song that gains special poignancy because of Hunt Lieberson's own premature death. Bishop might have been more eager to publish these poems if she could have heard Hunt Lieberson sing them.

A second new CD includes Peter Lieberson's *Rilke Songs*, from a 1994 concert at the Ravinia Festival, with pianist Peter Serkin providing the sensitive accompaniment. It's a setting of five of the German poet Rilke's "Sonnets to Orpheus"—poems that deal with more abstract ideas than Bishop's: the nature of human existence, the possibility of transformation, the nature of poetry itself, though the composer says they're really about love. The last song ends: "If what is Earthly forgets you, say to the silent Earth: I'm flowing. To the rushing water speak: I am."

One of Lorraine Hunt Lieberson last public appearances was singing her husband's *Neruda Songs*—a setting of five of the famous Chilean poet's *100 Love Sonnets*—with James Levine leading his revitalized Boston Symphony Orchestra. I think it's the composer's most beautiful and heartfelt work. And his wife is at her most radiant. I'm particularly moved by the third song, in which she repeats with greater and greater urgency the opening line: "Don't go far off, not even for a day."

Besides our memories of Lorraine Hunt Lieberson, her recordings are now what we have left, and these new ones are among her most moving and most ravishing. But I also hope that these are just the tip of the iceberg; that more of her live—living—performances will become part of a more permanent recorded legacy.

August 2, 2011

In the liner notes to a new CD of two live concerts by Lorraine Hunt Lieberson, the director Stephen Wadsworth, who worked with her, says what a lot of people who loved her and cherished her singing must also feel: "Her work has such immediacy," he writes, "is so alive, that I even dread hearing her sometimes, because it makes me miss her and feel the just plain awfulness of her absence."

I was very lucky to live in Boston around the time a young violist named Lorraine Hunt moved there. She also sang. One of the people who noticed her was Craig Smith, the late conductor of Boston's Emmanuel Music. She played in the Emmanuel Orchestra, then Smith started casting her in opera, and so she also caught the attention of the brilliant stage director Peter Sellars, Smith's working partner in some of the 20th century's most exciting opera productions. In 1985, she had a major breakthrough—as Sesto, the son of the assassinated Pompey, in the Smith/Sellars production of Handel's *Julius Caesar*. Her performance was ferocious, tormented, and terrifying. Decca finally issued the DVD of that production after her death and it remains a landmark.

Fortunately, much of her later concert work has been preserved. Conductor Nicholas McGegan's Philharmonia Baroque Orchestra label, PBP, has released two live concert recordings. One, from 1991, has Lieberson singing a selection of Handel arias, including two from *Julius Caesar*. But there's also a new addition to the Lieberson recorded repertory: her sublime singing, from a 1995 concert, of the Berlioz song cycle *Nuits d'été* (*Summer Nights*)—one of the most gorgeous pieces of vocal music ever written. Lieberson was a thrilling Berlioz singer—ask anyone who heard her at the Met as the tragic Carthaginian Queen Dido in Berlioz's epic *The Trojans*. The songs of love and regret in *Nuit d'été* are on a smaller scale, but Berlioz seems to have composed his long spun out melodies just for Lieberson's seamless legato and creamy tone.

Harmonia Mundi records has also released a couple of new Lieberson albums: a CD of excerpts from her Handel recordings and another live concert, this one exquisitely accompanied by pianist Peter Serkin at the Ravinia Festival in 2004. It's a very sophisticated and personal program, including songs by Brahms and Mozart, cantatas by Mozart—Masonic and noble—and Handel, and Debussy's erotic, sensual *Chansons de Bilitis*. A Brahms song ("Ruhe, Süssliebchen"), is a more grownup lullaby than the one we usually get to hear.

A special treat on this CD are the encores. One is a duet from Handel's *Julius Caesar* with her friend countertenor Drew Minter, who sings the role of Cornelia, the mother of Lieberson's Sesto. The two are weeping over what may be their permanent separation.

Lorraine Hunt Lieberson sang a lot as a soprano before she lowered her range to mezzo-soprano. Her husband, composer Peter Lieberson, who died earlier this year, apparently didn't want to release any of her performances as a soprano. I hope the Lieberson estate might reconsider. We need the full picture of this extraordinary, incandescent artist.

Stravinsky

April 20, 1988

Stravinsky said he didn't believe in interpretation. If musicians simply followed his scores, the pieces should come out right. But from fairly early in his career, Stravinsky began to record his own music so people could hear exactly what he intended. Some of his earliest 78s are fascinatingly awkward. Musicians weren't as familiar with his music (partly because there were few other recordings), and in those days Stravinsky himself wasn't such a good conductor. Unlike another 20th-century composer/conductor, Benjamin Britten, Stravinsky never made a commercial studio recording of anyone else's music. But like Britten, Stravinsky became his own best conductor.

No one has ever surpassed the spaciousness, the flow and color of his performances, the electricity of his phrasing. Not every attack may be razor-sharp, but Stravinsky's rhythmic bite is such a source of joy—and juice. On CD you can hear more details than ever, and there's the luxury of uninterrupted continuity in the complete ballets. The magic casements of these recordings seem to open directly onto the distant worlds of these extraordinary scores. This *Rite of Spring* shows not only the violent energy but also the deep solemnity and beauty of pagan Russian ritual. *Petrushka* places the pathos of the lonely artist, the puppet Petrushka, in the context of the breathtaking kaleidoscopic bustle of a turn-of-the-century Shrove-Tide fair.

On the other Stravinsky CD are three later works, cleverly packaged together because each has the word "symphony" in the title. The least well known is his major-key, neo-classical Symphony in C, composed during what he called the unhappiest period of his life: the diagnosis of his own TB and soon afterwards the deaths of his wife and his older daughter, Mika, from the same disease, and the death of his mother. Stravinsky wrote, characteristically, "I was able to continue my own life only by my work on the Symphony in C. But I did not seek to overcome my grief by portraying or giving expression to it in music, and you'll listen in vain, I think, for traces of this sort of personal emotion." There is something obsessive about the Symphony in C but it's also an exhilarating, exuberant work. One passage, Stravinsky wrote, "would not have occurred to me before I had known the neon glitter of the California boulevards from a speeding automobile."

The other two "symphonies" on this CD show two other important sides of Stravinksy—the religious and the political. The *Symphony of Psalms*, composed in 1930, is one of his major devotional works. The powerful Symphony in Three Movements, written during World War II, was inspired by newsreels of goose-stepping soldiers and Chinese scorched-earth tactics. The haunting slow movement, however, with its delicate passages for harp, was actually first intended as music for a vision of the Virgin Mary in the movie *The Song of Bernadette*.

COLH

June 8, 1988

How many great recordings are there? How many of the so-called great recordings live up to their reputation? When I started to collect records, one of the most important discoveries I made was that some scratchy old performances transferred from 78s were greater than anything I'd ever hear in hi-fi. I learned this mainly from a series called *Great Recordings of the Century*. They all had the same cloth-textured jacket with the same code letters (COLH), and each one included a gray booklet that told you just what you needed to know about the performers, their interpretations, and the works themselves. Angel Records has just begun to reissue them on a new CD series. The invaluable program notes are gone—the vocal discs don't include either texts or translations (how can a new listener tell how moving Hans Hotter really is in Schubert's *Winterreise*? Or Chaliapin's Russian songs and arias?). Still, the performances remain unequalled, they're inexpensive, and they've never sounded better.

There are several interesting surprises. A Wanda Landowska Bach disc includes her first—and far superior—harpsichord recording of the Goldberg Variations from 1933 (I think the first time it's been issued in this country), as well as her chilling version of the Chromatic Fantasy and Fugue. Some post-war recordings have also been newly elevated to the status of Great: these include such choice items as Dennis Brain, probably the greatest horn player ever recorded, in all four Mozart Horn Concertos; Claudio Arrau's Chopin Etudes; and Heitor Villa Lobos conducting four of his own *Bachianas Brasileiras*, with Victoria de los Angeles singing and humming along with the cellos in the famous Number 5. There's Kathleen Ferrier's heartbreaking version of Mahler's *Kindertotenlieder* under Bruno Walter (which first appeared in America on the Columbia label); there's Kirsten Flagstad as Dido in the Mermaid Theater production of Purcell's *Dido and Aeneas*, with the young Elisabeth Schwarzkopf in three different roles; and the first and more radiant of Schwarzkopf's two recordings of Richard Strauss's *Four Last Songs*.

There's an exciting recital album by Bulgarian Soprano Ljuba Welitsch, who was probably the most sexually uninhibited Salome ever to play the part. Her terrifying little nymphet voice could actually cut like a dagger through Strauss's huge orchestra. The version of Salome's final scene released here isn't the famous one conducted by Fritz Reiner, under whom Welitsch made her sensational American debut. It's an even more blisteringly erotic performance from five years earlier—a 1944 live broadcast on Austrian radio conducted by Lovro von Matacic. The uneven sound quality has nothing to do with transmission—it's merely Welitsch melting the microphone.

Of course, these are only the tip of a magnificent iceberg. When are we going to get Artur Schnabel's complete Beethoven sonatas, Joseph Szigeti's Bach, Landowska's Scarlatti? At least the landmark Pablo Casals recordings of the Bach Solo Cello Suites are already on the summer agenda, and I can't wait.

Annie Fischer

July 6, 1988

Annie Fischer is a small, elegant woman, but the first time I saw her I thought she was monumental. Shoulders back, arms swinging, she strode out on stage in an austere black floor-length gown and looked eight feet tall. She nodded to the audience, sat down, and began to play. No nonsense. No display. If it weren't for that nod, you might have thought she didn't know anyone else was there. And while she played, she was completely rapt—not in the piano, but in the notes themselves. Her performance was less an interpretation than the act of living through each note. Someone remarked afterwards that you could tell she thought it was the music that was great, and not herself.

Her playing is unmannered, with a glistening, pearly tone that could explode into passages of overwhelming power. Effortless transitions showed she knew exactly what the composer intended not only at that particular moment but how every moment fit into the grand architecture of an entire piece.

Her repertory tends to be unadventurous, mittel-European "standards" from Mozart through the major 19th-century figures, with a toe occasionally dipping into 20th-century waters. Until fairly recently her recordings have been pretty hard to find. But the Price-Les$ [sic] label has been releasing a number of Annie Fischer recordings on cassettes, and now there are also three CDs—glorious performances made in London in the 1950s and '60s. There are Mozart, Schumann, and Bartok concertos, and *Carnaval*, Schumann's masterpiece of Commedia del'arte—and split personality (the Apollonian Eusebius and the compulsive Florestan are surely a joint self-portrait)—for solo piano.

Typically, Annie Fischer worked with the best conductors. The Schumann Concerto is a 1963 performance with the Philharmonia Orchestra under Otto Klemperer. The introspective, melodic Bartok Third Piano Concerto under Igor Markevitch dates from 1955, barely a decade after Bartok finished it. Actually, Bartok never quite finished it—he died before he completed the scoring of the last 17 bars. Fischer turns the piano into nature itself—awakening, or dreaming—in a movement Bartok called Adagio religioso.

There's also a wonderful disc consisting of two Mozart Concertos with the Philharmonia, conducted elegantly by Sir Adrian Boult. Here Annie Fischer is at her most sublime, as in the heartbreakingly intimate slow movement of the 23rd Concerto. She said after her American visit last March that she probably wouldn't be returning. If that's true, then at least we'll have these recordings with which to hear and re-hear this cherishable artist.

Szigeti/Bartok

August 10, 1988

The friendship of Bela Bartok, who was probably at least as well known as a pianist during his lifetimes as he was as a composer, and violinist Joseph Szigeti dates back to the 1920s in their native Hungary. Szigeti was eleven years Bartok's junior and had already admired him for nearly twenty years. Szigeti was a champion of Bartok's music, some of which Bartok wrote for Szigeti, and they gave many chamber performances together all over Europe and even in New York. Both of them were strenuously anti-Nazi. Szigeti refused to perform in Germany after 1932. Bartok wouldn't allow his music to be broadcast in either Germany or Italy. Perhaps the most important concert they gave together was the one at the Library of Congress in Washington on April 13, 1940, shortly after Szigeti emigrated to America. Bartok returned to Hungary one last time but he had already decided to leave. What he called his "exile" in America began in October 1940 and lasted to his death only five years later.

This concert, part reunion, part renunciation, is both a personal and a political statement. It's played at white heat, with the ebullient abandon of musicians whose knowledge, and whose instincts, are profound and unerring.

The program begins with Beethoven's *Kreutzer* Sonata, and I've never heard a more exciting or heroic version. There's deep understanding of the drama inherent in the first-movement sonata form and of the way the variations of the second movement unfold. The Presto Finale is one of the great celebrations in music. Bartok and Szigeti pull out all the stops yet never lose their sensitivity or rhythmic precision. This is both their cry of joy and their assertion of freedom.

This recording shows what a great pianist Bartok was in music other than his own. He never made a studio recording of a large-scale work by any other composer, but here, beside the Beethoven, is also Debussy's extraordinary Sonata for Violin and Piano, one of his last works, completed in 1917. It's an intricate and intimate piece, moving and heroic, but in a more glancing, modern way than the *Kreutzer*.

There are also two wonderful works by Bartok himself—the First Rhapsody, which he dedicated to Szigeti, and the difficult Second Sonata, which Bartok and Szigeti played together many times before. They reveal both the conversational intimacy, the playfulness, and the daring adventurousness of this forbidding work.

The "live" sound from nearly a half-a-century ago is warm and vibrant. It's amazing that this recording exists at all. It opens a door to all the legendary great performances of the past. It lets us believe in giants. But there couldn't have been many figures quite as gigantic as these magnificent compatriots.

Szigeti on DVD

July 13, 2004

A recent scandal in the classical music world involved soprano Deborah Voigt, who was fired from London's Royal Opera because she was too big to fit into a skimpy costume. Voigt is an impressive singer. People want to hear her, not just look at her. But what performers look like is part of what they do. Voigt might be a more interesting artist if she were more interesting to look at—not thinner but more expressive, like Pavarotti, who is also not small, but you can read every flicker of feeling on his mobile face. Of course, some performers overdo it. I used to have a hard time with Leonard Bernstein, because all his reeling, writhing, and fainting in coils distracted me from the music. Sometimes I wish I were home listening to recordings than at a live concert.

Yet I still want to SEE a performance. With the great musicians of the past, artists whose recordings affect me deeply, but whom I was born too late to experience in person, I long to see how they play, to see them move. I love the great pianist Artur Schnabel, but I've never seen an image of him in motion. The most profound and searching violinist I've ever heard is Joseph Szigeti. He appeared briefly in the 1944 film *Hollywood Canteen*, playing a short encore piece, then doing a comedy bit with fellow violinist Jack Benny! But where was any filmed record of Szigeti performing the kind of substantial music he's most admired for? Now, bless their hearts, Video Artists International has discovered fifty-year-old kinescopes of Szigeti performing on Canadian television, and these have just been released on DVD. There's Szigeti in 1954, with Wilfred Pelletier conducting the Orchestra of Radio-Canada, in an 18th-century

Violin Concerto by Giuseppe Tartini. Suddenly, the great dignity and inwardness I hear on Szigeti's recording of this I can also see in his body language, in his expression of rapt concentration.

The other pieces of music on the Szigeti DVD are the first movement of Beethoven's Violin Concerto, a Czardas by the Hungarian violinist Jeno Hubay, one of Szigeti's teachers, and since Szigeti was a great champion of contemporary music, it's especially poignant to see him with pianist Arthur Balsam in 1960, playing Prokofiev's Second Violin Sonata, a piece Szigeti first performed in 1944, when it was still in manuscript.

The camera work may be primitive. The picture quality may by grainy. And by 1960, the perfection of Szigeti's technique was beginning to be affected by chronic arthritis. But these films are a rare and moving image of a beloved figure. Literally moving. Seeing films of this musician who's meant so much to me is almost like watching someone in my own family coming back to life.

Ravel's Bolero

January 4, 1989

What would have happened if Ravel had kept the working title of his *Bolero*? Would the Ravel *Fandango* have been just as popular? One of the generally overlooked milestones of 1988 was that it marked the 60th anniversary of Ravel's most popular work, the *Bolero*, which was commissioned in 1928 as a ballet score, choreographed by Bronislava Nijinska, Nijinsky's sister. It wasn't played as a concert piece until two years later, by Arturo Toscanini and the New York Philharmonic-Symphony. In fact, when Ravel heard Toscanini conduct it, he considered the fast tempo so "ridiculous" (that's Ravel's word) that he refused to take a bow, provoking an international mini-scandal. Four months later Ravel wrote him a conciliatory letter followed quickly by a letter suggesting that Toscanini conduct the premiere of Ravel's Piano Concerto for the Left Hand, which he didn't.

Ravel was certainly a complicated mixture of the modest and the self-important. "My *Bolero*," he wrote to a friend, "is an experiment in a very special and limited direction, and it should not be suspected of aiming at achieving anything different from, or anything more than, it actually does achieve." He called it "a piece lasting 17 minutes and consisting wholly of orchestral texture without music—of one long, very gradual crescendo. There are no contrasts, practically no invention except in the plan and manner of execution. The themes are impersonal," he goes on, "folk tunes of the usual Spanish-Arabian kind. The orchestral treatment is simple and straightforward throughout, without the slightest attempt at virtuosity. . . . I have done exactly what I set out to do, and it is for listeners to take it or leave it."

Ravel was certainly being modest about his orchestration, which includes a particularly dazzling array of wind instruments: two kinds of oboes, three kinds of clarinets, bassoon and contrabassoon, and three kinds of saxophones. I'm especially fond of the slippery writing for trombone.

"Insistent" is how Ravel characterized his two tunes, tunes never actually "developed" but doubled at unusual intervals and in unexpected timbres. When Ravel actually makes his one big dramatic modulation near the end, from C major to E major, the change is shocking but it's also been carefully prepared for—the perfect solution, a simultaneous explosion and implosion. The world falls apart yet you're left with a feeling of wholeness and inevitability.

Ravel's own gorgeously restrained performance was recorded in 1932, with the Lamoureux Orchestra, and who but a group of French musicians could make such insinuating, slightly hung-over sounds? Ravel's inexorable slow tempo is a convincing model of how the Bolero should be played, though it finally clocks in at a minute and a half shy of the 17 minutes he insisted on.

Dinu Lipatti

March 8, 1989

Every century has its artists who died tragically young. Mozart was 35, Chopin 39, Schubert 32; Keats was only 25. In our century one of the most tragic losses was Dinu Lipatti, who died of leukemia at 33. His recordings indicate not only what a supremely gifted pianist he was, but what a sensitive musician. Like Glenn Gould, another great pianist who died too soon, Lipatti seemed to hear the inner workings of a piece of music, what made it tick. But unlike Gould, whose fresh insights could sometimes cross the border into eccentricity and mannerism, Lipatti never deviated from tradition, from the main stream, from what was always considered the stylistic center. You couldn't imagine anyone else playing like Gould. But when you hear Lipatti, you're sure he's playing exactly the way Mozart did, or Chopin, or courtly Scarlatti.

There are two Lipatti CDs in the latest batch of EMI's budget-priced Great Recordings of the Century. One disc includes all the selections that have already turned up on a full-priced Angel CD, plus two marvelous Schubert Impromptus that were recorded in September of 1950 at Lipatti's last solo recital, less than three months before he died.

Also on the recording are dazzling performances of two Scarlatti sonatas, and among the very greatest performances ever recorded of Mozart's tragic A-minor Sonata (comparable in articulation and emotional depth to Artur Schnabel's great version, recently reissued on Arabesque); and Bach's first Partita—more lyrical and intimate than Glenn Gould's equally extraordinary but tighter, nervier performance. Gould bursts into the room with an urgent message to convey; Lipatti takes you aside and whispers it into your ear.

The second disc includes most of Lipatti's solo Chopin recordings: the 14 waltzes and a Mazurka from his last recording session, a Nocturne, and the greatest performance I've ever heard of one of Chopin's greatest pieces: the Barcarolle. One of its most remarkable qualities is its sense both of continuity and of constantly shifting moods. Each new dappled episode flows directly out of the previous one and builds toward a climax that is not only overwhelming but inevitable.

With Lipatti, there's a nobility, a seriousness of purpose, that's never self-important or vulgar. The Chopin pieces are especially powerful in this regard. Chopin may have been the greatest master of keyboard counterpoint since Bach. Lipatti's tribute to Chopin is that he plays him with the same devotion and respect with which he plays Bach. The poetry of Lipatti's playing lies in the quiet core of dignity and poignance he sees at the heart of even the most glittering waltz.

Comparisons

September 26, 1989

When I first started collecting records, I didn't care who was performing. I only wanted to hear the music. Of course, I knew that some musicians let you hear more of the music than others. Or made more of it sound beautiful. But how did you find the ideal recording, the one which allowed the most music to come through? At first, I used to think this sort of performance, what the record companies liked to call "definitive," meant the most impersonal and literal reading of a score, the performance with the highest level of technical finish—untainted by anything quirky or eccentric in the interpretation. Later, I came to realize that impersonal and literal didn't necessarily make a piece interesting or alive.

I remember a recording of Schumann's Third Symphony, the *Rhenish*, that a record store salesman had recommended. I'd heard the piece on the radio and wanted to hear it again, over and over. The recording I got was with George Szell and the Cleveland Orchestra, perfectly executed and in beautiful sound. Then one day a friend played me the version conducted by Toscanini. The sound was poor but the opening bars made my heart pound with excitement. The whole symphony was more exhilarating, more rhythmically daring than I'd ever imagined. The Szell performance seemed academic and bland in comparison. Was it really more faithful to Schumann?

I still thought a great piece of music could be embodied in a single performance. The definitive Schumann Third was surely Toscanini's. But I remember a listening session with my best friend in graduate school. He had a large collection and we were comparing three very different recordings of Mozart's

40th Symphony, the tragic G-minor. Which one was best? In Toscanini's version, the first movement, marked Allegro molto, had a powerful forward thrust, high speed tension with a suppleness of phrasing that characterizes Toscanini at his best. Wilhelm Furtwängler was even faster, but more interior, nervous, almost manic. In their different ways, Toscanini and Furtwängler were both doing what Mozart indicated. But what were we supposed to make of the perversely slow tempo taken by Otto Klemperer? How could that be Mozart's Allegro molto? It was more like an Andante. Yet I'd never heard anyone so vividly capture Mozart's profound pathos. Klemperer's slowing down was like an X-ray that revealed both the skeleton and the heart of the music. At the time, I disapproved. But I couldn't get the performance out of my head. I think it's still my favorite version of the G-minor.

Each of these conductors is obviously passionately committed to his own deep understanding of the music. And each view adds crucial elements to our own understanding. Aren't they all closer to the spirit of Mozart—to the spirit of music—than the anonymous perfection of a "definitive" performance? How can we choose only one when each one is indispensable? And definitive.

Beecham's Haydn

February 21, 1990

Among the most popular works in the entire symphonic repertoire is the 94th of Haydn's 104 symphonies, the *Surprise*. Yet, many of his greatest symphonies are not so well known. They certainly aren't played as often as the symphonies by Mozart and Beethoven they inspired. I think one reason for Haydn's relative neglect is that his symphonies are not as easy to play as they seem. At least on records, they have very rarely received the performances they deserve. Maybe the thing that Haydn is most famous for, his sense of humor, is what throws off many conductors. How can a work be funny and serious at the same time? So they either play down the jokes, so they won't stick out, or they exaggerate them, so the more serious elements of the symphony seem dull and pedantic in comparison. Maybe most conductors don't understand that one of the most essential qualities of Haydn's century is wit. If you look at some of the great 18th-century writers, like Alexander Pope and Samuel Johnson, you can see that the texture of their work is a complex mixture of word-play, jokes, and high moral and psychological seriousness. Pope can write with sly sexual innuendo, then in the next breath make you aware of the triviality of that same sexual game-playing. No wonder Haydn was so popular in England. His last 12 symphonies, which were among his greatest, were actually composed for London. So it shouldn't be surprising that one of the very greatest Haydn conductors of this century was a witty and sophisticated Englishman, Sir Thomas Beecham.

What's most wonderful about Beecham's Haydn performances is the quicksilver way they slip back and forth in tone.

The humor is rich—and funny—but droll, understated. Beecham's elbow doesn't bruise your ribs. The seriousness is deep but never ponderous, as in the profoundly tender introduction to the Symphony, No. 102.

Among Beecham's greatest achievements are his entire series of Haydn's 12 so-called *Salomon* symphonies, which were named after the impresario who brought Haydn to London. They've been long out of print, but I'm delighted to see them reappearing on compact disc. Angel has released two CDs so far in their budget priced Classics for Pleasure Series, so now five of the symphonies are available, including the *Surprise*, the *Clock*, the *Drum-Roll*, and the *Miracle* (which got its nickname because a chandelier is supposed to have fallen during a performance of it yet no one got injured—an incident that actually happened during the Symphony No. 102). Angel has also been issuing other wonderful Beecham performances on CD, including a heavenly album of early Schubert symphonies and perhaps his most famous recording of all, *The Magic Flute* with the Berlin Philharmonic.

Conchita Supervia

February 28, 1990

I remember the first time I heard the voice of Conchita Supervia. A friend played me a Supervia recording and it was one of the strangest things I'd ever heard. Her voice was remarkably high and light for a mezzo-soprano, with a vibrato so fast and fluttery it seemed almost comic. But once I got used to it, I fell in love with it. She could use it to do the most phenomenally expressive things. For one thing, long before Marilyn Horne, Supervia could sing the great coloratura roles written for mezzo-soprano, especially by Rossini. Her voice was so flexible she could sing with ease the trills and roulades a heavier voice couldn't begin to negotiate. This same lightness and flexibility allowed her to be uniquely adept at comic roles. Of course, comedy isn't simply a matter of vocal technique. Supervia's comic timing is a phenomenon unto itself, and her phrasing, her ability to color individual words, is rivaled only by Callas. Supervia's fast vibrato projects two almost contradictory qualities: sexual urgency and innocence. That lascivious throb in her voice made her one of the great Carmens. This new Club 99 disc includes the "Habanera" and "Seguedilla," in Supervia's less familiar versions, sung in Italian.

    Supervia was a dazzlingly glamorous woman, with brilliant eyes and a cherubic round face. In a film called *Evensong*, she's the seductive villainess and the only person you can't take your eyes from. But she also excelled in playing so-called trouser roles, that is, male characters, often mischievous boys, who were meant to be sung by women, like Octavian in *Der Rosenkavalier*, Hansel in *Hansel and Gretel*, and most wonderful of all, Cherubino, the oversexed adolescent in *The Marriage of*

Figaro. Conchita Supervia sings the greatest performance I know of Cherubino's "Non so piú cosa son cosa faccio." Cherubino is overwhelmed by his sexual drives. He's on fire one minute, freezing the next. Every woman, he sings, *every woman*, changes his color and his pulse-rate. He feels only one desire, a desire he finds impossible to explain. Supervia puts a subtle rhythmic pressure on the word desío." Yet her uncanny dramatic conviction never betrays the elegance of the Mozartean style.

Supervia was a much-loved celebrity of her time. She was born in Barcelona in 1895 and made her opera debut in Buenos Aires before she was 15. She sang some of her most memorable performances at the Chicago Lyric Opera. She died in 1936 at the age of 40 after childbirth. This remarkable Club 99 album emphasizes roles we don't usually associate with Supervia, including arias and duets from *Mignon, Faust, Samson and Dalila, Hansel and Gretel*, Musetta's Aria from *La Bohème*, and even "Solveig's Song" from *Peer Gynt*. It shows her remarkable range and proves what one critic once said and more than one has echoed, "She was incapable of dullness."

Roland Hayes

April 19, 1990

Roland Hayes was born in 1887 in Curreyville, Georgia, on the very plantation where his mother had been a slave. He did his first singing in the Baptist Church his mother founded. As a teenager, he heard a recording of Enrico Caruso and decided to be a singer. He was admitted to Fisk University on the basis of his singing, even though his formal education had stopped at the sixth grade. On tour with the Fisk Jubilee Singers, he decided to stay in Boston and study voice. Later, he studied in Europe. In 1921, after a concert at London's Wigmore Hall, the royal family invited him to perform at Buckingham Palace. A year later, Roland Hayes became the first black performer to sing with a major American orchestra, the Boston Symphony. He became his own concert promoter because couldn't find a professional manager to represent a black artist. In 1924, he gave his first concert in Berlin. When he walked on stage, the audience began to hiss. He stood there in silence until they finally calmed down, then he sang Schubert's "Du bist die Ruh" ("You are quietness"). At the end, they cheered. On a new Smithsonian album, *The Art of Roland Hayes*, he sings the same song, recorded at Boston's Symphony Hall in 1955. Hayes was 68 years old when that recording was made. But you can hear what impressed the Germans thirty years before. The hushed restraint of his pianissimos, the sustained rapture of his phrasing dissolve the boundary between prayer and love song.

    Hayes wanted to compete with the world's great lieder singers on their own turf. But he never neglected the music that first inspired him. He was surely the first serious artist to bring spirituals to the classical concert stage. *The Art of Roland*

Hayes includes a fascinating variety of material. Hayes sings elegant versions of English songs from the 16th-through the 20th-centuries, including Haydn's great setting of Viola's lines from *Twelfth Night*, "She Never Told Her Love." There are songs by Beethoven, Schubert, Schumann, and Berlioz, an exuberant Creole folk song called "Mister Banjo," an African fetish chant set by Villa-Lobos, and ten folk songs, slave songs, and spirituals, most of them in Hayes's own superb arrangements. The earliest of these recordings were made in 1939, the last at Hayes's 80th birthday concert at Boston's Gardner Museum in 1967. All of them are eloquently accompanied by Reginald Boardman. Hayes's daughter Afrika joins him in two numbers, including a charming Mendelssohn duet recorded in 1965.

Hayes has one of the warmest tenor voices ever recorded, a sound unmistakable even into his 70s. Occasional rough spots crop up, even on his earlier recordings. But his flawless diction, his stylistic assurance and integrity, and the utter conviction of his delivery set towering standards for future generations of American singers.

Hindemith

May 9, 1990

To celebrate the 40th anniversary of the Bavarian Radio Symphony Orchestra, the Orfeo label has released some extraordinary new compact discs of live broadcasts from the archives of that superb ensemble. One of the treasures is the great Annie Fischer playing Bartok's magical Third Piano Concerto under the direction of Ferenc Fricsay, the brilliant conductor who died in 1963 of heart disease at the age of 48. There's Dimitri Mitropolous conducting the Schoenberg Violin Concerto with Louis Krasner, the violinist who played it for the first time. There are superb live performances by Otto Klemperer and Clemens Krauss, and a marvelous recording of Stravinsky conducting two of his greatest ballet scores, *Apollo* and *Jeu de Cartes* (*The Card Game*), both of which inspired the inspired choreography of George Balanchine. There's also another of Balanchine's greatest ballet scores—in fact, a score he commissioned: Paul Hindemith's Theme with 4 Variations, better known as *The Four Temperaments*. Hindemith himself conducts on a beautifully recorded live performance of thirty years ago with the glittering solo playing of Roumanian pianist Clara Haskil.

The four variations take off from the medieval idea that each individual is governed by one of the four ruling humors or temperaments: Melancholic, Sanguinic, Phlegmatic, and Choleric. In Balanchine's ballet, these four psychological characteristics become a kind of cosmic clockwork. The music wasn't originally intended for a ballet. In 1940, Balanchine had a little extra money from his work on Broadway and in Hollywood. He paid Hindemith $500 to compose a piece for piano and strings for a small group of musicians who occasionally came to Balanchine's home to eat dinner—Balanchine was a great cook. Then they performed new music. It's a perfect example of how Balanchine loved music for its own sake—especially contemporary music.

A year later, Balanchine thought of using Hindemith's score for a ballet called *The Cave of Sleep*, but it was never produced. In 1946, *The Four Temperaments* had its world premiere at the opening of Balanchine's new company called Ballet Society, the immediate predecessor of the New York City Ballet. Hindemith's loving, beautifully shaped performance doesn't exactly reflect Balanchine's dance rhythms but has its own compelling authenticity, as when Melancholy tries in vain to cheer himself up.

Orfeo Records dates this recording of *Four Temperaments* August 28, 1961. That would make Clara Haskil's performance even more extraordinary than it sounds, since she died eight months earlier.

This compact disc also includes Hindemith conducting his own Symphony in B for Concert Band and Alban Berg's fascinating Chamber Concerto for Violin, Piano, and 13 Winds.

Opera Originals

August 29, 1990

A charming excerpt from one of the most popular arias ever written, "Mi chiamano Mimi," from one of the most popular operas ever written, Puccini's *La Bohème*, was recorded in 1903, just seven years after the world premiere. The soprano was Cesira Ferrani, who was both Puccini's very first Mimi and his first Manon Lescaut. I think it's amazing that we can actually hear the voice of a singer who created a famous operatic role in another century. So I'm thrilled that producer Ed Rosen has compiled this extraordinary collection for the label Standing Room Only. The selections fall into several different categories. There are unknown singers, like Ferrani, who appeared in the premieres of major operas: members of the original casts of *Pagliacci*, *Cavalleria Rusticana*, and *Tosca* (Mascagni's first Santuzza and Puccini's original Cavaradossi actually made recordings). There are also legendary superstars in some of their greatest triumphs: Francesco Tamagno, Verdi's first Otello; Victor Maurel as Iago and Falstaff; Sir Richard Temple as Gilbert & Sullivan's Mikado and Pirate King; and Mary Garden as Melisande in Debussy's *Pelleas and Melisande*. She recorded an excerpt in 1904, two years after the premiere, with Debussy himself at the piano.

Other famous singers represented here include Caruso, Melba, and Rosina Storchio, the original Madame Butterfly and Toscanini's long-time mistress. Some of them created roles in operas we no longer hear about. Did you know that in 1892 Nellie Melba was in the world premiere of an opera based on Tennyson's *Idyls of the King*, Herman Bemberg's *Elaine*? Some of the most fascinating items here are by the most obscure singers in arias and ensembles from the most long-forgotten operas. The particular highlight on this set is unquestionably Victor Maurel as Falstaff. He sings the little aria in which Falstaff reminisces to Mistress Ford about when he was a young page for the Duke of Norfolk. He was so slim, so nimble, he could have slipped through a ring. Maurel was nearly 60 when he cut this record in 1907, fourteen years after the opera's premiere. He's so charming and full of character, the small studio audience cheers him on to an encore, then yet a third encore in French!

By the time the phonograph was invented, many of the singers here were already well past their vocal primes. Some may never have had a vocal prime. And of course the sound quality varies with each rare original disc. But many of these recordings are magnificent. I wish some of the original Wagner or Strauss singers were also included. But there's something so moving about the whole enterprise, I'd hate to part with any of the truly historic material here.

Eleanor Steber

October 12, 1990

The great American soprano Eleanor Steber died last Wednesday, October 3, of heart failure, at the age of 76, two months after heart surgery. Between her Metropolitan Opera debut in 1940 and 1962, she sang 33 roles at the Met. I saw her in person only a few times, and think she was one of the very greatest singers this country ever produced.

I remember seeing her once at MIT, late in her career, in a concert performance of Mozart's *Idomeneo*. She was clearly past her radiant vocal prime, but her performance of the embittered Elektra was hair-raising. Steber never stinted, in her life or in her art. Even towards the end of her career, she sang with everything she had. Perhaps this was part of what it meant to come of age as an American singer in a world in which American singers were still not quite taken seriously. You never felt that she was saving herself, or protecting a precious commodity. So even though she was an elegant singer—one of the century's great Mozart singers—she could always convey the passion and urgency that lie just beneath the exquisite surface of classical formality. For Steber, elegance and passion were not mutually exclusive. One of her best recordings was the Countess in *The Marriage of Figaro*, from a live performance conducted by Bruno Walter at the Met in 1944.

Steber had a long career, and an impressive range, from the most delicate French arts songs to Puccini's *Madame Butterfly* and Marie in Berg's *Wozzeck*. She didn't make an enormous number of recordings, though. A handful of complete operas, several recital albums, including some on her own record label, Stand, and a late recording of the most notorious event in her career, the black-tie/black towel concert at the Continental Baths, the gay health club where Bette Midler got her start. Steber was one of the great non-French interpreters of French music, especially of Berlioz. Her landmark recording of his sublimely Romantic song-cycle, *Nuits d'Eté*, is the standard by which all other performances must be judged.

Steber also championed American music, and she put her money, quite literally, where her mouth was by commissioning Samuel Barber's elegiac setting of James Agee, *Knoxville: Summer of 1915*. She sang the first performance with Serge Koussevitzky and the Boston Symphony in 1948. Her 1963 Columbia recording of this piece is probably her most famous. Few of Steber's recordings are currently available. In 1958, Steber created the title role in Barber's opera *Vanessa*. The original cast Met recording, made shortly after the world premiere, is now an RCA Victor CD.

A video tape of some of Steber's appearances on the early TV opera series, *The Voice of Firestone*, has been released by Video Artists International. On it, she sings a wide selection from Mozart and Verdi to Victor Herbert, Rodgers & Hammerstein, and Cole Porter. The Steber video has been so successful that two more of her *Voice of Firestone* videos are already in the works. Steber called herself the "little girl from Wheeling, West Virginia." No one who ever experienced her glorious voice, the joy she took in singing, or her American generosity of spirit is likely to forget her.

Kathleen Ferrier

November 11, 1992

The British contralto Kathleen Ferrier was born in 1912 and died of cancer in 1953, at the age of 41. Her singing career lasted only ten years. I first heard her on an album of Mahler's *Das Lied von der Erde* (*The Song of the Earth*). She made it in 1952 with Bruno Walter, the conductor who led the world premiere back in 1911. It's a staggering performance—a farewell to the earth sung by someone who must have known she was dying. Ferrier's warm, rich, natural voice sounds like a force of nature—it seems to well up from the very center of the earth. So it shouldn't be surprising that she made a career of singing the most profound music written for the alto register: arias by Bach, Handel, and Purcell; songs and song cycles by Schumann, Schubert, Wolf, and Brahms; and of course Mahler. She was also a wonderful folk singer. She worked mostly in concert, but she was also famous for one operatic role, Orpheus in Gluck's *Orfeo ed Euridice*. Her last public appearance, only shortly before her death, was in a production of this opera at Covent Garden. My favorite of her three recordings of Orpheus's big aria about losing Eurydice is the one she made in 1946 with Sir Malcolm Sargent, in English.

London Records has just released a ten-disc Kathleen Ferrier set of both studio recordings and live performances (the discs are also available separately). One highlight is a never-before issued live recording of some Schubert songs with the composer Benjamin Britten accompanying Ferrier at the piano. In everything she did, you can hear the openness and spontaneity that everyone adored. Someone once played me a private recording that must have been taped at a party. She accompanies herself in a hilarious parody of a pompous British oratorio singer. Serious or funny, whatever she felt she seemed to feel completely. In one Mahler performance with Bruno Walter, she couldn't sing the last word because she was overcome by tears. In fact, you can always hear the tears—they seem to be inherent in the very sound of her voice, as in her singing the great Mahler setting of a poem by Friedrich Rückert, "Ich bin der Welt abhanden gekommen"("I have become lost to the world"), with Bruno Walter conducting the Vienna Philharmonic Orchestra.

Along with the ten-disc Ferrier set, London has also issued in its historical series two magnificent discs of live performances: including Mahler's *Kindertotenlieder* ("Songs on the Death of Children") and Ferrier's only recording of Mahler's Second Symphony. They're both conducted by another great Mahler disciple, Otto Klemperer. And in a lighter vein, she participates in Brahms's lilting *Love-Song Waltzes*. Ironically, while London has been reissuing all these discs, they have deleted from their catalogue Ferrier's landmark *Das Lied von der Erde* with Bruno Walter, her most famous recording and maybe her greatest of all.

Hollywood String Quartet

May 10, 1994

Hollywood doesn't usually suggest classical elegance or profundity, but what's in a name? The Hollywood String Quartet was one of the world's most profound and elegant chamber groups. Its members included the late violinist Felix Slatkin and the cellist Eleanor Aller, who are the parents of Leonard Slatkin, the conductor of the St. Louis Symphony. The other regulars were violinist Paul Shure and violist Paul Robyn. It was the movies that really brought these players together. They were studio musicians who formed a string quartet because doing film soundtracks didn't satisfy their craving for the classics. After World War II, California became an international musical center. Schoenberg and Stravinsky both lived there; Otto Klemperer conducted the LA Philharmonic. Before the Hollywood Quartet recorded Schoenberg's *Transfigured Night*, which was originally written for string sextet, they performed it for the hard-to-please composer. He was so impressed he agreed to write the liner notes—the only ones he ever wrote (and they're reproduced in this new album). *Transfigured Night* is Schoenberg's deeply felt realization of a moving poem by Richard Dehmel about a couple whose love transcends the agony of the woman being pregnant with another man's child. The Hollywood Quartet performance glows with an otherworldly sweetness.

The other piece on this album is the Schubert String Quintet. The Hollywood Quartet plays it a little faster than usual. Fleet and unselfindulgent, it's one of the most radiant performances I've ever heard of one of the most gorgeous pieces of music ever written.

In these pieces, the Quartet is joined by violist Alvin Dinkin and cellist Kurt Reher. This is the first compact disc devoted entirely to the Hollywood String Quartet. But it's not their first appearance on CD. You can also hear them accompanying Frank Sinatra on his album *Close to You*—one of the reasons it's the best album he ever made.

Benjamin Britten and Peter Pears

June 2, 1994

One of my rarest records is an old 10-inch 78 of an Irish folk song called "The Salley Gardens." The composer Benjamin Britten accompanies the extraordinary tenor Peter Pears, who was both his professional and personal partner, in Britten's own arrangement of the song. The actual words are an early poem by Yeats, "Down by the Salley Gardens," which was his "attempt," as he said, "to reconstruct an old song from three lines imperfectly remembered by an old peasant woman . . . who often sings them to herself." Britten made many elegant, harmonically surprising arrangements of traditional English and Irish folk songs. In a way, he did the same thing to Yeats's poem that Yeats did to the old woman's "imperfectly remembered" words. As far as I know, that 1944 recording was never reissued. But it's just appeared on a new two-disc set that includes all of Britten's early folksong recordings. Now you don't have to come to my house to hear it.

I love this song, but two other items on this set are probably of larger significance. They are reissues of the first, original cast recordings of extended excerpts from Britten's first two operas: *Peter Grimes* and *The Rape of Lucretia*, under the direction of the late British conductor Reginald Goodall. Pears is the rough outcast fisherman Peter Grimes who reveals his doomed poetic dream of a better life.

Both *Peter Grimes* and *The Rape of Lucretia* are available in magnificent complete performances conducted by the composer. But these early recordings are special in their own way. The voice of Peter Pears later grew darker and more strained. Here you can hear both the strangeness and youthfulness that inspired Britten to write so many great roles for him.

Brain, Kell, Goossens

September 15, 1994

Three of my favorite musicians from the past have turned up on a single disc. They're not playing together, although since they were all British and living in England in the 1940s and '50s, they could have been. These three wind players may be the greatest artists who ever played their respective instruments. The best known in this country is Dennis Brain, the son and grandson of distinguished horn players. His recording of all four Mozart Horn Concertos under Herbert von Karajan in 1955 is one of the best-selling classical discs of all time. Two years later, he was killed in a car accident—he was only 36. His intonation, his flexibility were not merely flawless, but profoundly expressive. His sound could be both intimate and heroic. And he was the perfect chamber partner, as he was with pianist Denis Matthews in Beethoven's F-major Horn Sonata.

The second player on this disc is Reginald Kell, who lived to be 75, but stopped playing at the age of 52, at the height of his career. He made a historic contribution to clarinet playing. By daring to add vibrato, he brought new color and warmth to an instrument that had been relentlessly monochromatic. He has the sweetest clarinet tone I've ever heard, with phrasing so nuanced you forget that his pitch is also perfect. He was an ideal Mozart player. And equally at home in a more Romantic vein, as in the first of Schumann's three *Fantasie~stücke* with pianist Gerald Moore.

The oldest of these three artists, oboist Leon Goossens, died in 1988 at the age of 90. Like Dennis Brain, he came from a musical family. His Belgian father and grandfather, and his older brother, all named Eugene, were conductors. His two sisters were superb harpists. In fact, a new biography of the entire Goossens family, by Carole Rosen, is about to be published by Northeastern University Press. Like Kell, Leon Goossens was one of the handpicked principals of Sir Thomas Beecham's London Philharmonic Orchestra. He was the voice by which you recognized that magnificent ensemble. It was Goossens's sound that inspired Kell to add that expressive dimension to his own playing. No wind player ever had a more "spoken" quality. But as he talks to you, he's also singing.

Each of these artists has a sound that is instantly identifiable, and very human. They're all individuals with a very personal response to the music. We admire so many of today's players for their technique. But there's got to be more to music than anonymous perfection. That's one of the reasons it's so important to hear these marvelous old recordings.

Karl Muck and Early BSO Recordings

May 22, 1995

The lively, charming Overture to Wolf-Ferrari's comic opera *The Secret of Susanna* might not be what you'd expect to hear from the first recording session of the Boston Symphony Orchestra, especially under the super-serious German conductor and Wagnerian specialist, Dr. Karl Muck. His recordings of excerpts from *Parsifal* ten years later are still considered to be among the greatest operatic performances of all time. For the Victor Talking Machine Company, he cut ten sides at that first session with the Boston Symphony in 1917, including works by Tchaikovsky, Berlioz, and Beethoven, as well as Wolf-Ferrari and Wagner, and they prove his astounding versatility. For all their sonic limitations, we can hear a rhythmic drive and technical polish that any of today's digital conductors should envy. It was the first time a full 100-piece ensemble had ever been recorded.

Muck first conducted the BSO between 1906 and 1908. He returned from Germany to conduct in Boston again from 1912 to 1918. The horror story of what happened to him, however, is one of the most frightening examples of American intolerance and how badly the government of this country treats artists. During World War I, anti-German feeling ran very high in the United States. Muck was under heavy suspicion, although he was actually a Swiss citizen. In 1917, several groups in Providence, Rhode Island, had requested that the Boston Symphony play "The Star-Spangled Banner" at a concert there. This message was not passed on to Muck, so the orchestra didn't play it. A national uproar ensued. Muck was exonerated by the founder of the BSO, Civil War Major Henry Lee Higginson, and Muck went on to conduct the national anthem to great cheers at all his remaining concerts. Nevertheless, on trumped up charges, he was eventually arrested as an enemy alien and sentenced to internment in the federal prison at Fort Oglethorpe, Georgia, till the end of the War. Victor released only four of the ten sides he recorded, and his name was removed from the label.

Now, thanks to Brian Bell of Boston's WGBH radio, all of Karl Muck's surviving Boston Symphony records have been gathered on this new CD, including a rejected first half of the last movement of Beethoven's Seventh Symphony, his only Beethoven recording. The rest of the disc is taken up with the first Boston Symphony electrical recordings, made at Symphony Hall in 1928 under Serge Koussevitzky—the great Russian conductor who, among other things, started Tanglewood. These include a sensual, exuberant performance of the Suite from Stravinsky's ballet *Petrouchka*, the melting pas de deux from Stravinsky's *Apollo*, and Ravel's passionate *Daphnis and Chloe* Suite No. 2—all works by living composers at that time.

This disc also includes two alternative takes that are quite different from Koussevitzky's official versions. Some of Koussevitzky's greatest performances have also been turning up on other labels. RCA Victor has just released a spectacular CD of Koussevitzky conducting Prokofiev. And there's more Prokofiev and a wonderful Sibelius disc on Pearl. But Koussevitzky's very first recordings, in amazingly vibrant sound, beautifully transferred by Ward Marston, capture a special moment in the legacy of what used to be called "the Aristocrat of Orchestras."

Maggie Teyte / Heddle Nash

November 13, 1995

The British soprano Margaret Tate was known to the world as Maggie Teyte. Debussy himself greatly admired her and coached her as Melisande in his opera *Pelleas et Melisande*. "She is Melisande," Debussy said. She was the second soprano ever to sing this role (the first was another British singing actress, Mary Garden). Teyte's recordings of Debussy chansons, especially the ones she made in 1936 with the great French pianist Alfred Cortot, are among the vocal treasures of the century. These have finally come out on CD. My favorite song is called "Colloque sentimental" (sentimental dialogue). It's the last of Debussy's six settings of poems by Paul Verlaine, *Fetes Galantes*. "Do you remember our old ecstasy?" one of the haunted figures says. "Why do you want me to remember it?" the other ghost replies.

> "Does your heart beat at my very name?
> Do you still see my soul in your dreams?" "No."
> "Oh, the wonderful days of unspeakable happiness when our mouths were joined." "It's possible."
> "How blue the sky was, and how great our hope!"
> "Hope has fled, defeated, into the black sky."

Teyte had one of the qualities I admire most in a singer, the ability when she's singing to sound as if she's talking.

If anything, the British tenor Heddle Nash had an even more purely beautiful voice than Maggie Teyte's. Yet he too sings with the intimacy of speech, a sung whisper. He's probably most famous for his roles on the very first complete recordings of Mozart's *Marriage of Figaro* and *Così fan tutte*, but he was a beloved figure in a wide variety of operas, operettas, and oratorios. My nomination for one of the most gorgeous recordings ever made is Nash's rendition of the languorous tenor aria from Bizet's *The Pearl Fishers*, which in English becomes "In memory I lie beneath the palms and dream of love." Nash makes even the Victorian diction sound intensely erotic.

There are, of course, other marvelous performances on these discs. There's even another CD on which Teyte and Nash appear together—a vocal summit meeting—in a live 1938 radio broadcast of scenes from Massenet's *Manon*. But these two recordings define my own personal ideal, rare examples of those moments that I wish all singing aspired to.

Four Saints in Three Acts

April 17, 1996

My vote for the best American opera goes to *Four Saints in Three Acts*, a collaboration between two of the most original voices of the century: Virgil Thomson and Gertrude Stein. They both wanted to break the mold of traditional sentimental operatic narrative. Like a Seinfeld episode, the opera is, as Stein herself wrote, about nothing. "A saint," she says, "a real saint never does anything, a martyr does something but a really good saint does nothing, and so I wanted to have Four Saints who did nothing and I wrote the *Four Saints in Three Acts* and they did nothing and that was everything. Generally speaking anybody is more interesting doing nothing than doing something." The major characters in the opera are St. Teresa and St. Ignatius, though there are in fact both more than four saints and more than three acts. Whatever action there is was suggested by Thomson's friend Maurice Grosser after the score was finished. One of my favorite parts is St. Ignatius's vision of the Holy Ghost, a passage that's infinitely more poignant because the words make far more than strictly logical sense. "The Pigeons on the grass alas."

The opera broke a lot of new ground. The first performance, produced by a group that called itself The Friends and Enemies of Modern Music, took place at the Hartford Atheneum in 1934, seven years after Stein wrote the words and six years after Thomson composed the music. The production team was a Who's Who of Modernism. The choreography was by Frederick Ashton; the staging by John Houseman. New York artist Florine Stettheimer created transparent scenery out of cellophane. Most daring of all for the time, the original cast, most of whom are on this 1947 recording, consisted entirely of black performers. They're all marvelous. Soprano Beatrice Robinson-Wayne as St. Teresa and baritone Edward Matthews as St. Ignatius are especially eloquent. It's a heavenly work in which the musical jokes perfectly match the verbal ones. Mock hymn tunes and Gregorian chants, mock Baroque and Gilbert & Sullivan, mock minstrel show and vaudeville all create an atmosphere of endearing but unsentimental sweetness.

After the Hartford premiere, *Four Saints* ran on Broadway for six weeks—unprecedented for an opera. When George Gershwin saw it, he was so impressed with the conductor, Alexander Smallens, and the Eva Jessye Negro Choir that he hired them for *Porgy and Bess*. Thomson's notes to this recording refer to a completely happy collaboration. But in fact, he and Stein fell out and were not on speaking terms at the time of the premiere. Stein eventually saw the production in Chicago.

Thomson himself conducts this recording, in his own abridgement so it could fit on a single LP. To complete the CD, there's a wonderful 1946 performance of Thomson's suite from his score to Pare Lorentz's dust-bowl documentary *The Plow That Broke the Plains*. Leopold Stokowski conducts the Hollywood Bowl Symphony Orchestra. Thomson's sense of American heroism here includes Sunday School doxology and honky-tonk sleaze. Both scores are irresistible. I want everyone I love to have a copy of this disc.

Budapest String Quartet at the Library of Congress

November 6, 1996

In 1940, after performing there on and off for two years, the Budapest String Quartet became Quartet-in-Residence at the Library of Congress, a position they kept for twenty-two years. Their concerts were special because they were allowed to perform on a unique set of Stradivari instruments that were not allowed off the premises. Bridge Records has recently acquired the rights to the Library's archives, where the recordings of these live performances—and others—have been languishing for half a century. One of the works on the Budapest's official opening concert, August 3, 1940, was Haydn's *Lark* Quartet—and it is a high point on a disc that includes two other works by Haydn and Beethoven's Quartet for Piano and Strings.

These performances of Haydn's *Lark* Quartet and his late Opus 76, No. 5, which were recorded in 1941, show the Budapest at its best—refined but energetic, lean but full of rhythmic grace and the most delicate nuance of phrasing. The playing of Beethoven's Piano Quartet and the Hungarian Rondo from Haydn's G-major Trio (an encore piece), from a 1955 concert, is a little rougher, but they have the benefit of that master chamber-pianist, the late Mieczyslaw Horszowski. In the Brahms Piano Quintet and the Schubert Trout Quintet, on a separate disc, the pianist is no less than George Szell, just around the time he was appointed conductor of the Cleveland Orchestra. How flexibly the Quartet adapted to such diverse ivory tickling as the exquisite lyricism of Horszowski and the classical restraint of Szell.

In some ways, though, the most remarkable of these releases is the one from 1952 devoted to Rachmaninoff. This disc includes both of Rachmaninoff's rarely-heard string quartets and the big Trio *Elegique* in D-minor, with pianist Arthur Balsam—luscious, insinuating works that date from the 1890s and all composed before Rachmaninoff turned 23.

The Budapest Quartet was founded in 1917 by four members of the Budapest National Opera Orchestra—three Hungarians and a Dutchman. By the time these recordings were made at the Library of Congress, the personnel had completely changed. In 1952, the players were Joseph Roisman and Jac Gorodetzky, violins, Boris Kroyt, viola, and Mischa Schneider, cello—not Hungarians at all but four Russian Jews. They never made studio recordings of Rachmaninoff, so these forgotten gems of Russian Romanticism surely never had better performances.

George Copeland

November 11, 1997; January 20, 1998

I'm an optimist about the arts. I want to believe that what's really good will eventually come to light. You'll see an old movie on television and say: Who was that actress?—she's so real. Then you begin watching for her. One of the most important things a critic can do is remind people of the existence of lost treasures. At dinner recently, a friend said that he'd been meaning to ask me for years if I'd ever heard of a pianist named George Copeland. I was astonished. When was the last time I'd heard that name, except from a few fanatic record collectors? George Copeland didn't record very much, but I've loved the few recordings I've heard. He had an extraordinary touch—feathery, pearly, glistening—and instantly recognizable. He specialized in French impressionism, yet there's nothing merely "impressionistic" about his playing. You can hear every note distinctly—nothing gets washed away in a watery blur. He also championed 20th-century Spanish composers. This music can be percussive, rhythmically charged, yet Copeland never pounds. He seems to caress the keys. You can hear layers in his playing, foregrounds, middle distances, and backgrounds. And the fingerwork is phenomenal. As in his recording of a dance by Manuel de Falla, from an old MGM LP, which was probably reproduced from even older 78s on RCA Victor from the late 1930s or early '40s.

There are only glancing allusions to George Copeland in reference books. He was born in Boston, in 1882. When he was seven, his mother took him to Spain. He made his recital debut in Boston, in 1905. He met Debussy in 1911, and introduced many of Debussy's major piano pieces to America. He died in Princeton, New Jersey, in 1971, at the age of 89. The reason my friend asked about Copeland was that his family knew him. Copeland spent summers with them in Maine. He was charming, my friend said, and "big in every way," my friend's hands reaching up then stretching out sideways. He'd even given my friend a few piano lessons. Copeland told my friend never to "hit" the keys but to "stroke" them. My friend compared Copeland's fingers on the keyboard to a delicate paintbrush moving across a canvas. This description fit my mental image of Copeland's playing exactly.

Why wasn't George Copeland better known? One answer may be that he suffered from terrible stage fright. He didn't perform much, and his bad nerves sometimes interfered with his playing in public. He may also have been a victim of homophobic critics. I've looked, but can't find any of Copeland's recordings in print. Unless some record company comes to the rescue, you might never get to hear more of his playing than the excerpts you've just heard. And that's as frustrating for me as it might be for you. But remember his name: George Copeland. He was a wonderful musician, and he shouldn't be forgotten.

* * *

Talk about serendipity.

George Copeland was an American pianist whose rare recordings I'd loved for years. The person who triggered my recent piece about him on *Fresh Air* was a friend who was curious if I'd ever heard of him. Copeland had known his family (he had even given my friend a few piano lessons).

After the broadcast about George Copeland, I got a note from a listener in Memphis thanking me for explaining the mysterious figure on an old concert poster he'd found years ago at a garage sale. I also got a call from another friend who knew someone who was working on a new George Copeland album. That album has just been released. The liner notes on it by Charles Timbrell tell me more about Copeland than I'd ever known before. That, for instance, he had toured with Isadora Duncan, accompanying her dancers and playing piano solos. That Copeland had played the world premiere of two Debussy Etudes and that he was playing the first American performances of Debussy as early as 1905. And who but Copeland would have insisted on placing the microphones under his piano to capture the particularly diaphanous quality of Debussy's prelude "Veils"? Debussy once said to him: "It is not my habit to pay compliments. But I wish to say, Mr. Copeland, that I never thought to hear my music played as well as that in my lifetime." The new album includes Copeland's own insinuating transcription of Debussy's *Prelude to the Afternoon of a Faune*.

Copeland's wealthy Boston father was opposed to his son's musical career, but his Spanish mother encouraged it, which helps explain Copeland's devotion to Baroque and modern Spanish music. This generous new album includes the expected variety of French, Spanish, and Latin American composers, but there are also some happy surprises, such as a breathless Bach Passapied.

I especially value the chance to hear Copeland perform live—on never previously issued recordings of a 1964 concert. In fact, his very last, at Yale, when he was 82 years old (he died at 89). I had no idea these recordings existed. He was still playing with his singular, instantly identifiable combination of delicacy and power. The exquisite touch (his trademark), teasing rhythms, and captivating phrasing that critics were already praising before the turn of the century were all still there more than half a century later.

Erich Kleiber

September 24, 2003

Here's a frequent scenario: I'm listening to the radio in my car, and some music grabs my attention, so I try to guess who's playing. I keep driving until I learn the answer. A few months ago it was a performance of Beethoven's *Pastorale* Symphony. Not a version I knew. But it was charming and fresh; very Viennese I thought—delicate without sounding precious, full of vitality without being aggressive. And fun. My wild guess was Erich Kleiber—the Viennese conductor I knew best from the recording I grew up with of Mozart's *The Marriage of Figaro*, and who is probably better known now as the father of the wonderful but very eccentric conductor Carlos Kleiber, who has inherited, among other things, his father's love for Viennese waltzes. Well, give me a gold star! I was right. That recording of the *Pastorale* has just been reissued as part of a series on Decca called Great Conductors of the 20th Century.

That Beethoven performance triggered a new interest in Erich Kleiber, and I've been trying to find as many of his recordings as I can. His most famous recordings are that Figaro, and Richard Strauss's *Der Rosenkavalier*, which are still in print after nearly half a century. The famous sextet from *Figaro* is one of the pieces of music that first made me fall in love with Mozart, an amazing moment—part slapstick comedy and part profound human drama. In it, Figaro and the elderly lady who's been trying to trap him into marriage discover that they are really mother and son.

One reason Kleiber may not be better known is that although he led the world's greatest orchestras, he left Europe before the Second World War and lived for a while in Argenti na, where he didn't record. He died suddenly, in 1956, at the age of 65. A number of his live opera performances exist, including an electrifying version of Verdi's *Sicilian Vespers* with Maria Callas. Kleiber was also deeply interested in contemporary music. In 1925, he led the world premiere of Alban Berg's *Wozzeck*, a landmark of 20th-century opera. He never recorded it complete, but in a live performance of a concert suite from *Wozzeck* thirty years later, Kleiber captures both the brutality and the beauty of Berg's score.

I'm glad the record companies are still interested in Kleiber. The Music & Arts label has just put out an exciting album of Kleiber conducting four previously unreleased complete live concerts with the NBC Symphony—Toscanini's orchestra—with a Strauss *Tales from the Vienna Woods* with a particularly magical ending.

Kleiber once said that "Routine and improvisation are the mortal enemies of art." There was nothing routine about Erich Kleiber. He was a demanding musician. And although his recordings have the spontaneity of improvisation, he obviously achieved this effect through hard work. He was one of the major artists of the 20th century and left behind only a fragment of his accomplishment. But we should be grateful that at least part of his legacy still exists.

Patricia Brooks

January 25, 2008

Some performances are so indelible that even after many years you can't forget them. I can still picture in my mind the way Patricia Brooks handled a champagne glass in director Frank Corsaro's famous 1969 production of Verdi's *La Traviata* at the New York City Opera. Brooks had an unusual background for an opera singer. She was both a dancer, with Martha Graham's company, and an actress. She studied with the great Uta Hagen and appeared off-Broadway in José Quintero's legendary Circle-in-the-Square production of Eugene O'Neill's *The Iceman Cometh*.

Violetta, the heroine of *La Traviata*, is a tubercular courtesan. Brooks played her as world-weary and cynical, threatened by the love of her naïve suitor, Alfredo. At the end of the first act, she resists her sentimental impulse to fall in love and tries to talk—or sing—herself back into her ruthless pursuit of sheer pleasure. Brooks sipped her champagne as if she were sipping at the well of love itself. Maybe, she sings, Alfredo is the one. But no, honest feeling is impossible, absurd. "I must remain free!," Violetta sings. And as if she had to shake off this temptation in the most violent way, Brooks smashed the champagne glass on the floor. Few sopranos ever sing this passage, ever act it, with such desperation. Or with greater theatrical skill. But Brooks never recorded this role. Most of her performances remain only in the memory of those who saw them.

Now VAI has released a CD of her 1971 New York recital debut, and we can hear again her extraordinary sweetness and sensitivity, as, for example, in an atmospheric Mahler song, "Ich atmet," in which breathing in the scent of a lime-tree twig becomes an act of love. Brooks could also rise to heights of tragic grandeur, as in an aria from Meyerbeer's rarely performed *Robert le Diable*.

Patricia Brooks's opera career was cut short in 1977 by the onset of multiple sclerosis, which affected her breathing. She died in 1993 at the age of 59. I'm not aware of any film with Patricia Brooks. I wish I could see again how gracefully and with how much character she moved. But this lovely new disc, with its un-clichéd selection of songs and arias in German, Italian, and French, stylishly accompanied by pianist Harriet Wingreen and oboist Bert Lucarelli, is a powerful reminder of what an extraordinary artist she was.

Discography

Alkan
-Alkan: Organ Music, Kevin Bowyer. Nimbus.
Arlene Auger and Dalton Baldwin
-Love Songs: Arlene Auger and Dalton Baldwin. Delos.
Samuel Barber
-Music of Samuel Barber. Vanguard.
Josephine Barstow
-Josephine Barstow: Opera Finales. Decca London.
Beecham's Haydn
-Haydn: Symphonies Nos. 99-104, Sir Thomas Beecham, Royal Philharmonic. EMI Angel.
Jussi Björling
-Verdi, Il Trovatore: Björling, Milanov, Cellini. RCA Red Seal.
-Jussi Björling: Live Recordings 1929-1960. Legato Classics.
Jorge Bolet
-Chopin: Ballades, Barcarolle, Fantaisie op.49. Jorge Bolet. Decca London.
Boston Chamber Music Society
-Brahms: Clarinet Trio, Quintet, Boston Chamber Music Society, Thomas Hill. Northeastern.
Pierre Boulez
-Boulez Conducts Bartok: Concerto for Orchestra / Music for Strings, Percussion & Celesta. CBS Masterworks.
Brain, Kell, Goossens
-Brain, Kell, Goossens play Schumann & Beethoven. Testament.
Patricia Brooks
-Patricia Brooks In Recital: Bach, Mahler, Puccini, Etc. / Wingreen, Lucarelli. Vai Audio.
Budapest String Quartet at the Library of Congress
-Great Performances from the Library of Congress, Vol. 5. The Budapest String Quartet;
-Mieczyslaw Horszowski, piano. Bridge.
-Rachmaninoff: String Quartets, Budapest String Quartet. Bridge.

Busoni Concerto
-Busoni: Piano Concerto. Garrick Ohlsson, piano, Cleveland Orchestra, Christoph von Dohnányi. Telarc.

Maria Callas
-Operatic Arias. EMI.
-Maria Callas at Juilliard—The Masterclasses. EMI.
-Legend: Callas. EMI.

Elliott Carter
-Elliott Carter & London Sinfonietta / Knussen Triple Duo / In Sleep, in Thunder. Nonesuch.
-Songs of America on home, love, nature, and death, Jan de Gaetani, mezzo-soprano, Gilbert Kalish, piano. Elektra/Nonesuch.
-Elliott Carter: The Works for String Quartet. Arditti Quartet. Etcetera.
-J.S. Bach/Elliott Carter. Thomas Demenga. ECM New Series.
-Three American String Quartets. Elliott Carter, Milton Babbitt, Mel Powell. Composers Quartet. Music and Arts Programs of America
-Carter: Eight Compositions: Group For Contemporary Music. Bridge.
-Piano Music (Complete): Oppens Plays Carter - Elliott Carter at 100. Cedille.

Pablo Casals
-Bach Suites for Unaccompanied Cello, Volumes I and II (Angel, Great Recordings of the Century).
-Beethoven, Ghost and Archduke Trios, Philips, Legendary Classics.

Casals Festival at Prades
-Bach Festival: Prades, 1950. Pearl.

Casals's Schubert
-Schubert - String Quintet in C: Isaac Stern, Alexander Schneider, Milton Katims, Paul Tortelier, Pablo Casals, Prades Festival Orchestra. Sony.

Conchita Supervia
-Conchita Supervia (1895-1936) - Opera and Song Recital by Conchita Supervia. Club 99.

Cortot, Thibaud, Casals
-Cortot Thibaud Casals. EMI References.
George Copeland
-Spanish Piano Music. George Copeland, piano. MGM.
-George Copeland: The Victor Solo Recordings. Pearl.
Ruby Elzy
-Ruby Elzy in Song. Cambria.
Ensemble Alcatraz
-Ensemble Alcatraz: Visions & Miracles. Nonesuch.
Kathleen Ferrier
-Mahler, Das Lied von der Erde: Kathleen Ferrier, Julius Patzak, Vienna Philharmonic Orchestra, Bruno Walter. Decca.
-Kathleen Ferrier Edition. Decca/London Records.
Annie Fischer
-Mozart: Piano Concertos Nos. 20 & 23. Price-Less.
Leon Fleisher
-Leon Fleisher Recital - Bach/Brahms, Scriabin, Saint-Saens. Sony.
Four Saints in Three Acts
-Virgil Thomson: Four Saints In Three Acts/The Plow That Broke The Plains. RCA.
Gubaidulina
-Gubaidulina: Offertorium; Hommage à T.S. Eliot. Deutsche Grammophon.
Leon Goossens
-Elgar Miniatures. Chandos.
John Harbison
-Mirabai Songs/Variations. Northeastern.
-Flight into Egypt/The Natural World/Concerto for Double Brass Choir and Orchestra. New World Records.
-Harbison: String Quartets 1 & 2 "November 19, 1828." Harmonia Mundi.
Hindemith
-Paul Hindemith: Symphonie in B; Die Vier Temperamente. Orfeo.

Hollywood String Quartet
-Arnold Schoenberg: Verklärte Nacht, op.4 (Original version for String sextet) Franz Schubert: String Quintet in C, D,956 The Hollywood Quartet, Alvin Dinkin, viola, Kurt Reher, cello. Testament.
Horowitz
-Horowitz: The Last Recording. Sony.
Mieczyslaw Horszowski
-Mieczyslaw Horszowski: Mozart / Chopin / Debussy / Beethoven. Nonesuch, 1986.
Lorraine Hunt Lieberson
-Faure: Pelléas et Mélisande, Dolly, Après un rêve, Pavane, Elégie, Hunt, BSO, Ozawa. Deutsche Grammophon.
-Handel: Ariodante. Harmonia Mundi.
-North and South. John Harbison Chamber Music, Naxos.
-Rilke Songs, The Six Realms, Horn Concerto. Bridge.
-Lorraine Hunt Lieberson sings Peter Lieberson 'Neruda Songs' [Live]. BSO. Handel, Giulio Cesare. Decca DVD.
-Berlioz: "Les Nuits d'été" and Handel: Arias with Lorraine Hunt Lieberson. Philharmonia Baroque Productions.
-Recital: Lorraine Hunt Lieberson at Ravinia. Harmonia Mundi.
-Handel: Famous Arias. Harmonia Mundi 2008.
Ives
-Charles Ives: Holidays Symphony, The Unanswered Question, Central Park In The Dark.
-Chicago Symphony Orchestra & Chorus, Michael Tilson Thomas. CBS Masterworks.
Erich Kleiber
-Great Conductors of the 20th Century: Erich Kleiber. EMI.
-Erich Kleiber: Complete NBC Concerts 1947 – 1948. Music & Arts.
Kleiber Waltzes
-Carlos Kleiber: New Year's Concert 1989, Vienna Philharmonic. CBS Masterworks.
Otto Klemperer
-Bruckner: Symphony No. 6, Brahms: Haydn Variations. Music & Arts.

-Mahler: Symphony No. 2 EMI Classics.
-Mozart, The Magic Flute: Otto Klemperer. Angel.
Kolisch Quartet
-Kolisch Quartet Plays Mozart. Koch Schwann.
Krenek
-Ernst Krenek: Jonny spielt auf. Decca London.
Kurtág
-György Kurtág: Messages of the Late R .V. Troussova / Scenes From a Novel. Adrienne Csengery, Ensemble InterContemporain, Pierre Boulez. Hungaroton.
Adriana Lecouvreur
-Cilea: Adriana Lecouvreur / Olivero, Domingo, Silipigni. Legato Classics.
Lutoslawski
-Lutoslawski Conducts Lutoslawski. Philips Digital Classics.
Karl Muck and Early BSO recordings
-The First Recordings of the Boston Symphony Orchestra. BSO Classics, 1995.
Opera Originals
-Creators' Records by Giuseppe Anselmi, Celestina Boninsegna, Gemma Bellincioni. Standing Room Only.
Arvo Pärt
-Arvo Pärt: Arbos. ECM.
Artur Schnabel
-Arthur Schnabel Plays Beethoven. Arabesque.
-Schubert and Schnabel. Arabesque.
-Mozart and Schnabel. Arabesque.
Joseph Szigeti
-Beethoven, Debussy: Sonatas; Bartok: Rhapsody, Szigeti, Bartók. Vanguard Classics.
-Joseph Szigeti. Video Artists International.
Stravinsky
-Stravinsky Conducts Stravinsky: Petrushka / Le Sacre du Printemps. CBS/Sony.

-Stravinsky Conducts Stravinsky: Symphony of Psalms/Symphony in 3 Movements. CBS/Sony.

Mravinsky Tchaikovsky
-Tchaikovsky: Symphonies Nos. 4, 5, 6 "Pathetique", Mravinsky, Leningrad Philharmonic. Deutsche Grammophon.

Klaus Tennstedt
-Mahler: Symphony No 8, Tennstedt, London Philharmonic. EMI Classics.

Dubravka Tomsic
-Bach: Italian Concerto / Partita No. 1 / Toccata In D. Stradivari.

Arturo Toscanini
-Berlioz: Harold In Italy, etc, Toscanini, NBC Symphony Orchestra. RCA Victor Red Seal

-Verdi: La Traviata (Complete Rehearsal) / Toscanini, NBS Symphony Orchestra. Music & Arts Programs Of America.

-Debussy: La Mer; Elgar: Enigma Variations, Toscanini, BBC, EMI Great Recordings of the Century.

Kurt Weill
-Kurt Weill: Die Bürgschaft. EMI Classics.

Benita Valente
-Benita Valente Sings Lieder of Schubert, Haydn and Mozart. Pantheon.

-Benita Valente, Soprano - Great Singers of the 20th Century, Vol. 1. Bridge.

About the author

Poet, music critic, literary scholar, actor, and teacher, Lloyd Schwartz has had an unusually varied career. He is Frederick S. Troy Professor of English at the University of Massachusetts Boston, where he teaches in the MFA Program; an editor of three volumes of work on and by Elizabeth Bishop (including the Library of America's *Elizabeth Bishop: Poems, Prose, and Letters*); and the author of three volumes of poetry (*Cairo Traffic*, the most recent) and a chapbook (*Lloyd Schwartz: Greatest Hits*). His poems have been honored with a Pushcart Prize and publication in *The Best American Poetry* and *The Best of the Best American Poetry*. He is the Classical Music Editor of *The Boston Phoenix*, for which he has received wide acclaim, including three ASCAP-Deems Taylor Awards and the Pulitzer Prize for Criticism. He began work in radio as a regular cast member of the children's program The Spider's Web. Since 1987, he has been the classical music critic for NPR's *Fresh Air*, with Terry Gross.

arrowsmith is named after the late William Arrowsmith, a renowned classics scholar, literary and film critic. General editor of thirty-three volumes of The Greek Tragedy in New Translation, he was also a brilliant translator of Eugenio Montale, Cesare Pavese, and others. Arrowsmith, who taught for years in Boston University's University Professors Program, championed not only the classics and the finest in contemporary literature, he was also passionate about the importance of recognizing the translator's role in bringing the original work to life in a new language.

Like the arrowsmith who turns his arrows straight and true, a wise person makes his character straight and true.

—Buddha

Books by **arrowsmith**:

Girls by Oksana Zabuzhko
Bula Matari/Smasher of Rocks by Tom Sleigh
This Carrying Life by Maureen McLane
Cries of Animals Dying by Lawrence Ferlinghetti
Animals in Wartime by Matiop Wal
Divided Mind by George Scialabba
The Jinn by Amira El-Zein
Bergstein edited by Askold Melnyczuk
Arrow Breaking Apart by Jason Shinder
Beyond Alchemy by Daniel Berrigan
Conscience, Consequence: Reflections on Father Daniel Berrigan
edited by Askold Melnyczuk
Ric's Progress by Donald Hall
Return To The Sea by Etnairis Rivera
translated by Erica Mena
The Kingdom of His Will by Catherine Parnell
Eight Notes from the Blue Angel by Marjana Savka
translated by Askold Melnyczuk
Fifty-Two by Melissa Green

Books by PFP Publishing

Blind Tongues by Sterling Watson
the Book of Dreams by Craig Nova
A Russian Requiem by Roland Merullo
Ambassador of the Dead by Askold Melnyczuk
Demons of the Blank Page by Roland Merullo
Celebrities in Disgrace by Elizabeth Searle
(eBook version only)
"Last Call" by Roland Merullo
(eBook "single")
Fighting Gravity by Peggy Rambach
Leaving Losapas by Roland Merullo
Girl to Girl: The Real Deal on Being A Girl Today by Anne Driscoll
Revere Beach Elegy by Roland Merullo
a four-sided bed by Elizabeth Searle
Revere Beach Boulevard by Roland Merullo
Tornado Alley by Craig Nova
"The Young and the Rest of Us" by Elizabeth Searle
(eBook "single")
Lunch with Buddha by Roland Merullo
Temporary Sojourner by Tony Eprile
Passion for Golf:In Pursuit of the Innermost Game by Roland Merullo
What Is Told by Askold Melnyczuk
"What A Father Leaves" by Roland Merullo
(eBook "single" & audio book)

www.ingramcontent.com/pod-product-compliance
Lightning Source LLC
Chambersburg PA
CBHW022101150426
43195CB00008B/215